SURFACE WARFARE OFFICER'S
DEPARTMENT HEAD GUIDE

TITLES IN THE SERIES

The Bluejacket's Manual
Career Compass
Chief Petty Officer's Guide
Command at Sea
Developing the Naval Mind
Dictionary of Modern Strategy and Tactics
Dictionary of Naval Abbreviations
Dictionary of Naval Terms
Division Officer's Guide
Dutton's Nautical Navigation
Farwell's Rules of the Nautical Road
Fighting the Fleet
Fleet Tactics and Naval Operations
General Naval Tactics
International Law for Seagoing Officers
Naval Ceremonies, Customs, and Traditions
The Naval Institute Guide to Naval Writing
The Naval Officer's Guide
Naval Officer's Guide to the Pentagon
Naval Shiphandler's Guide
Newly Commissioned Naval Officer's Guide
Operations Officer's Guide
Petty Officer's Guide
Principles of Naval Engineering
Principles of Naval Weapon Systems
The Professional Naval Officer: A Course to Steer By
Reef Points
A Sailor's History of the U.S. Navy
Saltwater Leadership
Shiphandling Fundamentals for Littoral Combat Ships and the New Frigates
Watch Officer's Guide

THE U.S. NAVAL INSTITUTE
BLUE & GOLD PROFESSIONAL LIBRARY

For more than 100 years, U.S. Navy professionals have counted on specialized books published by the Naval Institute Press to prepare them for their responsibilities as they advance in their careers and to serve as ready references and refreshers when needed. From the days of coal-fired battleships to the era of unmanned aerial vehicles and laser weaponry, such perennials as *The Bluejacket's Manual* and the *Watch Officer's Guide* have guided generations of Sailors through the complex challenges of naval service. As these books are updated and new ones are added to the list, they will carry the distinctive mark of the Blue & Gold Professional Library series to remind and reassure their users that they have been prepared by naval professionals and meet the exacting standards that Sailors have long expected from the U.S. Naval Institute.

SURFACE WARFARE OFFICER'S DEPARTMENT HEAD GUIDE

EDITED BY
RADM Fred W. Kacher, USN
CAPT Joseph A. Gagliano, USN
CDR Samantha A. O'Neil, USN

NAVAL INSTITUTE PRESS
Annapolis, Maryland

Naval Institute Press
291 Wood Road
Annapolis, MD 21402

© 2022 by U.S. Naval Institute
All rights reserved. No part of this book may be reproduced or utilized in any form or by any means, electronic or mechanical, including photocopying and recording, or by any information storage and retrieval system, without permission in writing from the publisher.

Library of Congress Cataloging-in-Publication Data

Names: Kacher, Fred W., author. | Gagliano, Joseph A., 1974– author. | O'Neil, Samantha A., author.
Title: Surface warfare officer's department head guide / RADM Fred W. Kacher, USN, CAPT Joseph A. Gagliano, USN, CDR Samantha A. O'Neil, USN.
Description: Annapolis, Maryland : Naval Institute Press, [2022] | Series: Blue & gold professional library | Includes index.
Identifiers: LCCN 2021050778 | ISBN 9781682477731 (hardcover)
Subjects: LCSH: United States. Navy—Officers' handbooks.
Classification: LCC V133 .K34 2022 | DDC 359.00973—dc23/eng/20211115
LC record available at https://lccn.loc.gov/2021050778

♾ Print editions meet the requirements of ANSI/NISO z39.48-1992 (Permanence of Paper). Printed in the United States of America.

10 9 8 7 6 5 4 3 2 1

CONTENTS

List of Photos and Figures	ix
Acknowledgments	xi
List of Acronyms and Abbreviations	xv

INTRODUCTION
RADM Fred W. Kacher, USN 1

PART I. THE BEGINNING 5

1. GETTING PREPARED
   LCDR Kurt Albaugh, USN 7

2. DEPARTMENT HEAD SCHOOL AND THE COMMAND ASSESSMENT
   CAPT Peter Halvorsen, USN 17

PART II. THE DEPARTMENT HEAD 31

3. DEPARTMENT HEAD LEADERSHIP
   CAPT Joseph A. Gagliano, USN 33

4. MANAGEMENT
   CDR Sam O'Neil, USN 45

5. SUPPORTING THE EXECUTIVE OFFICER
   CDR Robert C. Watts IV, USN 56

6. SUPPORTING THE COMMANDING OFFICER
   RADM Fred W. Kacher, USN 68

PART III. THE WATCH 77

7. TACTICAL ACTION OFFICER
   CDR Katie Whitman, USN 79

8. SPECIAL EVOLUTIONS OFFICER OF THE DECK
   CDR Christopher H. Bland, USN 89

9. SENIOR WATCH OFFICER
   CDR J. D. Kristenson, USN 100

CONTENTS

PART IV. **THE BILLETS AND FUTURE OPPORTUNITIES**   111

10. OPERATIONS OFFICER
    CDR Doug Robb, USN   113

11. STAFF OPERATIONS OFFICER
    CDR James Hagerty, USN   125

12. WEAPONS OFFICER
    LCDR Dylan Ross, USN   138

13. COMBAT SYSTEMS OFFICER
    LCDR Carleigh Gregory, USN   151

14. ENGINEER OFFICER
    CDR Sam O'Neil, USN   160

15. STAFF READINESS OFFICER
    CDR Rob Keller, USN   173

16. SHIPBOARD PLANS AND TACTICS OFFICER
    LCDR Ashley O'Keefe, USN   181

17. FIRST LIEUTENANT
    LCDR Audrey Herrington, USN   192

18. AIR DEPARTMENT
    CDR Jonathan "Shank" Lushenko, USN   203

19. PREPARING FOR EARLY COMMAND
    CDR Cameron Ingram, USN   213

APPENDIX 1
Notional Turnover Schedule   227

APPENDIX 2
"So You Want to Be a Department Head" Revisited
RADM Fred W. Kacher, USN   231

Index   237

PHOTOS AND FIGURES

PHOTOS

1-1.	Formal training	8
1-2.	A healthy workout routine can keep your mind sharp and lower stress	13
1-3.	Disciplined self-study and professional reading are essential	15
2-1.	The Surface Warfare Officers School department head class 254 takes a class photo	25
3-1.	Department heads should practice and hone their warfighting leadership skills	42
4-1.	A chief engineer provides damage control training	49
5-1.	Khaki call	57
6-1.	A commanding officer and department heads work together	69
7-1.	Tactical action officer must maintain situation awareness	85
8-1.	A department head practices navigation seamanship	93
9-1.	Sailor stands boatswains mate of the watch	105
10-1.	Operations officers in cruiser or destroyer units oversee deck and shiphandling special evolutions	119
11-1.	Ships assigned to Destroyer Squadron 23 transit the Pacific Ocean	129
12-1.	A weapons officer takes inventory of 5-inch ammunition	139
13-1.	A combat systems officer reviews a training scenario	157
14-1.	An assistant oil king inspects fuel oil samples	167
15-1.	Engineering department conducts operations around the clock on every ship	177
16-1.	Plans and tactics officers work with warfare tactics instructors to provide combat mentorship and tactical guidance on board ships across the fleet	188
17-1.	Deck department Sailors conduct amphibious operations	200

18-1.	MH-60R conducts practice vertical replenishment during initial ship aviation team training	208
19-1.	USS *Zephyr* (PC 8) conducts a live firing event	223

FIGURES

4-1.	Quad/tri chart	50
8-2.	Special Evolution References	91

ACKNOWLEDGMENTS

Like most endeavors in the U.S. Navy, this book is a product of superb and talented naval leaders working together in support of a shared vision—born of the desire to share tips and tools that made each of us successful department heads. While each department head experience will differ, leading Sailors and maximizing our ships' warfighting readiness are the core of our profession.

This book is a testament to the passion and resilience our team embodies. The global COVID-19 pandemic impacted all of us, especially as every single one of us juggles the demands of an important day job and a family life at home. Just as leadership is essential in the fleet, it is also a critical ingredient in the making of a book. Our writing team worked "after hours" while serving in sea and shore assignments all over the world. We are grateful for their time and contributions. In addition to our contributing authors, many others supported us in this endeavor. Together, we are grateful to the Naval Institute Press for its teamwork, specifically U.S. Naval Institute chief executive officer and publisher VADM Pete Daly, USN (Ret.), for supporting this title, and LCDR Tom Cutler, USN (Ret.), who has served as a super coach and believed in the value of publishing this guide.

Leading as a department head is both an art and a science. For many of you, your department head tour will be the most challenging assignment to date, and your ability to effectively lead and manage your department will influence your future command-at-sea opportunities. Successful department heads lead with confidence, work together, build their teams, think critically, and plan ahead. The strength of each department head impacts every facet of shipboard operations. We hope that this compilation of lessons learned and helpful hints provides you with a framework to build upon throughout your department head tour. This book is dedicated to department heads—past, present, and future—who by their service strengthen our Navy and make a difference in our nation and the world.

I am grateful to have worked for some senior surface warfare leaders who were never too busy to share their insights and mentorship—ADM Mike

Mullen (Ret.), VADM John Morgan (Ret.), VADM Doug Crowder (Ret.), VADM Tom Rowden (Ret.), RADM Charlie Williams (Ret.), and CDR Bryan McGrath (Ret.).

Most of all, I would like to thank my family for their support. My wife, Pam, has always been willing to read and reflect on my writing despite being an incredibly busy and dedicated wife and mother of Jen and Katie, who have perhaps had to sacrifice the most during their childhood while I have worked in a profession that I love. I also thank my parents, Fred and Nancy Kacher, for serving as the original examples of leadership and patriotism in my life.

—**RADM FRED W. KACHER**

Editing this book has brought back great memories of the very best department heads I have seen over the years, including seniors, peers, and subordinates.

The first department heads I worked for while in my division officer tour on board *Laboon*—George Lang, Rob Katz, and Chuck Marks—were incredible examples of dedicated officers in demanding jobs. Most importantly, they demonstrated that no one personality type is more successful than another during a department head tour. Instead, authenticity to one's own personality is the key to success.

I most fondly recall the peers with whom I served during my own department head tours—Derek Trinque, Lex Walker, Jim Storm, Brian Mutty, Denise Woodfin, Deb Courtney, and Tony Delatorre. They provided the invaluable and enduring lesson that teamwork overcomes individual accomplishment every time. Their selfless examples were critical in my professional development.

I had the opportunity to see some of our very best surface warfare department heads in action while serving as a ship's captain—Kevin Bacon, Larry Johnson, Ted Trevino, Brian Tyler, Ed Giron, and Elliot Kujat—and as a destroyer squadron commodore—Sean Hurley, Nick Heiliger, Andrew Cordrey, Josh Womack, Chris Zeller, J. P. Bertram, Joel Stoorza, Chuck Becker, Becky Miranda, and Rich Kachman. Across the board, they demonstrated that department heads can meet any challenge when given proper resources and enough room to lead their Sailors.

On a more personal note, I am grateful for the continued support of my wife, Stephanie. In every writing project I have tackled across the years, she has cheered me on, all the while knowing the personal time required to complete it. Writing and publishing have long been a source of my professional fulfillment, and her personal sacrifice has made this possible.

—CAPT JOSEPH A. GAGLIANO

This is my first book, and I owe a debt of gratitude to many people—too many to list here, but a few deserve special recognition: my U.S. Naval Academy Blue and Gold officer, BMCS (SW) Jerry Lewis, USNR (Ret.), for never giving up on me and cheering me on throughout my career; my second tour division officer commanding officer, CAPT Dave Guluzian, who believed in my leadership abilities and encouraged me to continue my journey in the surface warfare community; my former department head commanding officers RDML M. Scott Sciretta, CAPT Kurt Sellerberg, and CAPT Bob Bryans, and former executive officers CAPT Jeff Heames and CAPT Justin Harts, who trusted, guided, and empowered me as their chief engineer. I would also like to thank my extraordinary teammates on USS *Preble* (DDG 88) and USS *Cowpens* (CG 63), specifically Scott Carpenter, Brady Bentzen, Thomas Deeter, GSCS (SW) Jerry Amog, USN (Ret.), MMCM (SW/AW) Shawn Seabron, and my port engineer, Dave Sparkuhl—who all went the extra mile to make me a better chief engineer, and my peers Ben Herring, Dave Hollon, Katie Jacobson, Rob Keller, Corry Lougee, Antonia Shey, Parina Somnhot, Katie Whitman, and Tim Yuhas, who are simply the best.

Finally, I would like to thank my parents Carol, Greg, and Mary for instilling hard work and gratitude as core values. I am deeply thankful to my husband, Kieran, who embraces my continued naval service while balancing it with his own service in the U.S. Marine Corps and who is unconditionally supportive of all my endeavors. I would also like to thank my daughters, Kiera and Charlotte, who inspire me to be brave and vulnerable and to never give up.

—CDR SAMANTHA A. O'NEIL

ACRONYMS AND ABBREVIATIONS

1LT	first lieutenant
2M	microminiature electronics repair
3M	maintenance, material, and management system
AAWC	anti-air warfare coordinator
AFL	assistant first lieutenant
AO	action officer
ARG	amphibious ready group
ARPA	automatic radar plotting aid
ASW	antisubmarine warfare
A-SWO	assistant senior watch officer
ATFP	antiterrorism force protection
ATG	afloat training group
ATO	antiterrorism officer
AT TRASUP	antiterrorism training supervisor
BM	boatswain's mate
BMC	boatswain's mate chief petty officer
BRM	bridge resource management
CA	command assessment
CAG	carrier air wing commander
CASREP	casualty report
CCO	combat cargo officer
CDO	command duty officer
CEL	combat elements
CHENG	chief engineer
CIC	combat information center
CICWO	combat information watch officer
CMAA	command master at arms
CMC	command master chief
CO	commanding officer
CoC	chain of command, change of command

COMMO	communications officer
CONOPS	concept of operations
CONUS	continental United States
COVE	conning officer virtual environment
CPO	chief petty officer
CQA	command qualification assessment
CQE	command qualification exam
CRG	coastal riverine group
CRUDES	cruisers or destroyers
CSG	carrier strike group
CSMM	combat systems maintenance manager
CSMP	current ship's maintenance project
CSO	combat systems officer
CSOOW	combat systems officer of the watch
CSTT	combat systems training team
CVN	aircraft carrier
CVW	carrier air wing
CWO	chief warrant officer
DCPO	damage control petty officer
DDG	guided missile destroyer
DESRON	destroyer squadron
DETMO	detachment maintenance officer
DFS	departure from specification
DINQ	delinquent in qualification
DIVO	division officer
EDO	engineering duty officer
EDORM	*Engineering Department Organization and Regulations Manual*
EKMS	electronic key management system
EMI	extra military instruction
EOCC	engineering operations casualty control
EOOW	engineering officer of the watch
EXPSAF	explosive safety
FITREP	fitness report
FSA	food service attendant
HSM	helicopter maritime strike
ISIC	immediate superior in command
KMI	key management infrastructure
LCPO	leading chief petty officer

LCS	littoral combat ship
LCSRON	littoral combat ship squadron
LDO	limited duty officer
LHA	landing helicopter assault
LHD	landing helicopter dock
LPD	amphibious transport dock
LPO	leading petty officer
LSD	dock landing ship
LSO	landing safety officer
MCM	mine countermeasure ship
MMTT	multimission tactical trainer
MPA	main propulsion assistant
MRG	main reduction gear
N3	staff operations officer
N4	staff readiness officer
NATOPS	*Naval Air Training and Operating Procedures Standardization*
NAV	navigator
NAVFAC	naval facilities engineering command
NEC	naval enlisted classifications
NSFS	naval surface fire support
NSS	navigation, seamanship, and shiphandling
NSST	navigation, seamanship, and shiphandling trainer
NSTM	naval ships' technical manual
OIC	officer in charge
OOD	officer of the deck
OPTASK	operational task message
OPS	operations officer
PB4T	planning board for training
PBED	plan, brief, execute, debrief
PCO	plant control officer
PCS	permanent change of station
PEO	prospective engineering officer
PHIBRON	amphibious squadron
POD	plan of the day
POE	projected operational environment
PQS	personnel qualification standard
PST	personal storage data file
PT	plans and tactics

PTO	plans and tactics officer
QUAL/CERT	qualification and certification
R-ADM	relational administration data management
RAST	recovery, assist, secure, and traverse system
RIB	rigid inflatable boats
ROC	required operational capabilities
RSCA	reporting senior's cumulative average
RSO	range safety officer
SAR	search and rescue
SERT	ship's electronics readiness team
SEWBC	senior enlisted watchbill coordinator
SMMO	ship's maintenance and material officer
SMWDC	Surface and Mine Warfighting Development Center
SOH	safety and occupational health
SOP	standard operating procedure
SORM	*Standard Organization and Regulations of the U.S. Navy*
STO	systems test officer
STW	strike warfare
SURFDEVRON	surface development squadron
SURFRON	naval surface squadron
SWO	surface warfare officer, senior watch officer
SWOS	Surface Warfare Officers School
TAD	temporary assigned duty
TAO	tactical action officer
TRAINO	training officer
TTP	tactics, techniques, and procedures
TYCOM	type commander
UNREP	underway replenishment
VBSS	visit, board, search, and seizure
VLS	vertical launch system
VMS	voyage management system
WEPS	weapons officer
WTRP	watch team replacement plan
XO	executive officer
ZIDL	zone inspection discrepancy list

INTRODUCTION
RADM Fred W. Kacher, USN

LESS THAN A YEAR AFTER the attacks of 11 September 2001, I penned a short article for the U.S. Naval Institute's (USNI's) *Proceedings* that shared what I learned during a very fortunate back-to-back department head ride on USS *Princeton*. That article, one of the first that I ever wrote, seemed to strike a chord with many readers. For a number of years, it was used in department head school (technically a course, but colloquially known as a school) at the Surface Warfare Officers School (SWOS) and was included in a USNI leadership anthology, and it ultimately inspired the book this revised article appears in. Looking back almost two decades on the experiences that shaped that original article, I am pleased that many of my observations have withstood what time and experience have offered me since then.

Certainly, some things have changed. The information technology revolution we were so excited about as a new century dawned delivered both efficiencies and challenges. Today, young department heads are more likely struggling not to gain information but rather to focus on the right information in what is now a sea of data (and the same can be said of new admirals and the rest of society). Databases, web-based solutions, and advances in technology by our adversaries have also made the job of today's department head tougher than mine was. More profoundly, the attacks on USS *Cole* in 2000 and on our nation's own soil the next year forever changed the way we oversee and execute force protection—a mission area we dedicated far fewer resources to in the late 1990s. Finally, after enjoying uncontested control of the sea since the end of the Cold War, our Navy and our nation are engaged in Great Power competition with China and Russia.

On a positive front, our department heads are receiving much more comprehensive and state-of-the-art training than my department head classmates and I did. That is not to say our training was poor—quite the contrary—but the continuum of training that SWOS provides, the state-of-the-art simulators that teach surface warfare officers how to fight and drive, and a command qualification process that is much more rigorous all demonstrate that we are building a better department head and commanding officer today than in previous eras. Taking all that into account, however, I would contend that leadership and effort still make the most difference today at sea, as they did yesterday.

With these early observations in mind, it has been gratifying to update and expand upon the concepts in the original article with the assistance of other surface warfare officers who have more recently completed their department head tours. As I have grown more senior, I have found myself focusing more on the strength of a ship's department heads—and fostering that strength—as a key determinant in a ship and its captain's success.

No matter your billet or ship type, your job as a department head at sea will arguably be your most challenging assignment to date. You will be expected to think critically and plan for events six to twelve months in advance and, in some cases, even beyond your anticipated time in the job. Your ship's success will depend on how well you understand your role, how well your team works together, and how well your team collaborates with other departments, no matter the phase of the ship's lifecycle. Department heads are the backbone of all ship operations, delivering and executing the commanding officer's vision and accomplishing the Navy's mission.

This book is an anthology of best practices and helpful hints collected from successful surface warfare officers who have previously filled these critical department head roles. It is not a substitute for any official Navy guidance or instruction but rather is meant to provide a framework to be used in conjunction with other available tools and references. Each chapter begins with a basic overview of your responsibilities and ends with advice for a successful department head tour.

From preparing for department head school, to providing leadership and management tools, to suggesting how to best support the commanding officer and executive officer, along with offering some sound watchstanding practices, this book will help you build a strong foundation. Given that we have dedicated one chapter to each of the major department head billets, you may find certain chapters more relevant to you than others, but having a basic understanding of your fellow department heads' roles will give you a better appreciation for the work and effort that each of you must dedicate for the ship and crew to succeed.

Our hope is that you revisit this guide when you become the executive officer and commanding officer of your own ship. While instructions are updated and processes change, the fundamental principles and traits that will make you a successful department head remain the same. We encourage you to carry the best practices and lessons learned with you and share them with your teams, and we remain grateful that another generation of young leaders has stepped forward to lead our Navy's ships during this critical time in our nation's history.

PART I

THE BEGINNING

CHAPTER 1
Getting Prepared
LCDR Kurt Albaugh, USN

A Select Group

CONGRATULATIONS ON YOUR SELECTION to department head afloat! Your selection represents a significant vote of trust and confidence by our community leadership. It also represents a series of opportunities to enhance the combat effectiveness of a warship, to engage in personal and professional development in preparation for command, to mentor and guide division officers and Sailors, and to build close and lasting friendships with your peers—the foundation of a network that will make you a more effective leader in our Navy.

While the commanding officer ultimately sets the tone for any ship, a strong, collaborative, well-prepared team of department heads will energize the whole crew to deliver their best performance and strengthen the crew's morale, and liberate the commanding officer to think more deeply and strategically about the needs of the ship, integrate the ship into a larger force element, and train watchstanders in the art and science of navigation, seamanship, and tactics. The more prepared you are, the more fun you will have while you are "in the seat," as well. Being a department head can be so much more than a demanding tour that you need to survive to reach future career milestones; your level of preparation can help you thrive as a leader.

The Navy provides a robust series of formal schools to prepare officers for their department head tours, but as with any other career milestone, those formal schools represent only one aspect of preparation. To expand the frontiers of our knowledge and skills, on-the-job training and self-guided learning complement the formal schooling in the training pipeline provided en route to your first department head tour. This chapter will focus on self-guided learning—it is the best avenue to prepare before reporting to department head school.

While self-guided learning is highly personal by definition, this chapter offers some thought-provoking considerations as a point of departure. Good luck!

Self-Assessment

The ancient Greek aphorism "know thyself" is perhaps the best advice when preparing for department head school and beyond. In the past ten years, two trends have shaped the surface warfare officer career path, and they combine in ways that make a clear-eyed self-assessment of our individual strengths and weaknesses as leaders more important.

On the one hand, formal schooling in the surface warfare community, especially at the division officer level, has become far more robust. The continuing expansion of formal schools, including the basic division officer course and the advanced division officer course, watchstanding courses focused on developing skills as junior officer of the deck and officer of the deck, and increased billet-specific training have combined to "baseline" our experiences and strengthen the consistency of training across the surface force. However, these shared experiences also provide us with a great deal of insight into our respective areas of individual strength—and the areas where we can improve. We should capitalize on these opportunities and be especially attentive to the feedback from these experiences.

On the other hand, the Navy's sustained efforts to transition toward a more modern and flexible military personnel system has increased the diversity of experiences possible in a Navy career. This trend will likely continue. The surface warfare officer career path provides the most flexibility of any unrestricted line community when it comes to the first shore tour. As a result, each

1-1. **Formal training has become more robust, including the use of advanced simulators for shiphandling, navigation, and seamanship.**

U.S. Navy photo by Mass Communication Specialist 2nd Class Derien C. Luce/Released

cohort that reports to department head school contains an impressive breadth of experience: from instructors reporting from duty in seamanship and navigation, to warfare tactics instructors, to officers who have pursued graduate education in a wide array of disciplines, to flag aides and many others. Beyond this inherent level of diversity, however, the expansion of initiatives such as the career intermission program has only introduced more flexibility into what was once a far more rigid career path. This increased flexibility demands rigor from us in our own self-assessment of our strengths and weaknesses as a prospective department head.

Thankfully, we are no strangers to self-assessment. We engage in it in rigorous briefings and debriefings in special evolutions at sea and ashore. We also enable self-assessment and introspection through formal opportunities for 360-degree feedback, gathering the combined wisdom of others to aid us in our choices for further development. With a little modification, you can use similar techniques to help determine where to apply effort to prepare for your department head tours.

This book seeks to assist in that self-assessment process. The chapters dedicated to general aspects of being department head, common watch positions stood by department heads, and specific department head billets can all offer perspectives to assist you in determining where to apply your time and energy as you prepare for this career milestone.

Duty Preferences and Slating

One of the most anticipated moments in your career will be slating for your department head billet. Engaging in some self-assessment will prepare you to engage with your detailer regarding your next assignment. Of course, you should also reach out to friends, shipmates, and mentors, and—most importantly—engage with your family to help determine your preferences.

Although the process is very similar to detailing for second tour division officers, where you will list preferences for ship type, homeport, and billet, both between categories and within them, there are some key differences. There are simply fewer billet choices at the department head level. The current options for department head assignment, as listed on the surface warfare officer career assignments (PERS-41) website, are:

- guided missile cruiser (CG): weapons officer
- guided missile destroyer (DDG): operations officer/weapons officer/engineer officer

- littoral combat ship (LCS): engineer officer
- landing helicopter assault/landing helicopter dock (LHA/LHD): combat systems officer
- dock landing ship (LSD): operations officer/first lieutenant
- amphibious transport dock (LPD): combat systems officer
- mine countermeasure ship (MCM): operations officer.

For many classes of ship, only one or two billets might be available for first tour, unrestricted line department heads. In addition, there are certain billets that are "fleet-up" or "single longer tour" assignments:

- DDG: engineer officer (DDGs 51–71, spot-promote)
- DDG: engineer officer (DDGs 72–78, no spot-promote)
- LCS: combat systems officer (fleet-up to operations officer).

On cruisers and destroyers, the commanding officer can selectively fleet up any of the first tour department heads to either the combat systems officer or plans and tactics officer billets.

In addition to a narrower spectrum of choice, the overall pool of officers at the department head level is much smaller. According to recent PERS-41 surface warfare career briefs, out of more than 1,000 surface warfare officers accessed every year, around 275 officers will remain by the time department head slating occurs. Because of this, the overall population is more sensitive to the personnel issues that affect all levels of the military: medical issues affecting sea duty qualification, humanitarian reassignments, exceptional family members, performance issues, and disciplinary or legal issues. In each instance, these create unanticipated demand signals across the personnel system. As a result, while slating is a significant event in anyone's career, it is important to maintain some mental flexibility if your detailer contacts you to discuss changing your assignment. Many prospective department heads make significant family and financial decisions based on their initial slate results only to have their orders changed later based on one of these unanticipated events. You should think carefully about making choices that are hard to reverse early in the slating process, as the needs of the Navy can be more pronounced at this stage.

You will receive a lot of advice about which billets, platforms, and homeports are "the best." However, each possible assignment and each officer have unique circumstances, so no advice fits everyone equally. Above all, your career will be defined by your performance, not by which platform or billet you serve in, so approach your slating with an open mind. Board results consistently confirm that sustained superior performance as a department head afloat—not ship type, billet, or homeport—is the key factor in selecting officers for command at sea.

Department Head Administration: Study Ahead

While division officers certainly play a role in shipboard administration, the scope and scale of this important work increase significantly as a department head. We all want to focus on fighting and driving the ship—and there is a natural impulse to think of shipboard paperwork as the province of the yeomen in the ship's office.

There are at least three good reasons to think otherwise. First, your executive officer (XO) is a very busy person—they will appreciate it greatly if you can make the process of moving correspondence easier by providing "all-but-signature"-quality products. If you can remove even a small amount from the XO's workload, you will be demonstrating that you're ready for that level of responsibility. Second, small ships such as littoral combat ships are becoming a larger part of the Navy's fleet architecture. As with many other areas, the size and composition of these crews mean that administration is an "all-hands" evolution. The one personnel specialist or yeoman assigned to the ship will have plenty to do and will need everyone's help in drafting accurate and properly formatted correspondence. Third, punting low-quality products to the ship's office means that everyone will be working longer hours—including the cognizant department head. You do not want to be waiting on board while the yeoman and the XO are working through a long queue of correspondence to get to the bill or instruction you need to send to an inspection team ahead of their visit the following morning.

There are many initiatives afoot to reduce the administrative burden on ships—and everything we can do to reduce the overall administrative load is great for Sailors. However, there is another aspect to administration that we neglect but that can provide similar gains: drafting and processing correspondence more quickly and with less reworking. Department heads who can do so will enjoy more time to dedicate to the key responsibilities of leading their department and standing key supervisory watches on behalf of the captain.

The formal schooling provided to prospective department heads rightly favors tactics and billet-specific training over general administration. As a result, if you don't feel comfortable with your own level of knowledge and proficiency with administration, this may be an area worth some self-study. The following references can help with drafting correspondence:

- ▶ SECNAV M-5216.5 (series), *Department of the Navy Correspondence Manual*
- ▶ SECNAV M-5210.2 (series), *Standard Subject Identification Code Manual*
- ▶ William Strunk and E. B. White, *The Elements of Style*.

The SECNAV manuals should be your first two references on any correspondence or administrative matter, and it's worth having, at a minimum, the current electronic versions handy in your personal files. Per OPNAVINST 3120.32 (series), the *Standard Organization and Regulations of the U.S. Navy*, all department heads report to the XO on administrative matters.

Time Management, Personal Organization, and Self-Care

The time between your division officer and department head tours offers an excellent opportunity to take stock of what worked well in terms of individual techniques for time management, personal organization, and self-care. As with the narrow example of shipboard administration, these more general skills also allow you to make better use of the limited time in any given day, preserve opportunities for rest, and devote a proportionally higher amount of time to core department head functions.

Although personal organization is important for any division officer, it only becomes more important as a department head. Although you delegated tasks as a division officer, you will be delegating larger groups of tasks to your division officers and chiefs as a department head. The only general rule is to do what works best for you—there are many different techniques suited to different personalities and circumstances. Among them are tracking tasks via Microsoft Outlook, using Excel spreadsheets, and bullet journaling. Depending on your shore assignment, the technique that works ashore may not be best suited for when you return to sea. It is worth your time to explore the options available and think about what may work best for you.

Likewise, you probably have some sense of what works best to relieve stress, and these and other techniques will be critical to your department head tours. If your present assignment or life circumstances have allowed you to drift away from those habits, now is the time to build them back up.

1-2. **A healthy workout routine can help keep your mind sharp and lower stress.**
U.S. Navy photo by Mass Communication Specialist 1st Class Elizabeth Merriam/Released

Executing Your Orders

Unlike most training tracks, your orders to Surface Warfare Officers School (SWOS) are permanent change of station (PCS) orders, and you will need to find a place to live during the six- or seven-month period you are assigned there.

As you likely remember from previous time spent in Newport, Rhode Island, life in the city is highly seasonal, with a lot of tourist and sailing activity and summer residents. In contrast, the winter gives you the full run of the city without having to navigate the crowds of summer. Depending on the timing of your class, finding a short-term rental may be relatively easy or more challenging, and if you will class up in the warmer months, it is worth engaging with a real estate agent early to help you find a home. Naval Station Newport also has a wealth of resources for Sailors relocating to the area.

At either end of your assignment to SWOS, you may find significant periods of time in your orders devoted to other schools as intermediate stops. The Aegis Training and Readiness Center in Dahlgren, Virginia, provides a combat systems common-core course to prospective department heads, as well as specialized training for the Aegis combat system and the ship self-defense system. You may have other specialized training en route, especially for officers assigned to littoral combat ships.

Depending on your previous assignments, two PCS orders in relatively short succession combined with several prolonged intermediate stops may represent the most complex set of orders you have executed in your career, and you may be issued modifications to your orders en route to the ship. Make sure to save copies of all of your orders, the endorsements on them, receipts, and other paperwork. Fortunately, the administrative department at SWOS is accustomed to processing travel claims and other pay and personnel transactions at volume, and they will be a key resource both before and after department head school. The Navy's reforms of the manpower, personnel, training, and education enterprise, such as the MyNavy Career Center, are also resources to help assist you while executing orders.

Proactive communication with your detailer, SWOS, and the XO at your ultimate duty station will help smooth over the situations that inevitably arise during a training pipeline of this length and will demonstrate your organizational skills before you ever step on board your ship.

Professional Reading

As you become a more senior officer, you will understand the importance of professional reading. In addition to this book and others like it, there are other publications that are worth considering as part of your own self-study plan.

Biography and History

As a department head, you will be training and mentoring division officers and shepherding the surface warfare officer qualification process. While this is a qualification about professional competence in shiphandling, tactics, and engineering, there is an important component of preserving our history and heritage. All ships have a proud history, and each is worth exploring. Consider reading a volume on your ship's namesake, whether it is a person, place, or famous battle—or an earlier ship to bear the same name. As a department head, you will be a steward of the history and heritage of your ship, and reading about your ship's namesake will increase your level of investment in the ship and her success.

Strategic Documents

Part of professional development and crew morale comes from linking the day-to-day actions on board ship, which sometimes may seem mundane, to broader national policy. Sailors, like anyone, seek meaning in their work. Strategic documents, whether Navy or joint, provide the context needed to have those conversations on the deckplates. Your Sailors will look to you to understand how they fit into the larger Navy—and our national defense.

Command Qualification Exam Bibliography

After your first department head tour, you will report to SWOS for a five-day period to complete a command assessment. The command qualification exam demands quality preparation. Reviewing the current bibliography, which is posted to both the PERS-41 website and the MyNavy portal, will help direct your study efforts over the course of your department head tour. Reviewing key references early, especially in areas where you may have less exposure than your peers, will also help you succeed academically at department head school. One of your first examinations will be on the Convention on the International Regulations for Preventing Collisions at Sea, and refreshing your study of the *Navigation Rules and Regulations Handbook* is essential. While there is no substitute for studying from the book, there are a number of useful applications and online videos that are helpful adjuncts to pass your Rules of the Road examination.

1-3. Disciplined self-study and professional reading are essential to your preparation as an afloat department head and a future commanding officer.
U.S. Navy photo by Mass Communication Specialist 2nd Class Lyle Wilkie/Released

Conclusion

Do not wait for the Navy to make you into a department head; rather, embrace this next stage of professional development as a challenge for you to manage yourself—you will enjoy more success and build self-confidence if you do so. There are a number of things you can do before you start executing your orders to SWOS that will help greatly during both your training pipeline and your first department head tour.

Serving as a department head afloat is an exciting stage of your career, where your knowledge and leadership skills will directly translate to the operational success of the ship. You will also be looked to for your knowledge and judgment on day one. Preparation is the key to answering that call!

LCDR Kurt Albaugh served as a division officer in USS *McClusky* (FFG 41) and USS *Carney* (DDG 64). He was a distinguished graduate of the department head course and served as engineer officer in USS *Wayne E. Meyer* (DDG 108). Selected for early command, he served as executive officer and commanding officer in USS *Devastator* (MCM 6). Ashore, he served as an instructor at the United States Naval Academy and as a speechwriter for the Chief of Naval Operations. He is the recipient of the Surface Navy Association's Admiral Arleigh Burke Award for Operational Excellence.

CHAPTER 2
Department Head School and the Command Assessment
CAPT Peter Halvorsen, USN

CONGRATULATIONS ON ACCEPTING a place at department head school! If you are reading this prior to attending, thank you for the decision to stay in the Navy and serve in one of the most challenging billets in a naval officer's career. Although your department head tours will undoubtedly be demanding, they will also be incredibly rewarding as your shiphandling ability, tactical acumen, and leadership aptitude grow. The professional skills you will learn as a department head, together with the increased complexity, scope, and scale of the job, will serve as a solid foundation upon which to build the rest of your career.

History and Overview

Your journey to department head will begin, as it has for generations of surface warfare department heads before you, in Newport, Rhode Island. The flagship course of the Surface Warfare Officers School (SWOS), department head school began life in July 1961 as the U.S. Navy destroyer school. Initially conceived by ADM Arleigh Burke, the destroyer school, renamed the Surface Warfare Officers School Command in 1970, was intended by Burke "to improve combat readiness and tactical knowledge for junior naval officers on all ships." Since the initial class of 38 officers, department head school has grown far beyond its initial scale and has become a 27-week course training more than 275 officers annually for service on board every surface ship in the fleet. Because of this variety of eventual assignments, department head school does not train to specific platforms or systems; rather, it seeks to take officers from the baseline of a division officer focused on a specific aspect of a ship's operations to mid-level leaders responsible for one-fifth to one-third of a ship and trains officers on general warfare principles, leadership, and the knowledge necessary to succeed as both a department head and a tactical action officer (TAO).

Upon completion of department head school, you will continue on to subsequent training schools around the country focused on the specific platform and weapons systems you will employ on your ship. These schools—which may be in Newport, Dahlgren, or Norfolk, Virginia; San Diego, California; or any one of a half-dozen other locations—are narrowly focused on distinct systems and associated tactics, techniques, and procedures rather than being broadly focused on general principles such as those you will learn as a department head school student.

Department head school is composed of several distinct modules, including the TAO course; bridge resource management (BRM) and navigation, seamanship, and shiphandling; afloat safety; leadership; training and administration; antiterrorism officer; damage control; material readiness; and billet specialty training. Each of these will be briefly described below.

Preparing for Department Head School

The best advice possible for an inbound department head student is to arrive with an open mind, or to put it more bluntly—get over yourself! No matter what you think you know (and admittedly you probably know a lot) from your division officer tours and your post–division officer assignments, there is a lot more to learn, and you will undoubtedly have weak spots. Every one of us does, no matter how long we have been around or how many ships we have seen. Moreover, every one of the post–department head instructors training you has successfully completed at least two department head tours and come out the other end in the top half of their year group—many in the top 10 percent; if they had not, they would not be an instructor. You have not done the job yet, so sit down, open your ears, listen to your instructors—and learn!

You also need to recognize that you will likely have to invest some quality time studying after normal working hours throughout department head school. In the span of six short months, you will be inundated with important information. It is a tremendous amount of material to study, absorb, and apply—and when you graduate, you will be in charge of thirty to one hundred Sailors and the safety and security of a billion-dollar-plus warship on the front lines of conflict during your tour. The stakes are high, and you owe it to the Sailors you will lead to do your best. For those with families, before arriving in Newport, have conversations with your spouse and children about the amount of work department head school represents, so they too are prepared to deal with the time you need to devote to studying in order to succeed.

Department head school is made even more difficult due to the preparations you and your family need to make to get ready for the move to your ultimate duty station, especially if the move will be overseas. Between medical screening appointments, house hunting, and working through the move itself, all these items can take a toll in terms of time and attention and can distract you from the course. As you arrive in Newport, try to sketch out a timeline for getting ready for the next move, which, although months away, will arrive all too quickly.

Throughout your coursework, you are going to receive a lot of formal training, but you also will receive important pieces of leadership advice, lessons learned, and updates on operations and standard practices that are not part of the formal lesson plans. You should take copious notes on the formal training items but also keep notes on your thoughts on leadership, things you want to either investigate or put in place once on the job, and a list of questions you want to ask your departmental leadership when you get to your ship. In some cases, these informal lessons may be some of the most important you learn. In the midst of all the other personal and professional requirements, try to set aside some time for self-reflection, because once you are in the job, time will become an incredibly valuable commodity. Don't hesitate to reach out to the SWOS staff for mentorship. Each of the instructors has not only survived, but also thrived in their respective department head tours, and they are a great source of advice and knowledge on how to succeed.

It is also important to get yourself into a physical fitness routine, if you have not established that as a regular part of your day prior to arriving in Newport. Not only is this important in order for you to set the example for your Sailors, it also is both a personal and a combat readiness issue. Being a department head can be stressful, and physical training—in whatever form it takes—is an important part of coping with and reacting well to stress. Moreover, we are in the profession of arms, and should you find yourself in combat, the training regimen you have established may be the thin edge that gives you the ability to fight through adversity.

Finally, look around and get to know the wonderfully talented officers who are your classmates. Not only will they be the folks who help you get through the course itself, they also will be the team that you call for help once you are on the waterfront when you have a leadership challenge or a readiness concern or just need to vent to someone who knows exactly what you are going through. In the same vein, ensure that you are reaching out to the other classes resident in Newport, and if their training track coincides with yours, arrange meet-ups and social engagements with your future division officers attending division officer training or with your future executive officer and commanding officer.

Week One and Threats

When you get to department head school, you will get right down to work with a review of core surface warfare practices, such as the sound shipboard operating principles. Following this introduction, you will dive into rules of engagement, the law of armed conflict, and what many describe as the most difficult portion of the course (at least from the sheer amount of new information): threats. The threats portion of the course includes almost twenty hours of lessons covering the air, surface, subsurface, and electronic warfare capabilities and limitations of adversary platforms, weapons systems, and tactics. Understanding the threats posed to our own ships and operations is a necessary precursor to understanding how the surface Navy will employ our own systems to counter potential adversaries, and the threats module forms the basis of advanced discussions on tactics discussed during the later TAO portion of the course.

Navigation, Seamanship, Shiphandling, Bridge Resource Management, and COVE

Following threats, you will return to your officer of the deck (OOD) roots and receive refresher lectures on shiphandling, radar, electronic charting and navigation, and Rules of the Road. All these topics are delivered by SWOS master mariners, who are either retired Navy captains with multiple afloat commands, licensed commercial masters who have commanded merchant vessels, or retired senior enlisted quartermasters and operations specialists. Many of the master mariners have more than three to four decades of experience sailing or teaching navigation, seamanship, and shiphandling (NSS) topics.

A thorough review of the Rules of the Road prior to arrival at department head school will greatly improve NSS week, and students who pick up and review Nathaniel Bowditch's *The American Practical Navigator*, *Dutton's Nautical Navigation*, *Farwell's Rules of the Nautical Road*, Russell Crenshaw's *Naval Shiphandling*, James Barber's *Naval Shiphandler's Guide*, or any of the other great books on the Rules of the Road and shiphandling will be able to engage in the lectures from a position of greater understanding.

A word of caution on the Rules of the Road: while it is possible through routine repetition of the Coast Guard database to learn to identify the correct answers on Rules of the Road exams, the professional department head must realize that *recognition is not understanding*. For example, Rule 6 (Safe Speed) and its relationship to Rule 19 (Conduct of Vessels in Restricted Visibility) were shown to be particular weaknesses of division officers during fleet OOD competency checks in 2018. Gaining a mastery of the Rules and NSS topics requires being able to explain the topic and apply it during both hypothetical scenarios and traffic management sessions.

Even though you will normally stand TAO versus OOD as a department head, you *will* be the senior officer on watch during Condition III, and your commanding officer will expect you to be able to mentor the officer of the deck and take action should they be standing the ship into danger. Moreover, on some ships, the captain will require department heads as special evolutions OODs.

During BRM, students complete a U.S. Coast Guard–certified standards of training, certification, and watchkeeping course, again taught by SWOS master mariners. The BRM module culminates in a restricted waters transit planned, briefed, and executed by student teams using both paper charts and the voyage management system (VMS).

The final module in NSS is the conning officer virtual environment (COVE). Over several sessions in a COVE shiphandling simulator, you will practice pierwork and underway replenishments, including both maneuvering alongside and casualty recovery. With sessions stretching across the entirety of department head school, usually in the evening, the COVE sessions build to a final pierwork practical exam, where you will bring your prospective ship alongside using only one tug with moderate environmental forces acting upon the ship.

The pierwork assessment is a source of stress for many students, but it does not need to be so. If you struggle to make a landing after the first session, seek out the master mariners and ask for help; they will be more than happy to schedule extra time. Your fellow students who are former SWOS instructors are another resource. They will likely have been qualified as shiphandling instructors during their tours at SWOS and can assist you in your practice.

Afloat Safety Officer, Antiterrorism Officer, and Damage Control Training

The afloat safety officer course, antiterrorism officer (ATO) course, and damage control training provide the knowledge necessary to oversee a ship's safety program, force protection programs, and damage control training, respectively. The safety course includes refresher modules on all aspects of the naval occupational health and safety manual; ATO includes requirements for the use of force and proper watchstanding; and damage control training ensures that every department head student, regardless of division officer experience, is brought up to speed on the basic principles of damage control and every piece of portable and installed firefighting equipment carried in our ships.

While not every department head will be put into the position of direct oversight of these programs, every department head will be required to qualify as a command duty officer, and these courses do a great job in preparing you to know what right looks like, what wrong looks like, and how to enforce standards every day as you walk around the ship. Your future commanding officer will expect you to know, implement, and enforce demanding standards during every port visit, to act as a safety observer during every special evolution—whether on the watchbill or not—and to be the damage control expert ready to lead a coordinated response to any incident on board the ship.

Department Head Leadership Course

Often the most popular week of department head school, the leadership course reinforces the transition from division officer to department head with an expanded scope of responsibility. Your classes will be taught by naval leadership and ethics center staff as well as SWOS post–department heads and post–commanding officers, who will discuss how to lead your Sailors, chief petty officers, and division officers and how to maximize the performance of your department, as well as how to engage with your executive officer, commanding officer, and off-ship organizations.

During the course, do not be afraid to ask your instructors what worked for them, as well as what did not. The instructors will gladly explain the pitfalls or unexpected challenges they faced during their tours, and the former commanding officers will be more than happy to answer the most popular question: "What does my CO expect of me?" Prior to the course, you should review the thirteen specific duties of a department head outlined in chapter 3.5 of the *Standard Organization and Regulations of the U.S. Navy* (OPNAV-INST 3120.32 [series]), since these are the minimum assumptions of what you will have to do as a department head for most commanding officers.

Tactical Action Officer

The preponderance of department head school by both length and, arguably, importance is the TAO course. The TAO is the principal watchstation stood by department heads, where they are responsible for employment of the ship's weapons systems and are the senior officer on watch at any given moment. To be successful, TAOs must have an intrinsic understanding of all U.S. Navy platforms, sensors, and weapons, and also have a thorough knowledge of these same components in any potential adversary's fleet. Remember that the TAO course is not platform-specific and teaches the general principles of naval warfare common to all Navy platforms.

While those officers who qualified as warfare coordinators during their division officer tours may have a slight leg up in the warfare area in which they qualified, do not worry if you did not have this opportunity. The TAO course is designed to level the knowledge of all prospective TAOs and, when combined with post-Newport tactical training, gives every officer the knowledge necessary to rapidly qualify as a TAO. Commanding officers know the value of the course and place a great deal of trust in the product that SWOS delivers.

The TAO course comprises several submodules, beginning with information operations and then working through air and missile defense, surface warfare, undersea warfare, and expeditionary warfare and concluding with a series of practical exercises and assessments in SWOS's multimission tactical trainers (MMTTs). By the end of the module, you and your peers will have gained an extensive knowledge of the principles of each warfare area as well as a working knowledge of the associated Navy-wide operational task messages (OPTASKs). This knowledge is tested through both a written TAO final and a practical assessment in the MMTT.

Training Management, Naval Administration, and Material Readiness and Maintenance University

Even though every surface warfare officer worth their salt would rather be known as a leader than a manager, it is an undeniable fact that as a department head, you will not succeed unless you embrace both leadership *and* management. These modules of department head school will shore up those division officer fundamentals you may have forgotten on shore duty and then expand upon them to discuss the larger role you will take on as a department head.

Diving into the details of being a department head, the training management and naval administration module discusses evaluations, awards, message traffic, legal issues, and the day-to-day management of ensuring your department is current on all training requirements. In a very similar way, the material readiness and maintenance university module covers the fundamentals of your departmental maintenance and material management system program, eight o'clock reports, zone inspections, and other readiness management projects, including how to enter and succeed through a maintenance availability. Just as the TAO course teaches you to fight the ship, these modules will prepare you to succeed in the everyday managerial and readiness challenges of being a department head.

Billet Specialty Training

Upon completing the TAO course and other topics described above, the department head class will split into billet specialty courses to prepare you for the specific duties of your prospective job. The billet specialty courses are taught by senior enlisted subject matter experts and post–department heads who held the position for which you are being trained.

Each individual course focuses on specific systems and programs important to each billet. For example, prospective operations officers learn about scheduling and specific fleet directives, prospective weapons officers learn about ammunition management and missile systems, prospective first lieutenants learn about boat davits and well deck operations, and prospective engineers learn the plant. For the topside department head students, the courses will set you on the path to success in your future jobs. For the snipes, the prospective engineering officer (PEO) course is incredibly rigorous and will set you up to qualify or requalify as an engineering officer of the watch within weeks of arrival on board. In fact, the culminating event in the PEO course is a series of drills conducted on the plant you will be operating and conducted by fleet assessors from the engineering assessments team.

The First Department Head Tour

Although graduation from department head school is the end of an officer's general education in Newport, it is not the end of the training track. From Newport you will head off to Aegis training, ship self-defense system training, Tomahawk school, mine warfare training, littoral combat ship officer of the deck, amphibious warfare staff planning, or any one of a dozen tactical or technical schools where you will learn the specifics of systems and platforms before ultimately arriving at your ship.

Departure from department head school is not the end of a department head's association with SWOS. Throughout your first tour, SWOS will remain a resource, a training partner through provision of numerous enlisted engineering, damage control, and navigation schools, and, at the conclusion of your tour, the destination for the command assessment (CA).

2-1. The Surface Warfare Officers School department head class 254 takes a class photo in December 2019.
U.S. Navy photo by Intelligence Specialist Second Class Autumn Washok

The Command Assessment Process

After successfully completing the first department head tour, every prospective second tour department head will receive orders back to SWOS to take the CA as part of their permanent change of station orders and prior to reporting to their second department head tours. Officers fleeting up on board their ship will also receive orders to Newport but will often advance or delay the timing of their return to align with a ship's operational schedule.

The CA forms the sixth (of ten) career assessment and second (of four) go/no-go mariner skills assessment as outlined in the Commander, Surface Forces assessment plan announced in mid-2018. Introduced in 2013, the CA has become a formalized process managed by the command-at-sea department (N75) of SWOS. With requirements set forth in CNSP/CNSLINST 1412.2 (series), the CA occurs over the course of a single week and is formed of several constituent parts, including a seamanship assessment, which is often called the shiphandling assessment; a tactical assessment; a nonassessed 360-degree review; and the command qualification exam (CQE).

A typical schedule for the CA looks like this:

- Monday morning: Check-in to SWOS and discussion with the director of command assessment

CHAPTER 2

- Monday afternoon: Full mission bridge familiarization and independent study
- Tuesday morning: Shiphandling assessment
- Tuesday afternoon: Independent study and 360-degree review debrief
- Wednesday morning: Tactical assessment
- Wednesday afternoon: Independent study
- Thursday morning: CQE
- Thursday afternoon: CA debrief.

The shiphandling assessment occurs in one of SWOS's full mission bridges and assesses an officer's ability to make decisions in a high traffic density environment. Despite what many allege or have heard, there are no "gotchas" in the shiphandling assessment. An officer will be assessed on their application of the Rules of the Road, their ability to use all bridge tools, including the automatic radar plotting aid (ARPA) and the VMS, and their ability to direct an officer of the deck and conning officer to maneuver the ship. The shiphandling assessment is evaluated by a post-commander command or post–major command officer. Debriefs of the assessment occur immediately after completion and often utilize the replay function of the full mission bridge to show the candidate what they did right and, more importantly, what they did wrong, *and* how to improve.

The tactical assessment places an officer in command of their first tour platform using one of SWOS's MMTTs configured for individual evaluation. Do not worry about the platform you came from; there is no advantage or disadvantage based on platform. The tactical assessment evaluates an officer on their knowledge of Navy-wide OPTASKs and the ability to employ their own ship's sensors and weapons, build and maintain a tactical picture, identify and prioritize threats, and make tactical decisions under the stress of an unknown scenario. The tactical assessment, like the shiphandling assessment, is also critiqued by a SWOS post-commander command or post–major command officer.

The CQE comprises five individual tests: Rules of the Road, command management, material readiness, maritime warfare, and navigation, seamanship, and shiphandling. The Rules test is formed completely from the U.S. Coast Guard database, and the other tests are developed by SWOS staff in a combined multiple choice and essay format. The CQE bibliography is updated annually and posted to the PERS-41 splash page on the Navy Personnel Command (https://www.mynavyhr.navy.mil/Navy-Personnel-Command/) website.

The 360-degree review delivers an unvarnished and unfiltered review of a department head's performance during their first tour. The candidate's commanding officer, executive officer, several peers, and several Sailors working for the officer are required respondents. Marks on the 360-degree review will provide an officer a view of their general performance and leadership, and the comments provided will give direct and (hopefully) constructive feedback on the officer's strengths, weaknesses, and areas to improve upon in subsequent tours. If a candidate is humble and takes the facilitated discussion on board, the 360-degree review can be incredibly rewarding and lead to significant growth. Often, an officer finds out something about themselves they did not realize or chose to ignore. The 360-degree review is facilitated by a SWOS post–department head staff member.

Success in the CA qualifies an officer as eligible for command once the officer also completes an oral board of three or more officers who have held command at the rank of commander or senior, chaired by a current or former major commander. Upon completion of the board, officers will be eligible for selection to command at their scheduled selection board. Failure to complete the CA will preclude an officer from being selected to serve as a commanding officer of any platform.

Failure of any portion of the assessment does not obligate a retake. Rather, an officer must make the proactive choice to request another opportunity and must coordinate with their command and SWOS to schedule the specific portions of the test required to complete qualification, while considering their ship's operational schedule. Second attempts are funded not by permanent change of station orders but rather by an individual's command temporary duty funds. At least thirty days must elapse after a failed attempt before an officer may reattempt the failed portions of the CA.

It is no secret that the CA is difficult. Only slightly more than one-third of officers pass the CA on the first attempt. Of those officers who failed one or more portions of the CA, approximately half request a second attempt, and more than three-quarters of them successfully complete the portions of the CA they previously failed. Failure in a second attempt does not automatically preclude an officer from taking the CA a third time. For officers who screen XO-afloat or XO–special mission, a third attempt is allowed prior to the final look for command.

CHAPTER 2

Preparing for the Command Assessment

It is important to remember when beginning to prepare for the CA that its purpose is twofold. It is foremost an important career milestone to prove your knowledge and assess your individual performance so that you are eligible for selection for command. But the CA is also a primer for command. It is meant to ensure that officers aspiring to command learn the references they will ultimately utilize and be accountable for on a daily basis in command.

While being a first tour department head is a full-time job, it is not a winning strategy to wait to the end and try to cram in the complete bibliography in the few days after being relieved or, worse, upon arrival in Newport. The bibliography comprises more than sixty references, ranging from a few pages to the majority of a publication. You cannot hope to review all the references in only a few days. Even if you do, cramming stores knowledge in short-term memory. Almost none of the material you learn in that way will be retained months or years later when you need the knowledge to actually perform your job. Instead, education theory suggests that the best means of retaining knowledge is systematic study, including periodic revisitation on topics, followed by an examination that stresses purposeful recall.

Through study, officers who pass the CA and ultimately ascend to command are better prepared *because* of the CA process. In a perfect world, you should start preparing for the CA from the moment you step on board your ship and spend an hour or two a week systematically reviewing both your notes from department head school and references from the CA bibliography. One best practice offered by many of those who have been successful in the CA is to turn the CA bibliography into the larger part of your ship's training program, so that even as you do wardroom training, you are studying for the exam.

Several months before the assessment occurs, you should ramp up your preparations and review the requirements for command outlined in the 1412.2 (series) to ensure you have completed all necessary steps, and step up your review of the CA bibliography. As the end of your first tour approaches, you should seek out your executive officer and commanding officer to discuss your turnover timeline with your relief. If the operational schedule of your ship and the reporting timeline of your relief permit, seek to arrange a week or two to devote to full-time study prior to taking the CA.

Even if you feel very comfortable in your current position, do not neglect the section of the CA that relates to your specific job. In other words, chief engineers should not neglect material readiness; weapons and combat systems officers should not neglect maritime warfare; and operations officers should not neglect navigation, seamanship, and shiphandling. Neglecting your area of "expertise" is a losing strategy, and nothing spells embarrassment like a chief engineer failing material readiness!

Likewise, qualification as a TAO can (and sometimes does) cause an officer to enter the tactical assessment overconfident in their own knowledge and abilities. To succeed in the tactical assessment, you must have a very firm grasp of the Navy-wide OPTASKs, especially preplanned responses, as well as a total understanding of your ship's capabilities and limitations.

Finally, do not forget the threat exam you completed during department head school, because you also must recognize and understand the potential threats that will be used against you in the scenario. Combat systems officers and those department heads who spend the majority of their time during scenarios as part of the combat systems training team should remember that their role in the tactical assessment is not to be a coach or a mentor but rather to act as a decisive and knowledgeable watchstander who is driving their team to fight the ship.

Preparing for the shiphandling assessment, just as for the tactical assessment, is an investment in time and effort. Although the surface forces Navigation, Seamanship, and Shiphandling Trainer (NSST) instruction allows for individual instruction and practice at your local NSST, this time is best spent evaluating your readiness in assessment mode. You should not go to the NSST with the intention of relearning core surface warfare officer skills or making up for the fact that you may have spent inadequate time on the bridge during your first department head tour. Instead, when you are in your first tour, seek out opportunities to be on the bridge, whether standing proficiency watches in open ocean or coastal waters, or standing officer of the deck for special evolutions and sea and anchor details. The shiphandling assessment will evaluate your individual skills and performance, not the ability of the watch team to support you. You must find opportunities to apply the Rules of the Road, use all the bridge tools including the ARPA and the VMS, and practice your own ability to direct an officer of the deck and conning officer to maneuver the ship. Talk with your commanding officer and seek to act as the decision-maker or conn coach during high-density traffic situations and restricted waters transits. Also, seek out opportunities to take the conn during pierwork so that you become comfortable with handling the ship's rudders, screws, or water-jets and to practice the skill set you will ultimately need should you go on to command. It is not enough to merely have your shiphandling letter signed by your commanding officer; you must seize every opportunity to become comfortable in your shiphandling skills.

Finally, a wise officer should note that the desire for command factors most prominently in those who ultimately succeed in the CA process. Desire equals drive and determination. Officers committed to their profession who fall short in the first attempt but then realistically confront their shortcomings and work to correct them emerge better off for their study and succeed at a high rate during subsequent attempts. So study hard, and good luck!

CAPT Peter Halvorsen is a career surface warfare officer with service in cruisers and destroyers. He commanded USS *Carney* (DDG 64) from November 2016 to April 2018. During his tenure in command, *Carney* completed three forward-deployed patrols in Sixth Fleet and earned the 2015–16 Arizona Memorial Trophy and the 2017 Destroyer Squadron Sixty Battle "E." CAPT Halvorsen also served two tours at the Surface Warfare Officers School. As a lieutenant commander, he served as a department head school leadership instructor and navigation and shiphandling instructor. Following his command tour, he served as the director of fleet training (N72) and as a command assessment and prospective commanding officer assessor.

PART II

THE DEPARTMENT HEAD

CHAPTER 3
Department Head Leadership
CAPT Joseph A. Gagliano, USN

ONE DAY AT SEA during my first division officer tour, I was standing the antisubmarine warfare coordinator watch during an integrated training team scenario. It was a typical multiwarfare training environment, where the ship faced threats on, above, and under the water simultaneously. The tactical action officer (TAO) was a new department head on board, and the captain sat alongside him at the front table to observe his performance. As the inbound attack intensified, the TAO drew inward into a quiet paralysis. The experienced captain turned to him and said just one word: "Lead."

This powerful moment summarizes so much of your department head tour. Some challenges build very quickly, such as the multiwarfare attack that day. Others build slowly over time and create problems so large and entrenched that it takes months to recover. No matter the volume or speed of the problem set, paralysis in the absence of leadership is debilitating. You have many responsibilities during this tour, but none is more important than leadership.

The good news is that you are not beginning cold. You likely have already had two division officer tours, seen two ships, worked for three or four commanding officers, and had several chiefs reporting to you. The Navy has invested leadership training in you, and most importantly, you have succeeded as a division officer. You are a journeyman in the naval service, poised to grow in the next professional stage of your career.

Concept of Leadership

Volumes have been written about the purpose of leadership. There is a cottage industry designed for novice leaders built on concise phrases to sum up a very challenging job requirement: leadership is making people do things they don't want to do; leadership is empowering people to accomplish their goals; leadership is helping those who are doing poorly to do well and those who are doing well to do even better; leadership is adjusting the sails. As a department head, you are no longer a novice leader. You are a professional, experienced leader now, so we can chart a different course. With a purpose-driven approach, let's consider leadership in the specific context of running a successful department.

Leadership versus Management

There is a clear difference between leadership and management. Both are important for building a successful department, and you must understand when to apply the right skills to the right problem set.

In the Navy, we manage programs, but we *lead* people. A good manager studies a program's requirements and ensures compliance. They apply the right resources in the right places to reach the program's goals. Conversely, a good leader understands the enormously complex people who work for them. They understand an individual's strengths and weaknesses, their motivations and demotivations, their capabilities and capacities. A great leader studies how their people amplify or weaken each other's effectiveness. This leader can apply the right people in the right combination at the right time to the right problem. Managing programs is by its nature uniform; leadership involves variables that are complex and continuously changing.

Given these differences, you can see the shortcoming of limiting yourself to management alone. You can manage your department to compliance, but you must lead your way to excellence. Compliance stems from asking, "What is the requirement?" Excellence comes from asking, "After we meet the requirement, what more can we be?" No program tells you that.

Inborn Quality or Learned Skill

There is an eternal debate over whether leaders are born or made. We all remember children during our youth who had certain characteristics that inspired followers. More than simply compelling others, they had an intrinsic magnetism about them. Does that mean that we cannot develop into leaders? Certainly not. Everyone benefits from leadership development. With formal leadership training and on-the-job experience, mediocre leaders become good ones, and good leaders become great ones.

We often view great Navy leaders through this lens, assuming they were always that way. When we hear about contemporary leaders, we rarely learn about the training and experience they gained along the way. Instead of seeing leaders as a product of the Navy, we presume they possess some inborn ability or natural talent. Friedrich Nietzsche best captured this effect in assessing how people see Greek temples: "In the case of everything perfect, we are accustomed to abstain from asking how it became: we rejoice in the present fact as though it came out of the ground by magic."[1] At best, ignoring a leader's education and experience leaves us with an illusion of magic. At worst, it makes us disciples of mythology, where leaders appear with a miraculous suddenness.

In the final analysis, we serve in a professional Navy that centers on mission accomplishment. Our Sailors, when led by competent leaders, hardly care whether their skills are natural or developed. They simply want to be led well. For you, the debate of inborn quality or learned skill matters even less. You are beginning a job where leadership is a requirement.

Leadership as a Division Officer versus a Department Head

Your experience leading a division provides the foundation for leading a department. To be sure, there is a difference between leadership as a division officer and department head.

You are now leading officers. This charge might seem simple since you are one, but not all officers are the same as you. Using your own success as a model will not replicate in everyone, and your motivations, interests, capabilities, and weaknesses likely will be different than theirs. Additionally, officers' egos must be considered differently than those of chiefs and Sailors. Officers have education and experiences that make them confident in their abilities—oftentimes to a fault—and they value their professional reputation. When your words or actions question their abilities or threaten their reputation, particularly when done publicly, you may create long-lasting unintended consequences. The benefit derived from responsible, accountable officers carrying out your tasking far outweighs the cost of ego management, but this factor simply is too important to dismiss.

You also are leading with increased responsibility. Division officer leadership is something of a training ground, where your division leading chief petty officer was charged with training you and acting as a safety net. They likely had side conversations with your department head to ensure you did not fail catastrophically. You no longer enjoy this luxury. As will be noted in subsequent chapters on your relationship with the captain and executive officer, you are expected to perform consistently without this safety net.

Seeing how your first department head and chief kept you on track, you now have a responsibility to pay it forward. You must give your division officers every chance to succeed and develop into future department heads. Their successes are your successes; their failures are yours too. That certainly is true in day-to-day business, and nothing reflects your leadership more than their overall success as a division officer.

CHAPTER 3

Qualities of Department Head Leadership

Good leaders come in many shapes and sizes, and you should spend time contemplating some of the most important qualities of leadership required for your department head tour. You likely will not score yourself perfectly across the board, so self-inventory is valuable to consider areas for improvement ahead of and during your time in this important assignment.

Integrity

Integrity is the foundation of leadership in every capacity. I cannot emphasize this enough—your integrity must be absolute. You can make mistakes, and you are not expected to know everything, but your Sailors can never see your integrity waver. If you demonstrate a lack of integrity, they will take it as license to do the same.

The biggest challenge with integrity stumbles is that rebuilding your credibility after the fact is very difficult. Moreover, the effect of integrity lapses is not linear across multiple infractions. A pattern of integrity failures will be interpreted as your true character, and that perception is nearly impossible to reverse. John Paul Jones's "great truth" is eternal: "In one word, every commander should keep constantly before him the great truth, that to be well obeyed, he must be perfectly esteemed."

Fidelity to "Right"

Doing the right thing should be straightforward. What makes it complicated are the stories we tell ourselves to justify other choices. Behavior theorists refer to this as "cognitive dissonance," where the disconnect between what we ought to do and what we want to do causes us to alter one to match the other. In effect, when we choose to do the wrong thing, we convince ourselves that we had no other choice. Make no mistake about it—when faced with a choice between right and wrong, it is a choice.

Sailors want to do the right thing. Not all Sailors seek the more difficult road, but they want to have pride in their work. You can help them do both. For those lured by shortcuts, you clarify their options by establishing a reputation of accepting nothing less than right. We hope all Sailors would want the same, but if you cannot convince them to want it, you can foster an expectation that you demand it. When you set clear expectations, they will follow.

Authenticity

Department head assignments can make seemingly grounded officers do strange things. The transition from division officer to department head motivates some to begin role playing. They take on a different persona, doing an impression of a department head. For serious professionals, there is no room for role playing. Say what you mean, and mean what you say.

To be sure, you will change in the course of your department head tour, but in reality, this change is growth. This growth cannot be forced any more than a child can make themselves taller; it happens over time. In the meantime, there are two things you can do to facilitate this growth. First, start thinking about yourself as a department head before you report on board. Seeing yourself this way helps you acclimate to this role internally and exhibit it externally. Second, be yourself. You were selected for department head because of your strengths and qualities. Build on them, and you will become better than you can imagine. Besides, Sailors instinctively sense posing, which makes you more difficult to follow. "Fake it 'til you make it" is a fool's mantra.

Emotional Intelligence

As warfighters, we customarily see our ships as unemotional work environments. We cannot avoid the fact, however, that ships are manned by real people with real emotions. Your ability to understand these emotions and their effect on performance, decision-making, and interpersonal relationships is referred to as "emotional intelligence." These immeasurable factors have equally immeasurable effects on the success of your department.

Emotional intelligence comprises two parts. First, you must sense and understand the emotions of others. Emotional intelligence demands that you see the world through someone else's eyes. It requires you to discern what motivates others and what frustrates them. In effect, you must embody empathy. Second, you must lead by dealing with the emotions of others. Emotions can be assets or liabilities. Assets should be channeled toward accomplishing tasks, and liabilities should be steered away from certain areas to prevent them from becoming obstacles. Conquering these two parts—understanding and dealing with emotions—occurs serially. You must identify them before dealing with them. Developing the ability to channel emotions toward a common goal is an invaluable advanced leadership skill.

Emotional intelligence also includes the ability to understand and deal with your own emotions. Even-keeled leadership requires composure, which is not a passive skill. It requires you to identify emotions that threaten stable leadership and dispatch them. Your department head tour assuredly will be filled with its fair share of bad news. You will be disappointed, and you will disappoint. Some circumstances will be out of your control, and other mistakes will have been entirely avoidable. Average leaders react by emotional instinct; good leaders pause, think about their emotions, moderate hazardous ones, and accentuate beneficial ones.

Confidence and Humility

There is a fine line between confidence and arrogance. Sailors want to follow a confident department head, but they detest working for someone who is arrogant. Knowing the difference is an important leadership quality.

It is entirely within your capability to be both confident and humble. Knowing your own capabilities does not require you to brag about them. Moreover, you can possess certain skillsets without disparaging others for lacking them. One of the best parts of working in a professional organization like the Navy is that other professionals recognize you are capable. You need neither advertise yourself nor denigrate others.

There also are benefits to acknowledging your limitations. No one is good at everything, so there is no harm to admitting it. Letting your team know where you need assistance invites your subject matter experts to step forward and empowers them to contribute to collective success. Sailors take pride in their specializations; let them help you.

As you become more senior, fighting off arrogance becomes more challenging. By the end of your department head tour, you likely will be the "third in command" of your ship. The Navy is built on a tradition of rank and deference that underlies good order, extended to you even more so during this tour. They have an important place in our culture and organization, but you must keep them in perspective. These courtesies can be an arrogance trap, and the effect is compounded by a sense of entitlement. It is a human condition to inflate ourselves, so it takes discipline to resist haughtiness.

Skills of Department Head Leadership

The beginning of your department head tour is about mastering how to lead a functioning department. A successful department head tour is marked by leading your Sailors to a better place than where you began. You will require advanced leadership skills to get there.

Self-Assessment

In your first month as a department head, you should spend a great deal of time assessing your department. What do you do well? What is particularly difficult? Who are your star players? Who tries but struggles to perform? Who does not try at all? Your department leading chief petty officer should help you with this assessment. They can provide observations across paygrades—from E-1 to O-3—and relay how effective your khaki are in leading Sailors. The most important part of this assessment is honesty. There will be times when you must sell the performance of your department or the quality of your khaki leadership, but self-assessment is about determining what needs improvement.

Self-assessment should be a continuous process throughout your department head tour. Your department will perform tasks for the first time as a team, people will come and go and create new team dynamics, and even the most stable team will have to fight complacency at some time. As you conduct these continuous self-assessments, beware this fallacy: "We completed it safely, so we must have done it right." This logic fails every time. Just because you did not run aground does not mean you navigated well. Sometimes, we simply get lucky, and you do not want to lead your department based on luck. Every team has areas for improvement, so find yours.

Priority-Setting

As the department head, you hold the special position of setting your department's priorities. Think about that: you will establish what one-fifth of the ship will focus their time on, in both the short and long term. That authority should both energize and frighten you, and it is the reason priority-setting is leadership rather than management. You are leading people to apply collective effort in accomplishing your most important goals.

First, ensure your priorities complement those of the commanding officer (CO). They will not mimic them, but each should support the CO's intent. In some cases, your priorities will be a more detailed application of the CO's priorities. For example, the CO may say their top priority is to successfully complete the basic phase, so the weapons officer could say their top priority is completing the cruise missile tactical qualification, and the operations officer could say theirs is to complete the navigation certification. In other cases, your priorities will be below the captain's radar. The CO may not spend any time thinking about the oil analysis program, but if the chief engineer has an ineffective program, they know it will undercut every engineering certification.

Second, your priorities must be specific. Lofty platitudes can be attractive—who would argue against saying the highest priority is safety?—but if your officers and chiefs cannot actualize your top priority on a daily basis, it is not very effective. A good measure of effectiveness occurs at your department's daily officers' call. If your khaki leadership can articulate how they are applying manpower to pursue your specific priorities, then you are doing it right.

Third, your priorities must convey prioritization. This concept seems simple, but it evades many. It is much easier to say that everything is a priority than to say that important things are not. Doing so is lazy leadership that provides no guidance for your khaki leaders who live in a world of constrained time and manpower. As the department head, it is your responsibility to tell them what is a priority . . . and what is not.

Stephen Covey provides a useful model for assessing the priorities of your department. With his model, you will plot each task in four quadrants: quadrant 1, important and urgent; quadrant 2, important and not urgent; quadrant 3, not important and urgent; and quadrant 4, not important and not urgent. By outlining these quadrants, you can quickly identify where your department's time is best spent. Quadrant 1 identifies necessity, quadrant 2 highlights effectiveness, quadrant 3 represents distraction, and quadrant 4 identifies waste. You may need to write tasks in each quadrant at first, but over time, you will learn to use it simply as a lens to filter the urgent from crowding out the important and spot work to be ignored. Put another way, this lens helps you to carve out time for tasks that are important but not urgent and to discard tasks that are neither urgent nor important.[2]

Communicating Your Vision

You should spend a great deal of time examining the trajectory of your department. While you are in department head school, think about the department you want to lead, what it looks like, where you want it to go, what you want to turn over to your relief, and what you want your department to accomplish to get there. This is your vision for your department.

Vision without planning is an illusion. You must convey this vision to your officers, chiefs, and Sailors if you want them to pursue it for you. Lay out your vision, and return to it often. Measure your department's performance toward this vision, and tell them how they are doing. You will unleash unmapped potential within very talented people when you tell them what you seek. They will work in unexpected ways and uncover unexpected methods to contribute to team goals. Set them loose.

Culture-Building

The importance of building a healthy culture within your department cannot be overstated. All aspects of your department—personnel, maintenance, training, warfighting readiness—are affected by culture. A toxic culture tears apart your department from the inside, and a strong culture allows you to achieve successes that you do not even know are achievable. If the three most important factors in real estate are "location, location, and location," then the three most important factors for leading large organizations are "culture, culture, and culture."

Your department culture should foster a healthy work environment. Healthy work environments are characterized by trust between officers, chiefs, and Sailors, professionalism, a shared sense of purpose, professional development, mutual respect, and tolerance. Threats to your department's culture appear and reappear like weeds, widespread and often hidden, so you must thoroughly assess and regularly reassess your department to root them out. As the department head, you have a responsibility to identify those exhibiting toxic characteristics—abrasive leadership, discrimination, micromanagement—and realign them with our Navy's values.

During your incoming turnover, ask the executive officer for an opportunity to review the most recent command climate survey results.[3] This survey is required within ninety days after every change of command and annually afterward. The survey results are not categorized by department, but the anonymous comments usually reveal departments with areas for improvement. Even if it has been more than six months since the last survey, the comments remain relevant, because it takes a long time to alter command climates. In addition to building a strong culture for your department's success, your captain and executive officer will appreciate you contributing to a better overall command climate.

Building an effective department climate cannot depend on words alone. You must lead your department to adopt it as their own, so the culture becomes part of them. You are in a position now where you set the tone for "how we do things," which, when fostered consistently, turns into "how I do things." It becomes part of their identity, and this association creates an invaluable reserve during the toughest times. If you want Sailors to support your culture instinctively, you need them to make the right decision based on identity rather than whether it benefits them personally. The strength of their compass relies on a sense of who they are and the group to which they belong. In this endeavor, your success will be most apparent in new arrivals. New Sailors who quickly emulate your department's values indicate you have built a culture that is real and perpetuating.[4]

CHAPTER 3

Innovation

After you have mastered running your department efficiently, you will be ready to lead advanced change to make it even better. Good leaders run their department well; great leaders innovate their way to the next level.

In the arc of your naval career, you first learn the principles of our trade—how we operate ships and how we produce readiness. After you have conquered our time-tested methods, you should begin thinking about how we can make it better. You are at an important nexus in your career, where you are experienced enough to understand the foundational principles of operating ships but not so old that you are stuck in your ways. You will find opportunities to innovate in all aspects of your department, and your Sailors are a great source for what can be done better. Just ask them. In addition to improving your department, you will inject a good shot of energy into day-to-day shipboard life. People are invigorated when they are on the leading edge.

Your captain is looking for good ideas, so bring them. Your ideas, however, must be thought through. Ensure you take time to develop a plan that includes risk management. Change always involves some risk of failure, but

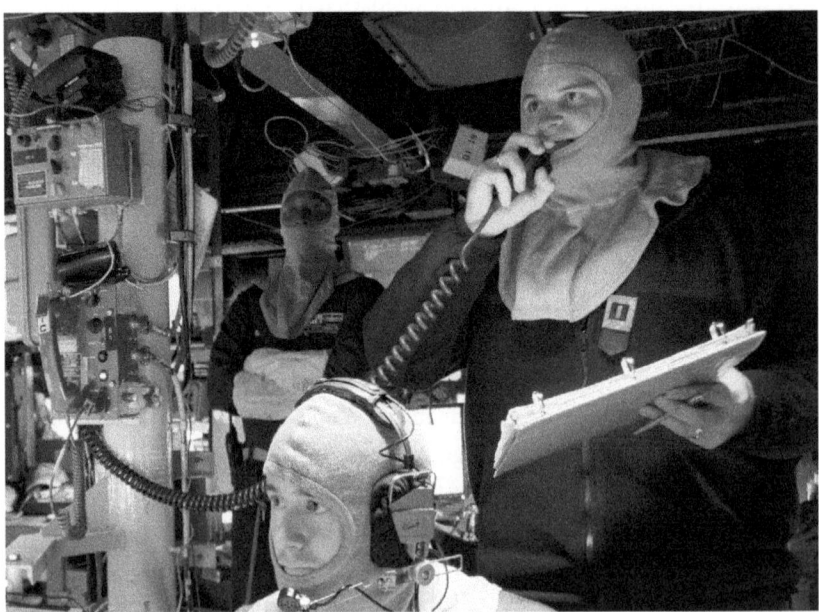

3-1. Department heads should take every opportunity to practice and hone their warfighting leadership skills.

U.S. Navy photo by Mass Communication Specialist 1st Class Fred Gray IV/Released

like investing, there is a relationship between risk and reward. As long as your plan includes methods to control risk, the captain will support your initiative.

Warfighting Leadership

Keep in mind that you are a warfighter first. If past is prologue, warfighting leadership will be the most important but least employed skillset of your department head tour.

Routine administration and management can make your department seem like a business, but you are not running a business. Your ship is designed to do one thing—fight and win naval battles—so your day-to-day work should be focused on manning, training, and equipping your department to be an integral part of your warship. You cannot run your department as a business manager and expect your Sailors to follow you instinctively as a warfighting leader. They need to see you as a warfighting leader first and a sound manager second.

For leadership in battle itself, the only way to become a better warfighting leader is to practice warfighting leadership. Take every opportunity to train with your team in the role your captain expects you to perform in combat. Whether you are the assigned Condition I TAO, officer of the deck, engineering control officer, or damage control officer, do not pass up an opportunity to stand that position during training. Hone your skills as a warfighting leader, and your Sailors will soon see you as one. During crisis, you want them to follow you without hesitation.

Final Thoughts

Pablo Picasso considered artwork ever-changing. He would not begin painting with the picture carefully thought out beforehand. He believed the picture changed as the painter's thoughts changed. Your leadership as a department head is much the same. Try as you might, you cannot know at the beginning of your tour how you will lead your Sailors at the end. Your leadership will evolve over time, undergoing changes inspired by real-life events. As long as you stay anchored in your principles and strive to do the right thing every day, you will leave proud of your leadership performance.

Your department head tour is not your first job in the Navy, and for the vast majority of naval officers, it will not be your last. This assignment is a journeyman position that sits amid a continuum of leadership development. It leverages experience from your division officer tours, initial shore duty, and college education, and it serves as a developmental tour toward future service as an executive officer and captain. So, invest time developing your leadership skills for more senior positions. Once your department head duties become second nature, talk with your executive officer and captain about their jobs. Observe how they lead you and your fellow department heads. Develop your whole-of-ship perspective and note the challenges of leading heads of departments in which you have no experience. You will soon find yourself in that very demanding role, and it is never too early to prepare.

CAPT Joseph A. Gagliano is a surface warfare officer, naval strategist, and politico-military specialist. At sea, he has served as the commander of Task Force 65, commodore of Destroyer Squadron 60, commanding officer and executive officer in USS *Independence* (LCS 2), and combat systems officer and weapons officer in USS *Cole* (DDG 67). Ashore, he has served as the director for defense policy and strategy for the National Security Council at the White House, a strategist on the Joint Staff in the Asia political-military affairs directorate, and the strategic planning team leader for OPNAV N00X. Captain Gagliano holds a PhD and a master's degree in international relations from the Fletcher School of Law and Diplomacy at Tufts University and a master's degree in national security and strategic studies from the U.S. Naval War College.

NOTES

1. Friedrich Nietzsche, *Human, All Too Human: A Book for Free Spirits* (Cambridge, UK: Cambridge University Press, 1986), 80.
2. Franklin Covey, "Habit 3: Put First Things First," Franklin Covey Co., 21 January 2021, https://www.franklincovey.com/the-7-habits/habit-3/.
3. The official name for this survey is the Defense Equal Opportunity Management Institute Organizational Climate Survey.
4. For an excellent discussion on the psychology of building culture, see Angela Duckworth, *Grit: The Power of Passion and Perseverance* (New York: Simon and Schuster, 2016), chapter 12.

CHAPTER 4

Management

CDR Sam O'Neil, USN

MANAGEMENT AND LEADERSHIP are often discussed as interchangeable skill sets. In reality, management and leadership exist in both a codependent and a mutually exclusive relationship. Not all managers are leaders, and not all leaders are managers, but without question, as a department head you will be expected to master the art and science of both. Although there is no single approach to effectively manage your department, this chapter provides a few suggestions.

As exciting as it is to finally lead your department, it can also be daunting. You may find yourself quickly overwhelmed by the sheer number of requirements you must balance—the emails you must read and respond to, the number of programs and projects that require your oversight, the countless checklists and certifications, all while managing personnel matters. You could work around the clock and still not tackle everything on your to-do list. Unlike when you were a division officer (DIVO), you cannot solely focus on divisional or departmental matters. You must be aware of requirements across all departments so you can effectively accomplish the mission. Planning for several contingencies and being organized will help you respond accordingly when there is a significant change in schedule or mission.

Where to Start

You may inherit a strong department that requires little rudder change to the way it already functions. Conversely, you may inherent a department that requires more attention, oversight, and direction. Regardless, as you progress in your career, how you manage one department will differ from how you manage your next department.

Know Your Responsibilities
The list below offers a starting point for understanding the scope of your responsibilities. No one document will completely capture all of your

responsibilities and requirements, so listing and organizing them will be helpful.

- Review the *Standard Organization and Regulations of the U.S. Navy*, which details your specific department head role and responsibilities.
- Walk your spaces and know your equipment.
- Understand your maintenance requirements.
- Familiarize yourself with inspection requirements and off-ship reporting requirements.
- Review the short-range and long-range schedules.
- Know your routine administrative requirements, such as evaluations and fitness reports.
- Identify items that require your attention daily and weekly.
- Identify tasks that only you can do and cannot be delegated.

Establish a Drumbeat

Regardless of whether you're in a maintenance availability, training cycle, or under way, establishing a routine will keep you focused and organized and help you prioritize your time. It will also help your department leadership manage their time, since they know that you will be routinely checking in on those items. Your commanding officer (CO) and executive officer (XO) may have specific priorities that they want you to incorporate into your drumbeat as well. Below are just a few examples of items you should include in your daily and weekly drumbeats.

No matter how busy your day, there are items that require your attention *daily*:

- Review eight o'clock reports.
- Review and approve well-written jobs.
- Walk your spaces.
- Review operating logs and identify discrepancies.
- Review status of casualty reports and critical parts.
- Tackle tasks that only you can complete and that cannot be delegated.
- Prepare your "must do" list for the following day(s).

It can be easy to want to skip these weekly items when something urgent arises, but do not make it a habit.

- Conduct maintenance and material management (3M) spot checks.
- Participate in zone inspections.
- Review current ship's maintenance project list and ship's force work lists.
- Review programs.
- Review plans of action and milestones.
- Review and update instructions.
- Review training reports and qualification statuses.

Best Practices

Communicate Effectively
Communication is a process, and you must continuously seek feedback. Effectively communicating up, down, and across the chain of command can make managing your department easier. Simply stated, when your team understands your expectations, they can not only meet them, but also exceed them.

Keep the Commanding Officer Informed
There are several ways to keep the CO informed, including informal face-to-face interactions and emails and formal on-ship and off-ship reports such as eight o'clock reports or casualty reports. Which methods of communication the CO prefers will differ from command to command, and communicating through several mediums will be important. When speaking or sending an email to the CO, it is helpful if you lead with a subject or a "bottom line up front" and offer a quick snapshot of the issue at hand. Be clear on whether you are only providing information or if you require a decision on a recommended course of action. Always offer the CO several courses of action along with your recommendation. Consolidate reports when you can so you can effectively manage your CO's time. Like you, the CO is juggling an endless list of tasks, so be clear about what you expect from them when sharing information. This will also help keep you and your CO organized.

Use the Executive Officer and Command Master Chief
The XO and command master chief (CMC) not only can help influence and shape how you deliver information to the CO and your department but also

can provide useful perspectives on how you manage your department, particularly regarding personnel matters. If you have concerns about your manning or personnel or have scheduling conflicts, the XO and CMC can help. Remember, the XO was in a department head role and can provide you with their best management practices and lessons learned. The CMC can offer you insight specifically about your chiefs' strengths and weaknesses, inform you on how your chiefs are managing in the mess, give you candid feedback about your management practices, and share how your department is viewed in the chiefs' mess.

Create a Department Triad
You may find it helpful to create a mini-triad comprising an assistant department head (often a chief warrant officer or limited duty officer) and departmental leading chief petty officer. Lean on them. Your triad can help you prioritize and reinforce your departmental requirements. They can help you identify potential roadblocks and offer ways to navigate around them. Similarly, your triad can provide backup for one another on important departmental and shipwide matters.

Walk the Deckplates
It is easy to get tied to your computer. However, walking your spaces throughout the day will give you the opportunity to observe how your team conducts maintenance and evolutions and executes the plan of the day. Are your Sailors busy, or are they sitting around waiting for instruction? Are your Sailors following strict procedural compliance? Are they following safety measures? Do your Sailors understand their role and the importance of their tasking? Talking to your Sailors informally and individually provides you an opportunity to spot-check information you and the command previously disseminated. Ask your Sailors how they interpreted the guidance they received. You will sometimes find that pieces of important information were misconstrued as it was passed down the chain of command. Walking your spaces and talking to your Sailors will provide you more opportunities to observe what, if any, adjustments you need to implement in your department.

Meet with Your Department Regularly
Whether you decide to hold monthly or weekly department head calls or to participate in a division's quarters is up to you. Providing a forum for your Sailors to openly ask you questions gives you an opportunity to reiterate and clarify departmental and command guidance, provide additional context to a decision or situation, demonstrate transparency, and validate their concerns.

MANAGEMENT

4-1. A chief engineer provides damage control training. Meeting with your department regularly is one way to reiterate and clarify departmental guidance.
U.S. Navy photo by Mass Communication Specialist 2nd Class Lyle Wilkie/Released

It also gives your Sailors an opportunity to offer you constructive feedback and useful ideas. Investing your time in face-to-face communications with your team can save you time elsewhere.

Streamline Communication
The CO prefers to receive consolidated reports from you; likewise, you should insist your DIVOs and chiefs provide you with consolidated reports. An end-of-day checkout does not need to occur exactly at the end of the day with Sailors waiting for you to give permission to their DIVO for them to depart for the day. Similarly, if there are things you must work on privately, it is okay to tell your leadership that you intend to work with your door closed and should only be interrupted in certain circumstances.

Make the Most of Each Meeting
Familiarize yourself with requirements and deconflict any issues ahead of formal meetings. Be prepared to discuss and confirm schedules, whether it be at a planning board for training, department head call, or routine maintenance meetings. The best department heads know the criteria to accomplish mission requirements and think through possible second-, third-, and fourth-order effects of a decision.

Be Responsive

Whether it is an email, a text, or a voicemail, do your best to respond to all correspondence, especially if it is directed to you specifically. A simple acknowledgment of receipt will go a long way. Managing your email inbox will be a constant battle, but it is something that cannot be ignored for any extended period of time.

Helpful Communication Tools

- Create a departmental philosophy that is tailored to your department and that complements and aligns with the CO's philosophy.
- Establish and post an easily accessible quad/tri chart (see figure 4.1). Highlight information that you are tracking, and share important departmental information with your team and other departments.
- Post an unclassified version of opportune times for leave periods outside of normal predeployment, postdeployment, or holiday stand-down periods.

ENGINEERING
15May15

Current Operations
- INSURV preps
- E-3/E-4 Evals- in progress
- Eng Standing Order Revision- with admin
- Safety Settings List
- Electrical Safety Instruction Update
- Tag Out Instruction Update
- Drain fluids from GTGs (support future removal)
- Special Tools Inventory- in progress
- IPDS/CBR Offload (ongoing)
- CSMP scrub
- Chill Water Assessment (10-15 May)
- Aluminum Superstructure Assessment (3-22 May)
- AFFF/CO2/Halon/CMWDS Assessment (15- 22 May)
- System secure plan (F/M, C/W, LP Air, A/C, etc)
- Start engine interference removal (11 May- 26 May)

Big Rocks
- Antenna Removal (week of 18 May)
- LAN Migration (18 May)
- GTE removal sked (26 May-17 July)
- Grenade Offload (29 May)
- MA-597 (Casualty Power Cable Replace to all SWBDs) install- (29-31 May)
- Change 2B F/O Recirc Valve (end of May/beginning June)
- INSURV (22-23 Jun)
- I-CMAV (15 Jun-30 Sep)

Future Operations/Events
- HPAC/LPAC/LP Air Assessment (17-23 May)
- MRG/Shafting Assessment (TBD)
- Main/Secondary Drainage Assessment (18-22 May)
- Seawater Systems Assessment (18-22 May)
- MHVC Stations and Valve Assessment (18-22 May)
- ERAT Visit (18-29 May)
- HVAC clean and survey/ Replace 4 FCUs (01 Jun start)
- ECSE equipment removal (15 Jun-3 Jul)
- CHT System Assessment (25-29 May)

Figure 4-1. **Quad/tri chart.**

Delegate, Delegate, Delegate

As much as you may want to, you cannot manage your department on your own. Delegate tasks to your team early and often.

Gainfully Employ Every Member of Your Team

Assign and empower officers, chiefs, and petty officers to manage your programs. Provide them with clear guidance and ensure your team is equipped with proper resources and authority to manage their program or complete their tasking. Routinely spot-check each program and hold the program manager accountable. Ultimately, you are responsible for the effectiveness of all your programs, but the program manager should oversee the day-to-day management of them.

Follow Up

Disseminating tasks to your team is not enough. You must engage in meaningful dialogue and follow up on those tasks. Ask thoughtful questions and allow for open communication. No one likes to deliver bad news to the boss, but how you respond to bad news will impact how much information your team will share with you and when.

Provide Timely Feedback

Your DIVOs or chiefs may need you to review an instruction, award, or other administrative work. Provide clear and timely feedback. Just as you look to the XO for guidance, your departmental leadership will seek feedback from you.

Build Strong Relationships

On-Ship Relationships

A cohesive team will contribute to your ship's success. Depending on your role, you may need to work with one department more than another, but no single department is more or less important than another.

Your Peers

On the best ships, department heads play on the same team and are not in competition with one another. Take care of each other. Share information, offer constructive feedback, and provide backup for one another. Likewise, if there is a meeting or training event that requires a representative from your department, do your best to support; showing up demonstrates that you support one another's requirements. You will observe large gaps of information exist across departments, and sharing information and deconflicting at the department head level will instill the XO and CO with total confidence that all departments are working toward common shipboard goals.

CHAPTER 4

Department Khaki
Similarly, build a strong rapport with your department khaki. Leverage your DIVOs' and chiefs' strengths, and seek their feedback. Sailors thrive in cohesive departments. You can realize some significant gains by occasional off-ship synchs over lunch to remove the distractions from the day-to-day events and allow for better communications. To recognize their commitment to you, offer to pick up the check!

Khaki outside Your Department
You should have open and fluid communication with other chiefs and DIVOs. You will require the support of other departments to accomplish your mission. This does not mean directly tasking someone from outside your department, but rather coordinating support through their respective department head. Coordinating support through the proper channels will strengthen your relationships and not convolute priorities. Likewise, offering support to other departments will go a long way when you need support from them.

Off-Ship Relationships
Take every opportunity to meet with key people face to face, and if you can't meet in person, call them on the phone and be responsive via email.

Peers across the Pier
No matter your role, you will find it helpful to build strong relationships with fellow department heads on other ships, particularly those who share your specific job. Establishing a supportive network will help inform you of best practices, share lessons learned, and connect you to a vast web of other important points of contact.

Off-Ship Chain of Command
Get to know your immediate superior in command (ISIC), including both the commander and the staff member whose portfolio aligns with your department. They can be the biggest advocates for you and your team, especially during the training cycle. Remember to keep your CO informed when you are reporting any items of concern to your ISIC, ideally before you report them off the ship.

Maintenance Team
Cultivate a strong connection with your port engineer, combat systems engineer, and project manager. Some department heads rely on communicating their maintenance issues solely through the 3M coordinator and the ship's maintenance and material officer (SMMO), but if these personnel don't fully

understand the critical action items, they can become reprioritized. The SMMO is often a collateral duty on a smaller ship, and the officer may not be familiar with a piece of gear or equipment in your department, so it is important to take the time to work with the maintenance team to ensure that you receive the right level of support.

Trainers and Certifiers

Get to know your trainers and certifiers. Almost every inspection is open book. There are no secrets, just untapped resources. Outside activities like the afloat training groups, Board of Inspection and Survey, readiness assessment teams, and type material inspection team can provide you with a multitude of references and lessons learned. Effectively managing means having the most updated reference material, knowing where to find it, and what to anticipate for the event.

Optimize Departmental Trackers

Trackers are important, but they can also be cumbersome. With that said, trackers are only as good as the quality of input, and if you have too many, your team may spend a disproportionate amount of time updating trackers that might become useless. Thankfully, you do not need to recreate the wheel. As a department head, you are required to routinely review and route many reports that are already generated.

Watch Team Replacement Plan

Your watch team replacement plan (WTRP) will go hand in hand with your monthly training report. Take time to critically assess each report and provide feedback to your team. You likely will find that keeping Sailors on track to earn qualifications is easier while deployed than in port. Use the WTRP as a shell for planning long-range, especially if your ship is scheduled for an extended maintenance availability with a significant number of seasoned personnel turning over. Look six months to twelve months downrange, and identify opportune times to send Sailors to required schools. Depending on your base location and ship schedule, it can be hard to request funding for schools at the last minute.

Leave/Temporary Assigned Duty Trackers

Develop a leave/temporary assigned duty (TAD) tracker and make it viewable to other departmental triads, warfare leads, and the training officer. A leave/TAD tracker can be critical in identifying potential personnel conflicts, especially during the training cycle. For example, the Repair 5 investigator might be in the supply department, but during light off assessment, they must be present to pass the main space fire drill. The message to the Sailor should not be "you cannot ever take leave," but rather, "You are a critical part of our team, and we would like you to take leave during a suitable timeframe instead."

Consider Developing a Plan of Action and Milestone
You may find it helpful to develop a plan of action and milestone (POA&M) as your ship is entering a maintenance availability, planning for an upcoming training cycle, or preparing for a periodic inspection (such as the Board of Inspection and Survey). Find a format that is easy to read and user-friendly. Often times, other ships will have a recently drafted POA&M that you can use as a starting point. One way to update and tailor your POA&M is to present it to your entire team and seek their candid feedback. What items or reminders need to be added to your plan? Rehearse the event in a tabletop format to identify any potential conflicts. What events can you run simultaneously, and do those events require the same personnel to support? A POA&M will help you identify critical path items and assess shortcomings so that you can address those issues early. Most importantly, a well-developed POA&M will help your team stay on target to meet major milestones.

Manage Stamina
Being a department head can be exhausting, and it may feel like you are in a sprint during your tour. However, the reality is that most of your Sailors are in a marathon. You might have eighteen- to twenty-four-month orders, but your Sailors could be in the same command for three to five years.

Take a Steady Strain
Successful commands do not "ramp up" for the training cycle or for deployment; they take a steady strain approach. A steady strain means that your department remains gainfully employed every day and benefits from department leadership preparing for upcoming events or evolutions well in advance. This helps ensure predictability in your department's daily battle rhythm. If there is time left in your day, start working on less urgent items.

Plan Ahead
Part of effectively managing your department is planning for each day. When Sailors report each morning, they should understand what is expected of them. There should be no surprises. For example, if you need your department to work late in support of an upcoming inspection, you should communicate that expectation in advance so they can make arrangements to support.

Go Home at a Reasonable Time

You may be tempted to stay well after working hours on board, but try to not make it a habit. Your team will see this and may also start working later because you are. If you must stay late to catch up on personal administration, ensure your team knows that you do not expect them to stay as well.

Incorporate Fun

You can quickly forget to have fun while managing your department. Find ways to incorporate fun into your schedule. Fostering camaraderie within your department and at divisional levels will build a more cohesive team that is easier to manage. It is also easy to drown in paperwork, but remember that how you handle stress and manage your department will influence your DIVOs' desires to one day be department heads. You are the best recruiter for your relief, so you want your job to be appealing.

- Plan for an off-ship departmental barbeque or bowling party.
- Eat lunch off-ship with your DIVOs and chiefs.
- Create a friendly competition between divisions.
- Find ways to publicly recognize individual team members for their hard work.

Conclusion

As with leadership, there is no cookie-cutter method to effectively manage your department. This chapter highlights a few tools and suggestions. There will always be too many requirements and not enough hours in the day to tackle every task. However, understanding your requirements, establishing a routine, effectively communicating, and building key relationships will assist you tremendously. Lean on your peers and other leaders on and off ship to help guide you. And remember to have fun!

CDR Samantha A. O'Neil served as chief engineer in USS *Preble* (DDG 88) and USS *Cowpens* (CG 63), where she was the recipient of the Navy and Marine Corps Association Leadership Award. Ashore, she served in the Commander's Action Group at Commander, Naval Surface Forces Pacific.

CHAPTER 5

Supporting the Executive Officer

CDR Robert C. Watts IV, USN

Working for Two Bosses: Captain and Executive Officer

AS A DIVISION OFFICER, you had one boss—your department head—but as a new department head, you will have two bosses: the commanding officer (CO) and the executive officer (XO). It may be tempting to view your relationship with the XO as secondary to your relationship with the CO. The captain is in command and signs your fitness report. Furthermore, your interactions with the captain will focus on your job's core functions, such as building the ship's schedule as operations officer, planning an exercise as plans and tactics officer, or managing repairs as chief engineer. Meanwhile, the XO will draw your attention and efforts toward some of the seemingly peripheral aspects of your position, such as editing your written work, evaluating the cleanliness of your spaces, assigning administrative tasks, and overseeing your maintenance program. But you should not consider one primary or secondary to the other. In other words, supporting the CO should not come at the expense of supporting the XO, and vice versa. Instead, supporting the XO goes hand in hand with supporting the CO and ensuring the success of your department and the command.

The relationship between a department head and the XO is critical to efficiently operating a warship and supporting the CO's vision; it is also important to one's development as a naval officer. The following sections will define the relationship between an XO and a department head, and then describe an XO's expectations of you as a department head, how to best support the XO, and how the XO can support you and your department.

Organizational Responsibilities and Relationships

Navy regulations define the XO's responsibilities and a department head's relationship with both the CO and XO. According to the *Standard Organization and Regulations of the U.S. Navy* (SORM, OPNAVINST 3120.32 [series]), the XO is "the direct representative of the Commanding Officer," "shall keep him/her informed of all significant matters pertaining to the command," and "shall be primarily responsible for the organization, performance of duty, and good order and discipline of the entire command." Within this wide remit, the SORM spells out specific duties, such as maintaining high morale, ensuring damage control readiness, overseeing personnel, administration, and training, promulgating the daily schedule, administering maintenance and security programs, and, as a catch-all, "[performing] such other duties as may be assigned." The XO is also colloquially referred to as the "second in command"; as the SORM articulates, "The Executive Officer shall assume command should the need arise."

The SORM outlines how a department head reports to both the CO and the XO. As "the representative of the Commanding Officer in matters pertaining to the department," each department head has "direct access to the Commanding Officer on matters specifically related to his/her department," such as operational readiness, equipment condition, and "any matters relating to the department which may affect the department, the command, or the Navy." Despite this broad relationship with the CO, a department head's organizational line of authority goes to the commanding officer via the XO. The

5-1. Khaki call is an important forum for the executive officer and department heads to communicate with ship leaders.

Photo by LTJG Marie Newkirk, USS John Paul Jones *public affairs officer*

SORM explains that department heads "will report to the Executive Officer for all administrative matters" but will also "advise the Executive Officer of all direct reports to the Commanding Officer." Elsewhere, the SORM reiterates that department heads "shall keep the executive officer appropriately informed" of reports to the commanding officer.

The Executive Officer's Expectations

As XO, I have three overarching expectations for my department heads: lead your department, work as a team with your fellow department heads, and manage time. Meeting these expectations is essential to running an effective ship and will set a positive example for your team to emulate.

Lead Your Department

As a department head, you will have the privilege of leading a team of professionals. To make the most of this opportunity, your XO will expect you to delegate tasks, know your people and equipment, manage your warfare areas, and own your spaces.

Delegate

Much like the XO, you will have too much to do, and you cannot do it all well by yourself. You must delegate. As a starting point, establish a departmental triad with your principal assistant (likely a second tour division officer or limited duty officer) supporting you like an XO would and your departmental leading chief petty officer serving as your senior enlisted advisor. Lean hard on them and share a common vision of the department's priorities and status. Lean hard on your division officers and chiefs, too. Assign tasks to them. Set clear deadlines and expectations for the final product. Follow up to check progress and ensure task accomplishment. Determine your priorities and articulate them to your team to help them manage their work. In turn, this will help you provide periodic updates to the XO.

Know Your People and Equipment

The XO will ask many questions about your personnel and the status of your equipment. You will work more closely with your Sailors and your gear than the XO ever will. Know your team, understand their issues, and advocate for them. The XO will depend on your judgment about their performance, discipline, training, and leave or special requests. With your equipment, the XO will similarly depend upon the technical expertise of you and your team. The XO likely will not have recent—or perhaps any—first-hand experience with your equipment; help them understand it.

Manage Your Programs

As a department head, you will be responsible for multiple warfare areas and programs. Delegate daily oversight of those programs to your division officers and chief petty officers, but do not neglect them. Use afloat self-assessment check sheets to help guide routine reviews of those warfare areas and programs. Start with your watch team replacement plan. If it is a vibrant and effective document, it will provide a foundation for enduring success and help you identify manning shortfalls, which is critical to program management. Early identification of manning gaps will enable you to work with the XO to find temporary and long-term manning solutions while there is time to correct them. The XO can best assist you if they know you will be updating an instruction, sending personnel to schools, or deconflicting schedules to conduct drills or exercises that will affect multiple departments.

Own Your Spaces

You will be responsible for many spaces, both topside and inside the ship. Own them. Walk them routinely and expect the XO will do the same. Evaluate them with attention to detail and a questioning attitude. Keep them clean, preserved, well lit, and secure for sea. Take the lead during cleaning stations. Show your division officers how you expect them and their Sailors to maintain their spaces. Embrace zone inspections and quickly fix any discrepancies found.

Teamwork

Effective cross-departmental cooperation at the department head level is a force multiplier, enabling a ship to more nimbly work through problems. The Royal Navy's equivalent of the SORM assigns responsibility to the XO for "activities which involve the co-ordination of two or more departments." In the U.S. Navy, your XO will expect you and the other department heads to cooperate effectively with minimal interference. The XO is well positioned, though, to see when department heads are not cooperating and, if needed, intervene.

Work Together, and Your Ship Will Succeed

Do not focus solely on your department. Work together with your fellow department heads. Help each other solve problems and provide fully developed options to the CO. Strive toward the overall success of your ship and its crew. Your cooperation, or lack thereof, will be apparent to the CO, XO, and your teams. Set the example; your department will follow your lead.

CHAPTER 5

Cross-Departmental Communications

Communicate often with your fellow department heads. Assume no one knows what you know. For example, one department head may not know to share specific and important details of an upcoming inspection with another department head and how the inspection could impact more than just their department. Share a common operational picture. Overshare. Include other department heads on emails that might pertain to them, but remember that speaking in person or on the phone could reduce confusion and ensure understanding.

Operational Example

Cross-departmental relationships affect mission readiness. For example, the relationship between the chief engineer, operations officer, and supply officer can be critical. The chief engineer will inevitably need repair parts and will know which ones are most important. The operations officer will know the ship's schedule, to include replenishments at sea or helicopter deck hits. The supply officer will know how to expedite parts and get them to the ship. The XO will expect all three to work together, communicate, share ideas, and think creatively to expeditiously get this mission-impacting part to the ship. If this coordination is not happening, the XO will hew closely to the Royal Navy's approach and compel cross-departmental communication and cooperation.

Help a New or Struggling Peer

Throughout your tour, you will evolve from being the new department head requiring or seeking advice from more experienced department heads to becoming the department head that new department heads seek. As you become a veteran department head, share best practices with a new shipmate learning the ropes and provide constructive feedback to a struggling peer. You and your command will not succeed when one of your fellow department heads stumbles, so take care of each other.

Manage Time

Time is a limited resource; use it wisely. The XO is responsible for the ship's daily schedule but will expect you to carefully use the time they allot. Plan thoroughly, execute effectively, and use your time efficiently. If you find it difficult to manage the time allocated, seek out the XO for help. It is better to lean forward and ask for your XO's assistance than to wait for the XO to notice you struggling.

Plan Thoroughly

Each week, you and your fellow department heads will meet with the XO to solidify the schedule of the weeks ahead in the XO's planning board for training (PB4T). Although the operations officer leads schedule planning, each department head should actively and cooperatively contribute. Provide schedule inputs early. Ensure these requests accurately reflect the resources required, such as time, people, equipment, and briefings. Communicate early with other department heads if your event will require their people or might inhibit an overlapping event. Devise, implement, and support a process that enables department heads and warfare leads to review the schedule, identify conflicts, and resolve them prior to the formal meeting. Advanced preparation will ensure that PB4T is the culmination of your coordination rather than a starting point for it.

Execute Effectively
The XO will measure your and your team's effectiveness by assessing the execution of an evolution. Start events on time with the right people and the right equipment. If a long period of time has elapsed or if you have newer watchstanders conducting the evolution, build additional time into your plan. Ensure your team is prepared to execute. Hold your people accountable if they are not timely and prepared. Finish on time. Aggressively enforce safety and procedural compliance, so your team can execute smoothly and correctly the first time without injuring Sailors or damaging equipment. Your own timeliness, preparation, and attention to safety and procedural compliance will set the example for your department.

Use Time Efficiently
The XO is responsible for maximizing efficiency throughout the ship, so how you use time either contributes to or distracts from that goal. Make the most of the time you have, particularly when it comes to leading your team or cooperating with other department heads. View routine events such as CO/department head meetings, XO/department head meetings, khaki call, and departmental meetings as forums for communicating messages to and receiving messages from other leaders or your own team. In these forums, listen attentively, take notes, and engage. Be prepared, and have a plan for what you want to convey. A few minutes of planning and a well-crafted and effectively delivered message can have a significant impact on maximizing efficiency.

Supporting the Executive Officer

Your XO will have a unique background, personality, and expectations. The CO's expectations of and relationship with the XO will also be unique to their own background, personality, and the circumstances of your ship. These factors are beyond your control, but you should recognize and understand them. As early as your check-in with the XO, you will assess their personality and learn about their background and expectations. If the XO does not lay out ground rules for working with them, ask questions. These questions could include:

- How do you assign tasking—email, verbal, face-to-face, multiple methods? What follow-up do you expect on tasking progress, obstacles, and completion?
- How accessible are you? What are your working hours in-port and under way?
- What information or contributions do you expect from your department heads at XO/department head meetings and khaki call?
- What is the process for routing administrative work to you and the CO?
- How do you prefer to communicate when you are off the ship?
- How do you manage the schedule? How should (and may) I provide short-notice inputs or changes inside the time frame of the normal scheduling process?
- What routine reports do you expect?
- How often and when should I speak with you during the day? Should I check out with you at the end of the day?
- How often and when do you meet with the CO on a typical day?

Although each XO may have different answers to these questions and different approaches to the XO/department head relationship, any XO will expect your support in three ways: keep them informed, dominate your assigned tasking and administrative work, and support ship-wide programs.

Keep the XO Informed

Your XO will prefer that you tell them more rather than less. Assume they do not know what you know. If you tell the XO too much, they will let you know. If you report something to the CO, tell the XO as well; both should have the same information about your department. This common operational picture will help them coordinate their efforts but will also ensure that the XO is always ready to act on the CO's behalf or to assume command. Also, if your XO and CO meet regularly during the day, the XO may relay your reports to the CO, so keeping the XO informed can be an efficient way to keep the CO informed about routine matters.

Use your best judgment about how quickly to "backfill" the XO on something you have discussed with the CO, but, at a minimum, inform the XO before the end of the day. If you make a report to the CO after normal working hours, tell the XO too. If it is important enough for a late call to the CO, it is important enough for a late call to the XO as well.

Dominate Taskings and Administrative Work

Your XO will give you ample latitude to lead your department and accomplish your mission, but if they assign a specific task to you, treat it as a command priority. If tasking conflicts with your departmental plans, voice your concerns to the XO and ask them to clarify the relative priorities. Your XO will also assign routine administrative work, such as writing evaluations and awards and creating or updating command policies. Write well and turn in assignments on time.

Write Well

Clearly expressing an idea to your reader is a valuable skill. Your writing represents you and your command. It should communicate your clarity of thought and attention to detail. Your XO will want to provide the CO with written work that is effective and error-free. Strive to provide the same to your XO. Pay attention to a few key points:

- Before writing, understand who the reader is and plan the message you want to convey.
- If writing an award, refer to specific shipboard, squadron, or strike group instruction for proper formatting and wording.
- Write in the active voice. Use a clear subject and action verbs. A helpful hint is that if the reader cannot tell who is doing something, you probably are writing passively.
- Eliminate redundant words.
- Be specific. Back up assertions with facts.
- Be brilliant on the basics. Spell and punctuate correctly.
- Know what words mean and use them accurately.
- Proofread!

Talk with the XO about their writing peeves. Ask to see the edits they made to your work and learn from them. Read and apply the lessons from a good writing guide such as *The Elements of Style* by William Strunk Jr. and E. B. White.

Meet Deadlines

An event or a decision drives a deadline. At best, a document submitted late compresses the time available for the XO and CO to review and sign it or make a decision. At worst, late submission (e.g., in routing an award to your immediate superior in command) could embarrass the command or, in other cases, make the document irrelevant. Either way, late written work detracts from the command's efficiency and effectiveness and reflects poorly on your leadership and management skills.

Plan your work backward from the deadline set by the XO. If you require inputs from your team, publish due dates early, and enforce them. Manage your time; work after hours if you fall behind. Your XO will not miss their deadlines; you should not miss yours.

Support Command-Wide Programs

As a department head, you are understandably tempted to focus on your own departmental work. If you are a combat systems officer, for example, you likely volunteered for this billet to lead the maintenance and employment of advanced weapons and sensors. Command-wide programs such as general military training, Navy family accountability and assessments system musters, damage control drills, force protection training, medical readiness, and zone inspections, to name a few, may not be as interesting to you as preparing for a missile shoot or running a combat systems training team scenario. Furthermore, some command-wide programs, such as providing a mess decks master-at-arms, damage control petty officers (DCPOs), or food service attendants (FSAs), draw away talent from your department. As a result, you may pour all of your efforts into your department and neglect or short-change command-wide efforts.

Instead, you need to support both your departmental efforts and command-wide programs with equal enthusiasm and vigor and spur your team to be similarly supportive. The time and talent devoted to command-wide programs may seem to detract from your departmental mission, but in reality, they build a broad foundation upon which your department's and the ship's success may be built. Help your khaki and your Sailors understand the importance of fulfilling their responsibilities to command-wide programs. Collaborate with your departmental triad to identify Sailors to serve as a DCPO or FSA, and plan how to best sequence and time their absences from your department. Support ship-wide programs as if they are your own. Expect the XO to hold you accountable if you do not.

Support from the Executive Officer

Just as you support the XO, they can support you in several ways. The XO will have an in-depth understanding of command priorities, unique leverage within the command and beyond the lifelines, and broad naval experience. You and your department will benefit from welcoming and even seeking the XO's support. Do not be too proud, too shy, or too busy to make the most of it. Your XO will never think poorly of you asking for advice or help.

Command Priorities

A good CO will state their priorities clearly, and the XO can help you align your plans with command priorities, especially when operating in a dynamic environment. No one in your command is likely to spend as much time with the CO as the XO. The XO will understand the CO's priorities backward and forward and will routinely communicate and reinforce them. Your XO will be glad to help you assess whether your efforts are consistent with those priorities or suggest how to "adjust fire" if they are not. For example, if you plan to present several courses of action to the CO for their decision, the XO can be a good sounding board to evaluate whether they align with command priorities and ensure they are ready to present to the CO. If they fall short of the mark, the XO can offer their insight into these priorities—and the CO's decision-making—to improve the options you provide.

Leverage

By virtue of their rank, position, and personal experience, your XO will have leverage within and beyond the command. Within the command, the XO has the authority to direct the crew's attention and efforts. They also have a bully pulpit that is second only to the CO's and many opportunities to use it, such as khaki call, one main circuit announcements, the plan of the day, and email. Outside the ship, the XO's voice and personal or professional relationships might carry more weight than yours and could help "shake loose" resources or cultivate support.

Ask for Help

The XO cannot help you if they do not know you need help. Never hesitate to ask the XO to advocate for your initiatives, particularly if you feel that you have been unable to make progress on your own. If the XO offers their help, do not reject it or assume the XO thinks your efforts have been insufficient. If they are, they will let you know. Instead, speak constructively with your XO about how they could best use their influence to support your department's efforts.

Experience

Lastly, your XO will have years of experience. Learn and benefit from it. They will have spent more years as a naval officer than you and will have been a successful department head.

Whether you want it or not, the XO will apply past experience in their relationship with you. They will be several years removed from serving as a department head but will have the most recent experience among the command leadership. I recall as a department head getting on edge when the XO started a conversation with "When I was a department head." This opening usually presaged what I felt was an admonishment of something I was not doing quite right. In hindsight, I appreciate that the XO was drawing upon past experiences to help me improve as a department head.

Mentorship

The captain will be an important sounding board and mentor to you, but the XO will offer valuable perspective as well. They will be more proximate to the department head tours and thus more recently will have faced personal and professional challenges and choices similar to those you will confront as a department head and work through as you think about your post–department head career. Do not hesitate to talk frankly with the XO about anything. They will be eager to mentor and help you, just as past leaders did for them.

Future XO

It is never too early to learn about your next afloat job and think about how you would approach it. Pay attention to how the XO does their job. What makes them effective? How do they fall short? Ask them questions about how they approach the job and execute its responsibilities. No two XOs are alike, and you will serve with several during your department head tours. Note the differences between them.

When you have the opportunity to serve as acting XO, act as the XO. Sit at the XO's desk, use a green pen, run khaki call, conduct messing and berthing, brief the CO on command issues, meet often with the command master chief, and so on. Spending time in the XO's chair will give you new insight into the XO-department head relationship and offer a glimpse of what a future XO tour may be like.

Conclusion

As a department head, you will work for the CO for all matters pertaining to your department, but you will work for the XO as well. Although it may seem at times like a zero-sum game, where supporting one comes at the expense of supporting the other, it is essential that you balance supporting both, and thereby accomplish the command's mission. All XOs are different, but yours will expect you to lead your department, cooperate across departments, and effectively manage time. Beyond meeting these expectations, you should support the XO by keeping them informed, staying on top of your administrative work, and supporting command-wide programs. Lastly, remember that the XO can also help you by providing insight into command priorities, leverage within and beyond the command, and mentorship. Establishing and maintaining a positive and productive working relationship with your XO will benefit you, your department, and the command.

CDR Robert C. Watts IV is the commanding officer of USS *John Paul Jones* (DDG 53) in Pearl Harbor, Hawaii. He also served as supply officer in USS *Raven* (MHC 61) in Bahrain, fire control officer in USS *Oscar Austin* (DDG 79) in Norfolk, Virginia, and operations officer in both USS *Fitzgerald* (DDG 62) in Yokosuka, Japan, and USS *Monterey* (CG 61) in Norfolk. Ashore, he served in the Navy foreign liaison office, the Office of the Vice Chief of Naval Operations, and U.S. Fleet Forces Command. He earned a master's degree in public policy at Princeton University through the Navy's politico-military master's program.

CHAPTER 6

SUPPORTING THE COMMANDING OFFICER

RADM Fred W. Kacher, USN

Fostering a Critical Relationship

IN THE NAVY, there is no more profound responsibility or privilege than command at sea. Today, the qualification process to attain surface command at sea has never been more rigorous, and today's commanding officers (COs) not only are well qualified, but the vast majority also are committed to do the right things for their ships, their crews, and the Navy. As they embark upon this life-changing command journey, some of their most important partnerships and relationships will be with their department heads. In turn, that relationship will help shape many of those young department heads into future ship captains.

A key aspect of your job will be to support your CO. This, of course, does not imply blind allegiance or supporting the captain's personal needs—having commanded several times at sea, I can promise you that your captain is far more interested in you doing your job to the best of your ability than in your being a "yes person" or "politician at sea." Put another way, as you do your job, you will be helping the CO execute their duties as the commander the Navy has entrusted with a warship and America's sons and daughters. By being the subordinate you would want to have as a CO, you will go a long way to helping your department and your ship succeed. With this in mind, I share a few observations and best practices that not only will help you and your commanding officer succeed together, but will also make for a better ship and relationship.

6-1. A commanding officer and department heads work together to conduct a lessons-learned critique.
U.S. Navy photo by Mass Communication Specialist 3rd Class Katie Cox/Released

Practical Advice for a Successful Tour

Command Your Department

Most department heads will be the leader of more than fifty (in some cases, more than one hundred) officers and sailors on a U.S. Navy ship. Carry yourself that way. Find opportunities to address your troops, set your agenda, and be a leader. I have yet to meet a CO or executive officer who wants to go back and do a third department head tour; make sure you leave them no doubt that you are on the job. More profoundly, when a ship deploys into a high-risk or combat environment, your commanding officer is going to expect you to lead your department in the fight with courage and competence.

Get Aligned

A big part of your job is executing the captain's vision as if it were your own. No one is asking you to check your own personality, style, or integrity at the door, but the reality is that it is the captain who mainly sets the course for the ship. In fact, the CO will look to their department heads as the prime managerial movers on the ship. Rest assured that you will look for this same quality in your department heads when you are in command.

CHAPTER 6

Lean Forward

Command is the greatest job in the Navy, but it is likely to be more successful and enjoyable when more than one person is leaning forward and anticipating future challenges. Captains by nature of the job will have more experience and more time to think about future challenges, but good department heads must develop this skill as well. Leaning forward and thinking about a ship's future challenges and opportunities, qualifications, and awards for your people and goals you have for your department not only will make you a more successful department head, but also will support your CO. Department administration trackers for requirements and their completion, a robust watch team replacement plan, and a plan to break down larger complex tasks and goals into more manageable ones are all tools that will help you lean forward for your department and your ship.

Expand Your Planning Horizon

A division officer who plans a month ahead may be exceptional, but a department head who only looks that far out will be a failure. As a leader, you will need to "unpack" the ship's schedule, understand what the command's broader goals are, and then ensure that the events you need executed to support those goals are scheduled appropriately. Within your department, factor in the essentials such as combat drills and training first and build the rest of your proposed schedule around them. Next, ensure that your department's needs and this schedule are integrated into the command schedule. Finally, make sure you find a way for your division officers and chiefs to understand your vision for the future so they can share it with your Sailors.

Do Not Just Focus on Your Strengths

We all tend to like the activities in which we excel, but you cannot afford to merely play to your strengths. Senior leaders have to focus on the entire spectrum of our jobs. For me, there were times that executing a maintenance spot check late in the week or performing a weekly zone inspection was not the first thing I woke up in the morning wanting to do. Nonetheless, I knew my involvement in those critical activities would help set the tone in my department. When I fell short and occasionally overlooked parts of the job I did not like, my department inevitably would pay the price, and I would wind up spending more time catching up in the area I underemphasized. Over time, you may even come to appreciate and even value the part of the job that felt like a chore.

See the World through Your Captain's Eyes

There is an old adage that your boss's problems are not necessarily your problems. Over the years, I have learned that viewing your CO's challenges with some professional empathy certainly helps. The vast majority of commanding officers want to do the right thing for the right reasons. They, and they alone, are most inextricably linked with their ship's performance and perception off ship. Most are doing everything they can to prepare their ship to fight and not let down the crew. Command at sea is the best job I have ever had, but it also could be a lonely one at times. Having another leader or two who understands and appreciates those challenges was worth its weight in gold.

Provide Your Commander Choices and Context

When sharing that you have discovered an issue, provide your CO context regarding impact and then offer courses of actions on how you believe the problem can best be addressed or mitigated. In other words, do not just bring your commanding officer problems. This skill never goes out of style. As a captain, you will find yourself needing to exercise the same skill at an even higher level as you share your ship's challenges and your plan to address them with your commodore.

Be Responsive

When the CO directly asks you a question, solicits feedback, or asks you to take something on, move that up to the top of your queue. Good COs will have a reasonable sense of timing and scale of what they are seeking, but if it is a relatively small task or request for information, answer it promptly. Over time, this builds the captain's confidence that you take their concerns seriously and that you do not let requests—even small ones—slip through the cracks.

Be Collaborative

The last thing a CO ever wants to do is serve as a referee for squabbles between department heads. Great ships are often great because the department heads managed to band together. The competitive aspect of the job is undeniable given our fitness reporting system, but cooperation and trust are the true coins of the realm at sea. Having served on a ship where every department head went on to make O-6, with five of six going on to major command, I can attest that the department heads who "cooperate to graduate" also win.

Honor Your Craft
You should be one of the lead warfighters and shiphandlers on the ship. As the captain, I took my role as the number-one warfighter and shipdriver seriously, but I was deeply appreciative to have department heads who embraced these competencies as well. Moreover, as I evaluated these leaders based on their potential to command at sea, these two competencies weighed heavily in my assessment. Very few of us were born both great shiphandlers or intuitive combat watchstanders; instead, this expertise comes with study, preparation, and training. Take comfort that these preparations are not just helping you and your current ship; they will be the two key competencies you will need to have when you take command.

Manage Your Equipment and Your Programs
Every department head will have equipment and programs to manage. In fact, for almost every department, you will have some absolutely core equipment and fundamental program to manage, with both having significant implications for the ship's ability to get under way or deploy. With material readiness deeply related to operational readiness, your CO will be reporting directly to their commodore and perhaps their strike group commander. You will almost certainly be the leader communicating the issue, impact, and path to correct that issue to your captain.

Focus Down, Across, and Out as Well
For all the talk about being aligned with the CO's vision and expectations (and that is legitimate), the captain is also expecting you to do all the right things and manage all the right relationships outside of their purview. In many ways, "managing up," while important, is far less fundamental than being a diligent and principled leader and partner to your Sailors, your peers, and your counterparts beyond the ship.

Take Care of Your People
Your CO is expecting you to care deeply for your people. The skills you learned as a division officer that helped you ensure that every facet of your Sailors' lives was managed so they could execute their job on the ship still apply. From physical fitness to pay to qualifications to performance, you may no longer be doing most of the actual hands-on work, but you need to ensure that your division officers and chiefs are.

Be Prepared to Make the Tough Call

As you balance the needs of your people and the needs of your department, recognize that your CO is trying to do what is right for the Navy and their ship. They will count on you to set the standard and say "no" when circumstances demand. On items such as leave and liberty, we as leaders want to "get to yes," but there will be a time during a critical inspection or deployment where elective leave, for example, will not be the right call.

Treat Your Division Officers Like the Young Leaders They Are

I believe that one of a CO's critical tasks is to engage the wardroom and inspire them to keep serving beyond this current tour. By design, this profession is not for everyone, but people remain our most precious resource, and the Navy's future leadership resides in your wardroom. As I thought about connecting with my wardroom, I viewed my department heads as the difference makers in how our division officers view their service. In a very real way, the executive talent you lead will ultimately be your relief one day. Treating division officers well, investing in them, and, most of all, teaching them are essential parts of a department head's job. Those who treat division officers as disposable talent that can be exhausted and then passed along to another ship do a grave disservice to our profession. Instead, do your best to inspire them, include them, and let them see you enjoying your job. If you cannot do those things, how would you expect our very best to ever want the job you have now?

Be Ready to Be Both an Advocate and Ambassador for Your Ship

As one of the five or six most senior leaders on the ship, you are going to help the CO represent your ship and your profession. Whether it is attending command events off the ship or leading the in-brief of a key inspection team, you will play an important role in setting the tone for the ship. In many ways, some of your toughest moments may be receiving feedback from inspection teams with equanimity and maturity. Polished department heads do not argue balls and strikes in outbriefs or bicker with each other in front of the boss, but regrettably, in thirty years of service, I have seen both occur.

Know Your Navy

Division officers are learning not only their jobs, but also about the Navy. As you may remember, one of the key leaders you learned from was your department head. Now it is your turn to teach your division officers and your young Sailors. To do that, you need to think beyond the blocking and tackling of your current job (which remain very important) and ensure you are up to speed on the policy and direction of the Navy. From visiting the www.navy.mil website to being on the lookout for updates from the Chief of Naval Personnel, the commander of Naval Surface Forces, the Surface and Mine Warfighting Development Center, and the Surface Warfare Officers School, you will be the leader who helps your folks understand their place in one of the great institutions of our nation.

Helpful Hints

- ▶ Get your personal life in order. A CO is going to be counting on you being fully focused on the job when you report as a ship's department head. While I worked hard to be compassionate as my key teammates dealt with the personal challenges that occasionally occur to all of us, work hard to get your life in order before starting the job. From finances to your move to your physical health, do all you can to have things settled when you walk up the brow for the first time.
- ▶ Write it down. As basic as this sounds, given that your span of control has quadrupled since your division officer days, this habit will save you repeatedly, particularly when the CO is providing you feedback verbally (often moving from topic to topic fairly quickly).
- ▶ Carve out personal planning time on the ship. You cannot lead a department if you do not have time to think, plan, and organize for the day. It is not very fun, but coming in early and setting thirty to forty-five minutes aside each day to read message traffic and plan will pay huge dividends.
- ▶ Take time to address your department formally and informally. Put simply, your CO needs your help in conveying their priorities and the ship's mission. Equally important, these departmental gatherings reinforce that each of the divisions is part of a broader departmental team that needs to work together.
- ▶ Set aside some time each day to "sharpen the saw." This will be a challenge, but this advice from Steven Covey certainly pertains to your position. There are times when your job will feel brutally busy, but setting aside time—even thirty minutes—to invest in your

professional skills will provide your CO a better leader, warfighter, and shipdriver.

- ▶ Work out every day. Your captain needs a healthy, resilient, and composed leader. As with many of the tips here, you may fall short every now and again, but pay yourself first by building your health into your schedule every day. You will look better, feel better, and set the right example for your department.
- ▶ Conduct a "planning off-site" with your leaders. Carve out a two- to three-hour period to paint the picture of the next three to six months for your division officers. This will give them a sense of what success looks like in your eyes and will provide them a vision to share with their teams. The excellent leader I saw first put this approach into action even provided drinks and refreshments to mark that this event was more important than the day-to-day meetings we attended, and two decades later I have not forgotten that lesson or that meeting.
- ▶ Read the news. As a Navy, we respond to the world events that impact our nation. By staying up on the news, you will not only gain a better understanding of our profession's purpose but will also be able to provide context to your team when current events intersect with your ship's mission and schedule. You can be sure that your CO is doing the same thing.
- ▶ Stay connected with your family and friends. With a job this demanding, this principle may seem impossible, but your friends and family will provide perspective and keep you grounded. On a professional note, some of your friends may very well be department heads on other ships, and I was amazed at how often those friendships helped me see an old problem in a new light. On sea duty, you will have to focus on quality of time versus quantity, so make your free time with loved ones and friends count. In the end, we all leave the Navy, but families and friendships remain.

An Enduring Partnership

As challenging as the job of being a department head is, rest assured your captain wants you to succeed. By doing so, it not only advances the ship under their command but also helps prepare you to take the captain's job one day.

CHAPTER 6

Having watched seven former department heads from my O-5 and major commands select for command at sea, I can promise you there are few things more satisfying in life than seeing one of your former departmental leaders commanding a U.S. Navy warship of their own. Whether or not command is in your future, by following some of these tips and helpful practices, you will be well on your way to supporting the CO, succeeding as a department head, and contributing to the success of your ship.

RADM Fred W. Kacher, USN, has commanded Expeditionary Strike Group SEVEN, Destroyer Squadron SEVEN, and USS *Stockdale* (DDD 106). He is a recipient of the Elmo Zumwalt Award for Visionary Leadership and the U.S. Navy League's John Paul Jones Award for Inspirational Leadership.

PART III

THE WATCH

CHAPTER 7
Tactical Action Officer
CDR Katie Whitman, USN

Responsibilities

THE TACTICAL ACTION OFFICER (TAO) is the leading tactical watchstander on the ship and sets the tone for the entire ship's watch teams. As a new department head, you have experience as a division officer driving the ship; you know and understand how the engineering plant provides critical systems with air, power, and water; and you have the benefit of tailored, tactical training specific to your ship's combat system. As the TAO, you will be required to synthesize those experiences and training together to proactively lead Sailors and, if necessary, to fight and win.

Organizational Roles and Responsibilities
The *Standard Organization and Regulations of the U.S. Navy* (SORM, OPNAVINST 3120.32 [series]) prescribes the TAO to be "the Commanding Officer's representative concerning the tactical employment and defense of the unit." The SORM specifically delineates the following duties, responsibilities, and authority:

- The TAO is responsible for the safe and effective operation of the combat systems of the unit (including aircraft under the unit's tactical control).

- The TAO is responsible for the smooth and efficient operation of the combat information center (CIC), including collection, display, and dissemination of tactical and other operationally significant data.

- Circumstances permitting, the TAO shall carry out promptly and precisely special orders and shall report any deviations to the commanding officer.

- The TAO shall keep the commanding officer fully informed of the current tactical picture and will immediately inform the commanding officer on any and all matters that pose a potential combat threat to the unit.

- When authorized by the commanding officer, the TAO will direct the employment of weapons and direct the officer of the deck (OOD) to maneuver as required to fight or defend the ship.
- The TAO will stand watch in the CIC.

The SORM also articulates organizational relationships between the TAO and other key watch stations.

- The TAO reports directly to the commanding officer concerning the tactical employment and defense of the ship.
- The TAO reports to the appropriate department head about any actual or potential problems in the combat system that may affect the unit's offensive or defensive capability.
- The TAO reports to the OOD for ship maneuvering and informs the OOD of the status of combat systems and of the tactical situation.
- The executive officer (XO) may direct the TAO in the general duties and safety of the ship.
- When the commanding officer is not present, the XO may direct the TAO in time of danger or emergency.
- The XO may relieve the TAO and will do so should it, in their judgment, be necessary, and the commanding officer will be promptly notified of such action.

Lead the Watch Team

Preparing for the Watch

Preparing for the watch as the TAO starts before entering the CIC. First and foremost, you should know and understand the commanding officer's battle orders and standing orders. As the commanding officer's direct representative and watchstander responsible for the defense of the ship, you must have a thorough understanding of your responsibilities and authority as well as your relationship with the other watchstanders.

A key element of knowing the commanding officer's battle orders and standing orders is understanding the commander's intent. While thorough and detailed, the battle orders and standing orders may not cover every situation you will face as the TAO. Most battle orders and standing orders are organized by warfare area or by threat (for example, preplanned responses or firing point procedures), but you will need to execute that guidance in a multithreat environment. Understanding which threats or warfare areas take priority over others and understanding the second- and third-order effects of your actions is extremely important.

Before assuming the watch as the TAO, you should also have a solid understanding of general operational, theater operational task, and operational task supplemental messages. These messages provide you with command and control, warfare-specific guidance, and preplanned responses. As the TAO, you are expected to know this guidance and provide forceful backup when necessary. You must know your immediate actions and the expected actions of your subordinate watchstations. You should also familiarize yourself with the plan of the day and schedule of events. Know what events are occurring when you have the watch and familiarize yourself with the watch team briefs before assuming the watch. Your job as a department head is a busy one, but it is imperative to dedicate time in the day to prepare for the watch. As the TAO, you should expect the same from your watchstanders and should set the example by doing it yourself.

Assuming the Watch

When you arrive in the CIC to assume the watch, you should arrive with enough time to observe the team on watch to gain situational awareness and get a feel for the tempo. Depending on your platform, you should have a screen or console you can use to observe ships, aircraft, and submarines operating in your vicinity. You also should take notice of the communications plan and subsequent channelization matrix to ensure you know which of your key communications circuits are programmed into which channels.

Look at the Plan of the Day and Schedule of Events and Discuss the Situation with the TAO on Watch

Understand the time/speed/distance plan to get your ship on station. Nothing is more frustrating than going to relieve the watch only to see that the watch team before you, while well intentioned, placed the ship in a situation where they cannot make a rendezvous location on time because of an oversight. A good mindset to have when preparing to assume the watch is to execute your watch, prepare the next watch, and plan two watches ahead.

CHAPTER 7

Review the Navigation Charts
While the OOD maintains responsibility for safe navigation, the TAO cannot effectively employ the ship ignorant of the navigational picture. Additionally, you should ensure that both combat systems displays and electronic charts have key overlays displayed and that those overlays are correctly entered into the system. Both the bridge and the CIC will make critical maneuvering and tactical decisions based on those visual aids, so it is imperative that overlays are accurate and up-to-date.

Understand the Current and Future Command-and-Control Relationships
You may assume the watch controlling aircraft during an air defense exercise but may end the watch conducting an antisubmarine tracking exercise. Know where your ship needs to be and for whom you will be working. Things may have changed since the plan of the day was published, so ensure you communicate those changes to the crew so they can plan accordingly.

Know the Status of Your Combat Systems and Engineering Plant
You should understand your radar configuration and what type of doctrine is active. From an engineering perspective, you should know which engines are on line and any maneuvering considerations or limitations you might have. If there is maintenance scheduled for combat systems or engineering, know the impact that it will have on your ability to employ the ship tactically. You should also know the impact of delaying that maintenance, if required, to maintain combat readiness.

Have a Turnover Log or Checklist
Some key topics to include are:

- events that occurred during the past watch
- upcoming events
- ships/aircraft/subs in company and any units/aircraft under tactical control
- any planned shifts in tactical control
- communications plan
- combat systems/engineering plant configuration
- any significant equipment maintenance that impacts propulsion or combat systems equipment or redundancies
- location of command leadership
- any specific instructions/guidance from the captain.

Following a set turnover checklist will help you keep organized and prevent a situation where important information is missed.

Stagger Turnovers in the CIC
Warfare coordinators and subordinate watches should turn over first, along with the bridge watch team. As the TAO, you should turn over last to ensure the off-going TAO maintains situational awareness and control during subordinate watchstation turnover. Once the turnover is complete, you should conduct a voice turnover on the internal net and provide your intentions as the TAO, then break to all warfare coordinators for their current status. This lets the oncoming watch teams hear your intentions and priorities and allows you to receive amplifying information from each warfare coordinator, the bridge, and engineering watch teams. It also can act as a backup to your turnover with the off-going TAO to ensure all critical information was passed.

Keep Professional Communications
Whether speaking externally or internally, covered or in the clear, the way your team communicates is critical. How you conduct yourself on the radio will set the tone for your watch team. When speaking on internal nets, brevity is key. Depending on your ship's mission, communications in the CIC may vary from routine reports to defense of the ship. You need to keep the watch team focused by encouraging net discipline. Operations in the CIC cover a multitude of warfare areas, and at times, one warfare area may take priority over another. For example, if your watch team is conducting a detect-to-engage scenario and the anti–air warfare coordinator (AAWC) is requesting batteries release, it is not appropriate for the surface warfare coordinator to interrupt the communications flow to report a merchant vessel twenty nautical miles away. Yes, the surface warfare coordinator is required to report the contact, but that information can wait until the more pressing event has concluded or until there is a tactical pause in the event. Providing your intentions and priorities ensures your watch team is on the same page and will help them work more effectively together.

Special Evolutions
Whether you are coming alongside for an underway replenishment, conducting a sea and anchor detail, or operating aircraft, your role as the TAO can ensure the entire watch team, both in and out of the CIC, is successful. Depending on the special evolution, you may need to secure radars and/or sensors to be in compliance with specific operations. While your situational

awareness might be limited, you are still in a position to provide the bridge and ship with critical information. For example, if your ship is planning to pull into port on your watch, you can back up the bridge by ensuring the combat information watch officer (CICWO) or other watchstander provides the bridge with an updated harbor movements message and a lineal list. Even more importantly, you can drive your watch team in the CIC to proactively support the bridge by anticipating what information they will need before they have to ask for it. The bridge should be concerned about safely managing shipping and restricted waters transit, not about which warship should initiate rendering honors when passing in the channel.

Consider a likely scenario where you are forward-deployed on a guided missile destroyer in the Mediterranean and just set flight quarters to recover a helicopter. The bridge calculated winds and recommends a course to recover the helicopter based on the wind direction. While the bridge's recommended course is mathematically correct, turning to that course might result in your ship's sensors not being optimized to detect potential threats. As TAO, you should ensure that the CIC and the bridge alternatively work a wind solution or calculate a flight quarters course that ensures winds remain within the required limits for safe recovery, and also allows for sufficient sensor management with regard to the threat.

If operating aircraft, both the bridge and the CIC should be monitoring the wind envelope to ensure winds remain in the envelope throughout launch and recovery of aircraft. As the TAO, you should look ahead at the surface picture and think about contingencies. If you anticipate that the ship will need to adjust course to open closest point of approach from another ship operating in the area, make recommendations to the bridge for alternate courses that still allow for flight quarters. Looking ahead and considering what could go wrong keeps your watch team engaged and can highlight potential problems before they become in extremis. Being proactive as a watch team ultimately buys you more time to make critical decisions.

The TAO should drive their watch team to be proactive and look for ways to support other controlling stations. The CIC, in conjunction with the bridge, can bring multiple sensors to bear to assist the bridge in identifying surface contacts. For example, when operating close to land at night, it may be difficult for the bridge to distinguish between shipping traffic and background lighting. The CIC can use gun cameras and/or electro-optical sighting systems and received emissions to help distinguish and identify shipping and help the bridge maintain situational awareness.

7-1. The tactical action officer must maintain situational awareness at all times and is responsible for leading the combat information center watch team and providing forceful backup to the officer of the deck.
U.S. Navy photo by Mass Communication Specialist 1st Class Fred Gray IV/Released

Practical Advice for a Successful Watch

Communications and Data Links Are Critical

Your ship cannot meet the mission without functional communications and data links. Often, your ship's reputation within the strike group and theater will be measured by your team's ability to not only maintain communications but also shift quickly between circuits and configurations. Familiarize yourself with the communications plan to ensure you know which of your key communications circuits are programmed into which channels. Depending on the mission or situation, there may be more communications circuits in the communications plan than you have circuits to listen. Look ahead at the events that will occur on your watch and ensure you have the right circuits patched. If your ship is scheduled to control aircraft, conduct a communications check with an adjacent ship or platform an hour prior to event launch. Also, take note of your secondary and tertiary communications circuits. Ensure they are operational and ready to use if the requirement arises.

Know Your Watch Team's Strengths and Weaknesses

Just as a good leader should know their people, you should know your watch team's strengths and weaknesses. For example, if a newly qualified AAWC is now standing watch in your section, be cognizant of the fact that their reports may lag those of more seasoned watchstanders. Delayed reports may not indicate lackadaisical watchstanding. Be patient, if the tactical situation permits, and allow that watchstander to work through the situation. Likewise, if you have a very seasoned watchstander, you may find yourself in a situation where the watchstander is so comfortable that they fail to have the required checklist next to them. Enforce the standard regardless of watchstander level of proficiency.

Back Up the Officer of the Deck
The OOD is responsible for the safe navigation of the ship. There may be times when you need to direct the OOD to maneuver for the tactical situation, but in most cases, there is time to discuss maneuvering intentions between the bridge and the CIC before the ship is in extremis. There may be times when the bridge and the CIC do not agree on the maneuver or the CIC does not fully understand the bridge watch team's intentions. In those times, if the tactical situation permits, the best course of action might be for you to leave the CIC and go to the bridge. This can be especially true if you are operating in an area with an abundance of small surface ships (e.g., a fishing fleet). The CIC might not have the best surface picture if the ships in the vicinity are too small to be seen on radar. Going to the bridge can allow you to get a better understanding of the situation, and it may also provide you with an opportunity to mentor and assist the OOD. If you have a newly qualified OOD, you also may consider calling the navigator or the senior watch officer to assist the OOD before calling the commanding officer, if the situation allows.

The CIC should back up the bridge with communications and vice versa. Your ship's standing orders or battle orders should prescribe which communications circuits will be guarded and/or covered by the bridge and the CIC. Back up the bridge by logging communications received on bridge to bridge and fleet tactical—even when bridge has the guard. This will provide essential backup to the bridge watchstanders, enhance situational awareness in the CIC, and allow CIC watchstanders to benefit from additional training.

Keep Fellow Department Heads in the Loop
The SORM and commanding officer's standing orders require you to inform respective department heads about the status of their key equipment. From a tactical perspective, you will need to inform the commanding officer when equipment casualties impact the tactical performance of the ship. However, if you feel there is sufficient time to inform the respective department heads so they can take action, it may be more appropriate to notify them first. For

example, if communications circuit shifts are taking longer than normal, you might call the operations officer or combat systems officer to inform them. Another example includes maintenance requests. If the engineering officer of the watch calls the bridge and/or CIC to request maintenance outside of the approved plan, you may want to call the chief engineer to ensure they are aware of the request. As much as you can, and situationally permitting, you should provide your peers with advanced notice so they can engage their departmental leadership to provide oversight.

Communicate Changes to the Crew
The plan inevitably will change while you are on watch. For example, the plan of the day may call for the replenishment detail to station at 1300, but the oiler might need you to come alongside earlier. You often will be the first to learn of these changes, and you will need to notify the operations officer, XO, and supply officer to adjust meal hours and communicate to the crew to ensure the ship is ready to support. Ensure key leadership is informed as the changes occur, as there may be additional background information to which you are not privy.

If You Do Not Know, Ask
You are expected to lead the watch team, and your Sailors and subordinate watch teams will look to you for clarity and guidance. If you do not understand your tasking, rules of engagement, or requirements, you should ask for clarification. If time permits, employ your watch team to find the answer. But if time does not allow, do not hesitate to pick up the circuit and directly ask for further guidance when things do not make sense. There are times when your ship and strike group may be operating with restricted emissions; during those times, you may not be notified of changes due to minimized communications. As the TAO, you are expected to take immediate action to defend the ship or take offensive actions in protection of the force. You cannot do that if you do not understand the full picture.

Know That You Cannot Do It All Alone
Empower and encourage your subordinate watchstanders to execute their roles autonomously and report to you. The layout and manning in the CIC support decentralized command and command by negation. Watchstanders should be proactive and accountable to their specific areas of responsibility. They should push information and recommendations to you instead of you pulling information from them. As the TAO, you will be busy, and you need to remain focused on the tactical situation. Empowering your watch supervisor and the

CICWO to take care of routine watch team requirements will allow you to keep your eyes on the scope and keep situational awareness. If you feel like you need help on watch, do not hesitate to augment the watch with additional qualified watchstanders or increase the condition of readiness (e.g., Condition II).

Guard against Complacency
Depending on your ship's current mission or assignment, you may be conducting routine training operations in your local operating area, or you may be escorting an aircraft carrier engaged in flight operations in the Arabian Gulf. Regardless of how comfortable you or your watch team become in executing these duties, you must guard against complacency in both your watchstanders and yourself. A great way to fight complacency is to think about contingencies on your watch. Your ship may not have a primary warfare commander role, but you may be called upon to act as secondary or tertiary warfare commander. Be prepared to assume those roles. For example, if you know that the air defense commander's ship has been struggling with maintaining communications and you are listed alternate air warfare commander, notify the on-call watchstanders, have necessary communications patched, and develop a draft version of your required reports so you can readily and smoothly assume the duties.

Conclusion

As the TAO, you are responsible for the tactical employment of the ship and the safety of the crew. You also have the responsibility to develop, mentor, and lead subordinate watch teams. Understand your governing instructions and expect the same from your team, but also know when to ask for help. You have an entire crew of officers, chief petty officers, and enlisted Sailors, so do not hesitate to call on them for help if the situation requires an extra set of hands or a seasoned Sailor's experience.

CDR Katie Whitman is a surface warfare officer who has served as strike officer and navigator in USS *Russell* (DDG 59) and weapons officer and combat systems officer in USS *Mobile Bay* (CG 53). Ashore, she served as a company officer at the United States Naval Academy, as a warfare tactics instructor at Surface and Mine Warfighting Development Center, and as a post–department head detailer and assistant community manager at Navy Personnel Command. She currently serves as the executive officer of USS *Gridley* (DDG 101).

CHAPTER 8
Special Evolutions Officer of the Deck
CDR Christopher H. Bland, USN

Two Perspectives on the Special Evolution

THROUGHOUT YOUR DIVISION OFFICER TOURS, you likely stood watch on the bridge as the officer of the deck (OOD) while getting the ship under way and while taking the ship alongside during an underway replenishment on numerous occasions. As a department head, you will be required to requalify as OOD, maintain watchstander proficiency by completing specific special evolutions, and be included on the bridge watchbill at regular intervals. By the time you report for your first department head tour, you will have spent two to three years on shore duty, followed by an additional year of training in the department head "pipeline." Your simulated and classroom training will be a good refresher, but your adrenaline undoubtedly will be pumping the first time you take the deck as a special evolution OOD as a new department head. The *Standard Organization and Regulations of the U.S. Navy* (SORM, OPNAVINST 3120.32 [series]) states that as OOD, "you are designated by the commanding officer to be in charge of the ship including its safe and proper operation." The difference between a special evolution during your division officer and department head tour is notable. As a department head, you are responsible for an entire department of personnel and their training and for ensuring that your equipment operates safely and effectively, undoubtedly affecting the success of the special evolution regardless of whether you are the designated OOD.

The information that follows is divided into two sections and is designed to help you prepare for a shipboard special evolution. The first section will discuss how to prepare for and execute a special evolution as the OOD, while the second section will provide suggestions for how to contribute to the success of the evolution in your role as a department head. Throughout this chapter, a special evolution refers to any ship evolution that necessitates a specific watchbill with supplemental watchstanders and includes entering or exiting port, underway replenishments (UNREP), and anchoring evolutions, to name a few.

The Department Head as the Special Evolution OOD

Your role and responsibilities as the special evolution OOD as a department head will be no different than they were when you were a division officer. However, you will be more experienced and will approach the evolution with a more discerning eye for identifying risks and situations that do not feel right. As the OOD during a special evolution, there are ways to prepare yourself prior to, steps to take during, and items to think about and record after the event that will significantly improve the chances of your watch team conducting a safe evolution.

Prior to the Evolution

Read the Brief and Thoroughly Know the Plan

The requirements for navigation brief attendance and content are defined in the *Surface Ship Navigation Department Organization and Regulations Manual* (NAVDORM, CNSPINST 3530.4 [series]). These requirements are extensive but are also the minimum. The navigator is specifically charged with preparing the navigation brief, and the first lieutenant typically prepares an UNREP brief, but as the OOD you own the evolution and owe it to yourself and your watch team to do your due diligence. Conducting a formal brief prior to executing an evolution is a useful tool to ensure every participant understands what is expected, and it affords everyone the opportunity to ask pertinent questions and discuss the variables that could impact the event, such as weather, equipment degradations, or newly qualified personnel standing a watch for the first time. You should be thoroughly familiar with the contents of every special evolution brief for which you will be OOD prior to briefing it to the commanding officer and the team.

Review Lessons Learned

Following every special evolution, controlling watchstations debrief each other on what went right and wrong. It is a best practice to catalogue these debriefing notes and include them as lessons learned in the next evolution's brief. When preparing for a special evolution as OOD, focus your review of lessons learned to similar events conducted with the same conditions. For example, if you are preparing for a night evolution, focus your review on lessons learned during previous evolutions conducted at night. If your ship has not previously conducted the particular evolution, it may be useful to reach out to other department heads on the waterfront to ask for their lessons learned. Three years may have passed since your ship last pulled into Singapore, but another ship may have done so three months earlier. And there are many resources to use when researching previous lessons learned: the Navy's Lessons Learned Library, Type Commander Near Miss Reports, and case studies of previous mishaps are all worthwhile resources.

Think about What Is Different and Consider the Risks
It is important to identify what about the upcoming evolution is different from previous evolutions. Perhaps your ship has gone alongside an oiler during the day but has not made an approach at night in recent memory. There are several differences despite performing the same evolution, and additional training is warranted prior to conducting the brief. You may want to highlight those differences in your brief by providing a picture of the ship and oiler's light scheme, the phone and distance line chemical light distribution, and lights that will be used in lieu of signal flags. Conversely, a key difference in the same evolution may have nothing to do with the time of day or the weather but instead could involve a watchstander. For example, a master helmsman has transferred since the last time the ship conducted the particular evolution, and it will be a newly qualified master helmsman standing the watch in their place for the first time. This factor should be taken into consideration, and ways to mitigate any potential concerns should be discussed. Take the time as OOD to consider all potential risks to minimize surprises during execution of the evolution.

Review the References
Every special evolution has a number of references that govern the preparation, timing, and execution of the event. There are technical manuals, type commander and Navy-wide instructions, government publications, and record message traffic to help you plan and prepare. You should be familiar with each

Table 8-1. Special Evolution References

Entering/Exiting Port	Underway Replenishment	Anchoring
CNSPINST 3530.4F NAVDORM	CNSPINST 3180.2 Fleet UNREP Guide	Ship Information Book
Navigation Rules & Regulations Handbook (COLREGS)	NSTM 571 – Underway Replenishment	NSTM 581 Anchoring
NSTM 582 – Mooring & Towing	NTTP 4-01.4 – Underway Replenishment	
LOGREQ	OPSTAT RASREQ	

of them, but there is no need to commit them to memory. The prebrief should cover any questions and clear up any uncertainty, but do not rely on the brief alone. Review the references (see table 8-1) on your own and refresh aspects of the special evolution with which you are unfamiliar.

Conduct a Walk-Through, Talk-Through

This is a simple way to increase the confidence of inexperienced or "rusty" watchstanders (including you!) conducting an evolution for the first time or for the first time in a long time. As a department head, you probably took the deck as OOD during many special evolutions throughout your division officer tours. However, it may have been several years since you last stood watch on the bridge, or you may have done so on a different class of ship, and a walk-through, talk-through exercise can help put you back in the right frame of mind to take the deck. Walk-through, talk-throughs can be accomplished in a variety of places using many different tools.

- ▶ Table top. One simple method is to "table-top" or white-board the evolution, using the wardroom table or a dry erase board in a classroom to draw the evolution and talk through, step by step, what you expect to happen during it.

- ▶ Muster on station. Alternatively, you can "muster on station" on the bridge, the forecastle, the boat deck, or a fueling station and talk and walk through each step using the actual equipment for better familiarity.

- ▶ Utilize the Navigation, Seamanship, and Shiphandling Trainer. Every Navy homeport has a Navigation, Seamanship, and Shiphandling Trainer, also known as the simulator, that can be reserved to conduct a harbor transit, an underway replenishment approach, or an anchoring evolution. In the simulator, you can choose the location, manipulate the environmentals, and pause and start over if things have not gone according to plan—a luxury you will not have during actual execution of the evolution. This quick and safe way to test several different responses to different shiphandling and maneuvering situations will bolster your confidence prior to standing the real watch.

Be Prepared Mentally and Physically

A special evolution may be scheduled to begin or end at any time of day. You may be asked to stand OOD while exiting port early in the morning or while

8-1. **One of many ways a department head can prepare for a special evolution is to practice in a navigation, seamanship, and shiphandling trainer.**
U.S. Navy photo by Mass Communication Specialist 1st Class Diana Quinlan/Released

conducting a refueling at sea that begins and ends after sunset. The length of the evolution also will vary. A typical underway replenishment might last two hours, but a harbor transit might last as little as one hour or as long as ten or more. Some special evolutions are long enough that you will turn over the deck to another OOD midway through the evolution. Consider all of these variables in the days and hours before taking the watch. Being well rested, well fed, and mentally prepared will improve your physical and mental performance on game day. Deciding when to go to bed the night before and what to eat and drink before taking the deck will have an impact on the evolution.

During the Event

Arrive on Station Early

An important part of setting yourself up for success is reporting to the bridge early to start gaining situational awareness. If getting under way from the pier, this extra time allows you to make sure communication circuits are dialed in, radars are properly tuned, and ready references are on station. Special evolution and pre-underway checklists usually begin at least ninety-six hours prior to the event, and everything up to two hours prior to taking in all lines should already have been accomplished before you take the deck. However, as OOD you should not take for granted that everything is ready to go. When entering port, arriving on the bridge early allows plenty of time for you to get comfortable with the surface contact picture and to assess environmental factors before turning over and taking the deck. There are also physical reasons for arriving early, which include letting your eyes adjust if you are conducting an evolution at night or ensuring you are properly dressed in case the temperature is cooler or warmer than anticipated.

Parse Your References and Have Them on Station
Even though you reviewed the references prior to the brief and before taking the watch, it is useful to have them available on station. The most useful format for these references will depend on the watchstation, the type of evolution, and personal preference. As OOD, decide what format works best for you. If conducting a harbor transit while entering port, a binder that includes the full navigation brief, a copy of the logistics requirement message, pages from the Coast Pilot or Sailing Directions that include pictures of important navigation aids, and a list of the VHF radio calls that need to be made would be useful for the OOD. However, a simple track sheet with courses, speeds, distances, and turn bearings might be all that is required to make the conning officer feel comfortable. Having reference material available on station and in a format that suits you and your watch team can help you and your team conduct a smooth evolution.

Leverage Your Watch Team and Bridge Resource Management
Bridge resource management (BRM) is the process of getting the most out of the resources you have available to break the "error chain" and ensure a safe evolution. Your resources include all of the qualified watchstanders and equipment at your disposal. Bridge watchstanding is accomplished as a team led by the OOD, and during a special evolution, the watch team is expanded to include additional key watchstanders. If you have not established a watchstander's responsibilities, it is imperative that you assign them specific tasks. The OOD must set priorities, delegate tasks, and ensure the watch team is working from a shared mental model. You can foster a shared mental model by taking a deep breath and communicating any changes to the plan to the entire team, should any arise.

SPECIAL EVOLUTIONS OFFICER OF THE DECK

Understand the Commanding Officer's Direction and Style

You will be required to prove that you have a deep understanding of the commanding officer's standing orders before they trust you in this position of leadership. During a special evolution, the commanding officer may remain on the bridge throughout, and you will have to learn to manage the watch in a way that best supports and complements the commanding officer. You may find your commanding officer interacts no differently with the special evolution OOD than they do with the OOD during open-ocean steaming, expecting the OOD to manage the evolution, provide recommendations, and execute in a "command by negation" relationship. There are other commanding officers who will take a more direct approach and make most of the decisions and expect the OOD to provide forceful backup. If you have an opportunity to observe a special evolution on your ship after reporting but prior to making your way onto the watchbill, you should pay close attention to how the commanding officer interacts with the OOD. However, if you are unable to observe an evolution before standing the watch and are unsure how the commanding officer expects you to work with them, simply ask the question.

Issues That Would Normally Require Your Attention as a Department Head

Taking the deck as OOD requires your undivided attention. Equipment casualties or personnel issues that involve your department should be handled by watchstanders, and your involvement should be limited to matters that involve the safe handling and employment of the ship. As chief engineer, you will likely be the plant control officer (PCO) during most special evolutions. In the event of an equipment casualty, as PCO you would immediately consider the specific actions required to limit equipment damage and quickly and safely restore the plant to a stable condition. However, the chief engineer serving as special evolution OOD during an equipment casualty should immediately consider how to alert nearby vessels of your situation and to determine the location of the closest and safest place to anchor. Potential issues that specifically involve your department and your role in their resolution should be discussed with the commanding officer prior to being assigned the primary duty of OOD during a special evolution.

Take Notes

Mental or written notes taken throughout the evolution to use as debriefing topics and lessons learned are key to improving as an OOD. Prior to the evolution, think about the most efficient way for you to catalogue your thoughts and observations in a way that is minimally distracting. You can write your own notes in a notebook or on the back of your copy of the brief, or ask the junior officer of the deck to take notes for you.

After the Evolution

Debrief and Capture Lessons Learned
Whether accomplished immediately following the evolution on station or more formally in a brief in the hours or day after the event, it is important to discuss the high and low points. The more watchstanders that are involved in the debrief, the better. Make it a point to be critical of yourself and anything you observed that did not go as planned. Push back against watchstanders who observed a safe evolution and have "nothing to report." You can set yourself up for success during the next evolution by capturing both the good and bad lessons learned.

Reflect
Separately from the watch team debrief, take the time to replay the evolution in your head and consider what you could have done better. Summarize your critique in the notes section of your Mariner Skills Logbook.

Supporting the Special Evolution as a Department Head

Every department head is responsible for something that will directly affect the success or failure of a special evolution. The following suggestions will help you maximize your contribution to the team.

The Prebrief, Again
It is important to give each brief your attention, as no matter the evolution, every department head will have an area for which they are specifically responsible. A single department head failing to do their due diligence could negatively impact the outcome. Being engaged and knowing the plan can prevent "churn" when it comes time to execute. For example, the operations officer will brief expected harbor movements at a navigation brief, but a list of ships and departure times does not suffice. Explaining the second-order effects is where a department head earns credibility. Do we expect to render honors to a ship encountered along the outbound transit? Will we use the same tugs or pilot as a ship under way before ours so that we can anticipate a delay? Thinking through all of the potential questions and having answers prepared ahead of time will raise the level of awareness for

everyone involved. This questioning attitude is squarely in the department head's wheelhouse.

Ensure Your Team Understands the Plan for the Evolution

The department head is not a one-man or -woman show, and failure is more likely if one attempts to prepare for a special evolution in a vacuum. Consider the BRM model and apply it to your department. Your job is to build a shared mental model for your department and get the most from the resources available. Department heads are required to have a better understanding of the big picture so they can identify the important role their department will play in the evolution and then communicate that critical role and the plan to their subordinates. The importance of the evolution and the extra level of attention and/or urgency required must be explicitly communicated. A routine task such as routing the ship's draft report, which is typically due to the OOD before noon, can become a distraction during a special evolution if the bridge is waiting for it to be delivered prior to getting under way. The individual Sailor responsible for preparing and routing the draft report should not be faulted for failing to recognize the urgency of a daily task if the plan was not properly communicated. They might not be aware that it is part of the pre-underway checklist and that the OOD requires it prior to taking in all lines. This is an example of how communicating the plan to your departmental leadership, who in turn can communicate the plan to every Sailor who will play a pivotal role in the evolution, can limit distractions and foster an environment where everyone is on the same page.

Walk Your Spaces and Trust, but Verify

One specific department head duty described in the SORM is to "ensure proper cleanliness and upkeep of departmental spaces" and to "inspect daily and report the condition of the department to the executive officer." The report the department head makes to the executive officer is not a "check in the box" and cannot be taken lightly. The department head is reporting that all assigned personnel, material, and spaces are ready to go for the evolution, and if there are any known discrepancies, they are reported as exceptions to the department's readiness and include a way forward.

No one should know the status of the department better than the department head. This is accomplished by putting into practice two oft-quoted maxims: *Trust, but verify* and *expect what you inspect*. If a repair or maintenance was accomplished on a critical piece of equipment in the days or hours leading up to a special evolution, you should make a point of checking it yourself. This extra effort not only will confirm the report but will also show the personnel in your department that you are engaged and tracking the important work they are doing. Before any special evolution, a department head should make a point of visiting every assigned space to confirm that everything is in order, including being secured for sea.

Provide Inputs to the Watchbill and Review Meticulously
The SORM designates the senior watch officer (SWO) as the officer responsible for the assignment and general supervision of all deck watchstanders. Department heads, per the SORM, "recommend qualified enlisted personnel of their departments for departmental watches and assign personnel to stations and duties within the department." As with assigned spaces and equipment, no one should know more about the personnel within the department than the department head, and the correct application of this knowledge can improve the chances that a ship executes a safe special evolution. For example, a last-minute change to the personal situation of an individual watchstander from your department may mean they can no longer stand the watch. Only departmental leadership may be aware, especially if something happens just prior to a special evolution. Do not let the ship conduct an evolution without a solid and discrepancy-free watchbill.

Effectively Manage the Watch Team Replacement Plan
Set up the ship for success in future evolutions. Tours of duty in the Navy are short, and turnover is high. It is typical for at least one-third of a ship's company to be new every twelve months. This turnover makes it extremely important to rotate your qualified watchstanders through different watchstations and always include under instruction watchstanders on the watchbill so that the ship maintains a deep bench of qualified personnel. A good time to address the next evolution's watchbill is immediately following the debrief of the current evolution, while observations about how each watchstander performed are still fresh. These observations can be used, assuming all other prerequisites have been met, to determine if a watchstander under instruction is ready to stand the watch alone. You also may decide that a qualified watchstander is ready to move on and train to stand a different and/or more advanced watchstation. The debrief is also a good time to assess your qualification process. For example, if a qualified watchstander did not perform competently, you may decide it necessary to revisit a certain area of the qualification process and provide additional training to all of your qualified watchstanders.

Conclusion

Both the OOD and each individual department head play an important role in the preparation and execution of a ship's special evolution, and there are times that you will shoulder both responsibilities at the same time. Every evolution is governed by an instruction and tracked by a checklist, and it has been successfully executed by your ship or a colleague's ship in recent memory. Going above and beyond in your preparation will pay dividends and contribute to your department being ready to support the evolution and to you being ready to effectively lead your team as the special evolution OOD.

CDR Christopher H. Bland is a surface warfare officer who has served as an auxiliaries officer, navigator, chief engineer, chief staff officer, and flag secretary with the Forward Deployed Naval Forces in Japan and Europe. He is also the recipient of the Surface Navy Association's Admiral Arleigh Burke Award for Operational Excellence. He most recently served as the executive officer in USS *McCampbell* (DDG 85) and is currently serving as the executive officer in USS *Mobile* (LCS 26).

CHAPTER 9

Senior Watch Officer

CDR J. D. Kristenson, USN

CONGRATULATIONS, YOU HAVE BEEN SELECTED as the senior watch officer (SWO)! While it can feel like a thankless job at times, you will gain valuable experience in shipwide administration and management, and you will have an even larger role in increasing your ship's overall effectiveness than you currently have within your department.

Organizational Roles and Responsibilities

The *Standard Organization and Regulations of the U.S. Navy* (SORM, OPNAVINST 3120.32 [series]) outlines the functions, duties, authorities, and organizational relationships of both naval unit leadership positions and shipboard billets. The SORM's description of the responsibilities of the SWO follows:

a. BASIC FUNCTION. The senior watch officer, under the direction of the executive officer, is responsible to the commanding officer for the assignment and general supervision of all deck watchstanders, both underway and in port.

b. DUTIES, RESPONSIBILITIES, AND AUTHORITY. Maintain a data file of officer underway and in-port deck watchstanders, including watch standing qualifications, assignment to watches, and section assignment. Assist the executive officer by coordinating training of watchstanders, preparing watchbills and scheduling of the command's in-port duty rotation.

c. ORGANIZATIONAL RELATIONSHIPS. The senior watch officer reports to the commanding officer, for approval of officer watchbills and to the executive officer for the training of deck watch officers. Department heads recommend qualified enlisted personnel of their departments for departmental watches to the senior watch officer.

Being "the SWO"

The senior watch officer is generally the officer with the most seniority in the watch rotation that is assigned responsibility to generate in-port and at-sea watchbills and to maintain watchstanding standards throughout the ship.

Suggestions from the department heads as to who makes the most sense for the ship are generally welcome, but the ultimate decision of who will serve as the SWO is made by the executive officer (XO) and commanding officer (CO). The SWO is often, but not always, the senior department head. Tour timing or other primary or collateral duties (such as when assigned as board of inspection and survey coordinator or maintenance availability coordinator) might sometimes mean that it makes sense for a more junior department head to serve as SWO.

Build Your Team

Not every unit is large enough to have a "training department." You will need to build a team of Sailors who likely have other significant responsibilities. The SWO, training officer, and senior enlisted watchbill coordinator (SEWBC) are the three primary people who support the XO in making sure that the ship is well trained. It can also be effective to recruit a motivated petty officer first class to the team as well. You will need his or her assistance in coordinating support from duty section leaders and duty section watchbill coordinators for in-port watchbill construction and routing.

Training Officer

A great training officer can make the XO's and SWO's jobs much easier. The SORM makes clear that the training officer (TRAINO) reports to the XO regarding their assigned duties. In practice, many ships find it helpful for each division officer (DIVO) to fall under a department head who can provide advocacy and mentorship. You may find that the TRAINO works directly for one of your peers (probably the operations officer), and you will need to manage those relationships as you task the TRAINO and provide direct oversight for watchstanding and training-related tasks.

Senior Enlisted Watchbill Coordinator

This is the single most important person in producing watchbills that work. Do not let this fall to a chief or senior chief who does not want to do it. Look to chiefs you know and with whom you work well—perhaps in your duty section or department. Work with the command master chief (CMC) to identify who is eager to do the job well and has the support of their fellow chiefs.

Junior Watch Officer

You will not find the junior watch officer in the SORM or on any watchbill, but most ships have one. It is an informal position but is the secret to success for keeping officers on track for qualifications. Some ships have formalized this position as assistant SWO (A-SWO). Perhaps it is a qualified first tour DIVO coming up on the end of their tour or, more commonly, a second tour DIVO who can whisper to the SWO at the right time. This is a DIVO who has the pulse of the wardroom and can let you know who still needs to conn alongside one more time before their officer of the deck board. They also can be instrumental in helping to arrange cross-decking opportunities. Frequently, they will know fellow junior officers on the waterfront from their commissioning source, basic division officer's course, or social circles. The officer chosen for this role should be one who genuinely cares about helping ensigns qualify; this trait makes them the most effective in this role.

Your Fellow Department Heads

You cannot know every Sailor's qualification status personally. You will need to rely on and demand accountability from each department head for all of the Sailors for whom they are responsible. You are not directly responsible for every watchstation. For example, if you find yourself lacking qualified line handlers, you need to discuss with the operations officer why deck division is not running an effective watch team replacement plan, and the SEWBC should be having the same discussion with the boatswain's mate chief petty officer. Hold the khaki responsible for the watches they own, and, in turn, they will hold their Sailors accountable.

Executive Officer

There will be times when you will be asked to provide support to other ships or will need to prevail upon the goodwill of other ships in order to get your officers qualified. Some of this communication will be XO-to-XO, but keep in mind that your XO is even busier than you are. You can set up your XO and officers for success by knowing the other ships' schedules and who can provide temporary assigned duty (TAD) underway time while your ship is in the yards.

Your Relief

Commanding officers have increased flexibility as to which first tour department head to retain on board for a second tour. On most ships, the operations officer, weapons officer, or chief engineer could go on to become either the plans and tactics officer or combat systems officer. There is a good chance that, if you are the senior watch officer, you know already who the SWO after you is going to be. Work with them to make the transition as seamless as possible for the ship; everyone will be better for it.

Practical Advice

This section offers some suggestions and best practices for senior watch officers.

Finding of Fact One

Not all poorly constructed watchbills result in mishaps, but nearly all mishaps begin with an unqualified watchstander, inappropriate watch condition, or other watchbill error. You can break the first link in the error chain with a watchbill that works.

The R-ADM Permissions Problem

The relational administration data management (R-ADM) system is the Navy's software program to manage qualifications and construct watchbills. Use of R-ADM is required on every ship that has it as part of their naval tactical command support system software suite. While the software could use a refresh to improve user interface, it has some very powerful features that are underutilized across the fleet due to a lack of formal training and unfamiliarity with its robust capabilities. Spending time on a duty day becoming more familiar with R-ADM will pay dividends throughout your tour as SWO, as the system will consistently output a watchbill in direct relation to the quality of inputs that you provide. There is no "R-ADM Monster," and do not let anyone tell you otherwise.

R-ADM permissions are prescribed in the 43100 personnel qualification standard (PQS) unit coordinators guide and in various afloat self-assessment check sheets. Your ship training instruction should cover system permissions, including who will enter PQS indoctrination, assignments, and final qualifications. Keeping the permissions too tight will result in a significant time burden for the few individuals who are responsible for managing R-ADM, and the larger team may lack sufficient permissions to build effective watchbills. If you set the permissions too loose, it becomes difficult to ensure the integrity of the qualification process. If you find someone to be incorrectly listed as qualified, it becomes easier to identify how that happened and how to fix the process when three people have that permission, not thirty. A best practice is to spell out who has which R-ADM permissions in the ship instruction and to conduct periodic audits to ensure that people with the necessary permissions have not transferred and there has not been diffusion of access over time.

CHAPTER 9

Qualifications

The PQS program is designed to be progressive and build sequentially. In general, one qualification in the following categories is the most that a Sailor should work on at any given time: damage control, force protection, duty section, in-rate, and warfare qualification. This mandate will not be appropriate for every Sailor, but limiting the amount of PQS assigned simultaneously will prevent Sailors from becoming overwhelmed and helps in holding them accountable to appropriate qualification deadlines.

Delinquent in Qualification

Not every qualification is achievable throughout the ship's lifecycle. For example, it will be very difficult to obtain engineering officer of the watch if your ship is in an extended drydock. Sometimes, due to extended TAD or assignment of other significant responsibilities, extending a qualification deadline is prudent and just. The SWO must guard against the arbitrary rolling of qualification deadlines simply because it is easier than assigning extra military instruction (EMI) or delinquent in qualification (DINQ) study.

There are several legitimate reasons why a Sailor might not be pursuing an assigned qualification. Occasionally, a Sailor will be "assigned" PQS in R-ADM, but no one in their chain of command has communicated that expectation to them. Even when Sailors are aware of qualification deadlines, there are a lot of demands on their time, to include watchstanding and maintenance—neither of which can normally be deferred or delayed. As a result, even motivated and mission-oriented Sailors can find PQS qualifications pushed to the bottom of their personal priority list. Helping Sailors prioritize their qualifications is an important part of their professional development and growth and yields an effective watch team replacement plan.

Accountability is hard, but even great Sailors need external motivation from time to time. Work with the CO and XO to discuss the application of EMI and a DINQ study program as necessary. You must avoid inconsistency where no one seems to care about delinquent qualifications until liberty is threatened, and then a wave of PQS comes rolling in. Your consistency in enforcing qualification standards can set the conditions where the decision to "gun deck" is an individual integrity violation, not a pressure brought about by a failure of the system.

Templates

R-ADM bogs down when building watchbills for which there are a large number of qualified watchstanders (line handler, lookout, etc.). It can be faster to work with an Excel file as each watch section or department submits draft inputs. Feel free to use Excel as a planning tool but insist on using R-ADM as the only source of official watchbills. Building versatile templates within R-ADM will minimize rework and the number of pen-and-ink changes. Retain all signed watchbills in a three-ring binder for two years. This is a legal requirement for many programs and will be a lifesaver if the R-ADM server crashes or is inaccessible during a network upgrade or local area network migration.

Watchbills

Watchbills are the essence of the SWO responsibility. You are responsible for them all even if you do not write them. You must establish a system for writing and routing them effectively. You need a trustworthy member of the engineering department to edit the engineering section and a member of the operations department to be responsible for the deck section. Once all of the inputs are submitted, you need to review them thoroughly to make sure people are not doubled up or standing watch back-to-back. For example, a master helmsman standing the 0200–0700 watch before getting under way is not good risk management, but it can happen easily. You are the person who needs to catch that. Having the watchbills done early will make this process much easier.

9-1. A Sailor stands boatswains mate of the watch. The senior watch officer is responsible for all watchbills on the ship.

U.S. Navy photo by Mass Communication Specialist 2nd Class Justin R. Pacheco/Released

CHAPTER 9

Fast Cruises

The joint fleet maintenance manual has specific requirements for a "fast cruise." In practice, the term often is incorrectly used in place of what is akin to a "watchbill verification drill." A watchbill validation is particularly useful prior to getting under way after a prolonged in-port period. It makes sense to cycle through all the watch conditions and have each controlling watchstation sight muster every watchstander and conduct comms checks. By limiting the scope from a typical fast cruise, it can go quite quickly but can be instrumental in identifying holes in the watchbill that would be difficult to detect if it were built on paper.

Pen-and-Ink Changes

A best practice is to have a "clean" watchbill whenever possible. The captain may elect to switch the helm safety officer with aft steering at the navigation brief and be perfectly fine with a pen-and-ink change. Your follow-through in bringing a clean copy "for the record" whenever possible will demonstrate your commitment and attention to detail. I recommend only extending pen-and-ink privileges to the captain. Incorporating all of the changes, including the XO's edits, in the printed version you bring to the captain will have the added benefit of not drawing their attention to errors caught in routing.

Circadian Battle Rhythm

The SWO community has perhaps been slow to recognize the dangers of fatigue on watchstanders but is beginning to embrace the situation in a big way. In the last few years, the concept of circadian rhythm has changed from something a few ships were trying based on Naval Postgraduate School theses and *Proceedings* articles to a mandated practice throughout the fleet. There are a number of ways to implement this. My recommendation is that you take inventory of how well your current system is working and areas in which crew rest could be improved. Under way on Monday and back in on Friday is not enough time to determine if a routine can be effective. The longer underway stretches are a good opportunity to try a new routine by giving it enough time to settle out and see how it works. However your ship decides to implement circadian rhythm, it is essential that you have complete ship-wide buy-in for it to actually improve crew endurance and watchstander effectiveness. For example, if you decide that the workday will start at 0900 under way, then you cannot default to scheduling meetings at 0800 every time the schedule starts to fill up. It is challenging, but it can be done. The only way it works is by having the discipline to commit to it.

Surface Warfare Mariner Skills Logbook

The mariner logbook is a very useful, and perhaps long overdue, addition to surface warfare. We are jacks-of-all-trades by nature, but driving ships is the sine qua non of our profession; we all need to develop and maintain this expertise. SWOs are required to log the hours spent standing bridge watch, conducting special evolutions, and training in the simulator. The CO must sign the logbook at the end of every quarter. As with every requirement, compliance will vary. Some DIVOs will diligently fill it out each watch, and others will try to recall it days or weeks later. My recommendation is to check them yourself monthly (after wardroom training is a good time) to ensure that the DIVOs are regularly maintaining them. Then, at the end of the quarter, have the A-SWO or navigator collect and bring them to the CO for signature, along with the deck log. Routing them with the deck log will allow the captain to quickly spot-check them as they see fit.

Equally important to the logbook, the command must send a letter to PERS-41 at the end of every officer's tour detailing the number of hours of bridge watch they stood. This number can be simple enough to calculate, but it is better to track it by quarter along with the logbook. In order to ensure fairness in opportunity to qualify, a best practice is to keep a spreadsheet where you or the A-SWO tracks which special evolutions they have completed and which ones they still need to complete in order to qualify. Using this when you write watchbills will help ensure that you are not accidentally overlooking anyone and leaving them behind in the qualification process.

Watchstander's Liberty

The practice of allowing watchstanders to stand their watch and then go on liberty on a duty day varies widely by ship. For example, a Sailor might be allowed to stand an in-port deck watch in the morning and, not if strictly required for security or fire party watches, be allowed to leave the ship after watch. Every Sailor that should be on duty but is not degrades a ship's overall readiness. Furthermore, this practice can reinforce perceptions of favoritism and erode unity among the crew. I recommend the following business rules:

- ▶ Section leader and command duty officer (CDO) can allow Sailors to leave the ship on duty with permission to perhaps retrieve something from their car or pick up food on base.
- ▶ The CDOs from both sections along with the SWO can approve all duty swaps to ensure equivalent qualifications and that no one is abusing the process.

- Only the XO or CO can grant "watchstander's liberty" or excuse someone from a duty day entirely on a case-by-case basis.

Keeping these permissions at a consistent and well-publicized level will protect you as SWO, the duty section leadership, and the Sailor. Too many Sailors end up at captain's mast because of poorly managed enforcement of duty section requirements.

Who Stands Duty
It should be very clear who does and does not stand duty. Generally, the CO, XO, and command senior enlisted leader are exempt from duty by virtue of their position. If you are going to extend exemptions to others, such as the senior medical department representative because they are "always on watch" for medical emergencies, that should be made clear in the ship's SORM.

Duty Section Rotations
Just as there are a number of ways to build an at-sea watchbill, there are a number of different approaches to duty section routines. The number of duty sections that a ship maintains will vary by crew size, level of qualification, and threat condition. While it would be preferable to have the entire ship in the same number of duty sections, that is often not possible. The ship may be in six-section duty, but there may not be enough senior, supervisory positions such as engineering duty officers (EDOs). Often the EDOs will understand and voluntarily agree to maintain their own four- or five-section rotation to avoid having the ship collapse on their account. This can go the other way as well, where the CDO, as the senior watchstander and the captain's direct representative while in port, is afforded the luxury of a more forgiving rotation. Duty section rotations are a good vessel for lessons in leadership. As with many things in life, not everyone will be happy with the system you choose to implement. Dog the weekends, or don't dog the weekends; you will have grumblings and dissent either way. The best you can do is work with your SEWBC and CMC to build consensus and keep your XO and CO informed of your plan.

Communication as SWO
If you are going to implement an unusual practice, such as personally standing a fixed duty schedule and having the whole ship rotate around you so you can see all the duty sections and maintain standards, you need to make this clear to both the XO and CO so they can be prepared to answer questions about the plan for the duty sections. Keep in mind that they are removed from

the day-to-day duty section routine and largely will allow you to run it, but you need to keep them informed. Generally, Sailors will tolerate hardship, but they hate surprises. Communicating the plan well to the whole ship will go a long way in preventing any frustration about the operating policies.

Timing and Publicity

Having a business rule such as keeping the same watch team for the inbound and outbound sea and anchor teams is often a good practice. For short port visits, this approach can build upon the lessons learned from the previous under way, serve to establish expectations, and simplify watchbill routing. The watchbill should be posted along with the underway checkoff list. In order to hit that timeline, you need to have watchbills submitted a week before the intended ship's movement. This will allow time for them to be routed, revised, signed, and posted. Your effective planning will allow other shipboard leaders (DIVOs, leading chief petty officers, work center supervisors, maintenance technicians) to make their own plans. If no one knows who is going to be on watch, it becomes difficult to write and execute a maintenance plan and the rest of the shipboard routine suffers. Do not be the weak link—be the lead domino.

Add Value

If you are going to employ an A-SWO, you need to be prepared to recognize—and publicize—when the good work you are bringing the XO and CO is that of your assistant. You also need to own any mistakes that they made and you did not catch. If your A-SWO is writing the watchbill and you are merely routing their work, you are not adding supervisory value to the process. Watchbills are the commander's business. Never route a watchbill that you did not at least read. You should aspire to route perfect watchbills and not rely on your XO or CO to catch your mistakes.

Funny Business

Be alert for watchbills that contain practical jokes. Watchbills are a military appointed place and duty. Sea and anchor detail is the wrong time for it to be revealed that someone assigned the XO a watch in the vacuum, collection, holding, and transfer pumproom. While this may have been amusing as a junior officer, your assignment as SWO often means that you are, in terms of seniority, third in command. You are at a point in your career where you need to not only resist participating in, but also guard against pranks that reduce readiness and erode good order and discipline.

CHAPTER 9

Conclusion

Despite what your fitness reports may have been saying for years, your assignment as SWO might be the first time that you truly have "command-wide influence." The SWO job can feel like one more thing to do, but, if done right, it can have an enormous effect on the professionalism of your ship. It also can be enjoyable and rewarding as you see your plan put into action.

By the time you have been selected as SWO, your apprenticeship in surface warfare is nearly complete. The next time you will return to sea will likely be as XO or CO. Be the senior watch officer that you would want backing you up when you are in command.

CDR J. D. Kristenson is a career surface warfare officer and Olmsted Scholar (Beijing, China). He has commanded "a damn fine crew of Iron men on a Wooden ship" in USS *Champion* (MCM 4). He also served ashore as special assistant to the commander of United States European Command and Supreme Allied Commander of NATO. His next assignment will be leading Sailors in USS *Michael Murphy* (DDG 112).

PART IV

THE BILLETS AND FUTURE OPPORTUNITIES

CHAPTER 10
Operations Officer
CDR Doug Robb, USN

Being "the OPS"

NO MATTER THE METAPHOR—stage manager, third base coach, or straw that stirs the drink—the operations officer (OPS) is at the center of planning a ship's schedule. You are, as the name implies, an operator who choreographs the ship's operations. Nearly everything—personnel matters, qualifications, ship movements, drills, operations, all manner of meetings—filters through the OPS department. Officers who enjoy collaboration with colleagues involving long-range planning, short-term execution, shiphandling and deck evolutions, and advising the executive officer (XO) and commanding officer (CO) on how the ship will meet its tasking would find the duties of the OPS fulfilling—indeed, the best job on board.

Every Navy ship, submarine, squadron, or company has an OPS; however, in the surface fleet, expectations differ based on ship class. For example, operations officers on board cruisers or destroyers (CRUDES) are responsible for deck division—the boatswains mates charged with preserving topside spaces, executing special evolutions, operating small boats, etc.—which is led by a first tour division officer (DIVO). Conversely, on amphibious ships or aircraft carriers, deck is not a division but an entire department—one with added responsibilities for flight and well deck (landing craft) operations. Furthermore, the OPS on a littoral combat ship is typically a more senior second tour department head who has ascended, or fleeted up, after completing a first tour as the combat systems officer. Although they share many tasks, differences do exist between these assignments.

But the differences do not end there. Even within CRUDES ships, the OPS department's organization and the job's scope can vary from hull to hull. For example, the creation of the plans and tactics officer—a second tour department head position—may, at the captain's discretion, alter the exact divisional, programmatic, and planning duties for which the OPS is responsible. Additionally, operations officers on board newer Flight IIA *Arleigh Burke*–class destroyers—those constructed with hangars capable of carrying two embarked MH-60R helicopters—must factor in flight deck certifications, drills, and daily air schedules to complement the ship's broader training and operational requirements; also, those serving on board *Ticonderoga*-class cruisers must balance their ship and departmental responsibilities with added duties that include serving as a carrier strike group's air warfare commander.

Finally, differences exist between operations officers serving in afloat units and those serving within staffs afloat or ashore. This chapter is tailored to guide first tour department heads bound for an OPS tour on board a "gray hull" ship. After listing some of the OPS's more prominent job responsibilities, the chapter will offer some best practices to consider for a successful tour.

Organizational Roles and Responsibilities

The *Standard Organization and Regulations of the U.S. Navy* (SORM, OPNAV-INST 3120.32 [series]) outlines the functions, duties, authorities, and organizational relationships of both naval unit leadership positions and shipboard billets. The SORM prescribes the OPS to be "responsible for all operational aspects of the assigned mission, such as maintaining operational readiness in support of battle plans or other instructions as may be directed by higher authority." The SORM's specific functions inherent within the OPS position and the collateral duties typically assigned to OPS include:

- the conduct of surface and air search
- the execution of anti-air warfare, antisurface warfare, antisubmarine warfare, electronic warfare, strike warfare, and intelligence and/or cryptologic operations as directed
- the control of assigned aircraft when airborne
- the preparation of operational plans, orders, and other reports and directives
- the collection, interpretation, display, and dissemination of meteorological and oceanographic information
- the collection and transmission of requests for operational and logistic services required by the command in support of operations
- the preparation and issuing of training schedules

- the maintenance and dissemination of the ship's or unit's operating schedule
- in units without a deck department, the functions prescribed for the deck department
- if assigned as the collateral duty safety officer, serve as the principal advisor to the commanding officer on safety and occupational health matters; oversee the unit-wide elements of the safety program; ensure timely and accurate submission of required mishaps reports; and conduct training on safety-related issues.

Practical Advice for a Successful Tour

The following information describes some helpful tips for those currently serving, or seeking assignment, as a ship's OPS.

Represent the Ship—and the Captain

Build Your Off-Ship Network

Because the OPS is central for planning and executing the ship's missions, it becomes necessary to communicate and coordinate with many different people and organizations almost daily. This can require not only skill but also a healthy helping of diplomacy. It may be necessary to call others with whom you work—the port operations officer, ship's training liaison officer, port engineer, immediate superior in command (ISIC) operations officer (e.g., destroyer squadron or strike group N3), fleet scheduler, and your local fleet area control and surveillance facility, to name a few—on short notice or under emergent circumstances. Therefore, make a point to get to know these colleagues. Ideally, meet them face to face before you report on board the ship to establish a bank of mutual trust that can help foster successful working relationships.

Familiarize Yourself with Key References

To represent the command well, you must be competent in the guiding references. In department head school, develop a broad list of required reading and references to keep in your personal (or electronic) library. Take time to read these sources, and be able to reference the principal documents governing the profession on an as-needed basis. This will prove its value the first time you need to consult them. Examples include the *Surface Force Training and Readiness Manual, Fleet Operational Order*, the *Department of the Navy Correspondence Manual*, the *Standard Subject Identification Code*

Manual (SECNAV M-5210 [series]), *Standard Operating Procedures for Special Incident Reporting* (OPNAVINST 3100.6 [series]), *Navigation Rules and Regulations Handbook*, *Navy Performance Evaluation System* (BUPERSINST 1610 [series]), and ISIC-delineated guidance. Doing so will help you to perform your job better, be able to support (or provide forceful backup to) your Sailors, demonstrate your interest and competence to your chain of command, illustrate a desire to grow professionally, and represent the command authoritatively.

Know—and Anticipate—Reporting Requirements
One reason it is so vital that you internalize the key references mentioned above is that ships have no shortage of operational reporting requirements. Such reports include: movement reports, situation reports, operational reports, casualty reports and updates, operational tasking orders, logistics requests, environmental spill reports, operations area waterspace requests, fuel management, and fleet in/out change of operational control messages. Some are situational, but there are also recurring requirements (i.e., updated messages transmitted on a set periodicity). You should know the redlines that would necessitate sending the more common reporting messages. Create templated documents in advance to make the task easier. Be aware that these reporting requirements may differ slightly among the numbered fleets when you deploy.

Be Cognizant of Changes to Your Chain of Command
Shifts in operational and tactical control are common at sea—especially during the high tempo periods of basic, intermediate, advanced, and sustainment phases, including deployed operations. Be aware of who your ship's officer in tactical command is for the exercise or operation in which you are participating and communicate expected or emergent changes in your chain of command to the tactical and controlling watchstations. Disseminate your new boss' reporting requirements and ensure that your ship (and, by extension, your captain) is only being tasked by the commander who has the requisite authority to do so.

Insert Yourself in All (or Most) Off-Ship Communications
"Representing the ship" means more than simply being physically present at a meeting or conference. It also means projecting an image (hopefully a positive one) on radio circuits, in email, and through message traffic. Fair or not, in the naval service, where units operate apart from one another often at very long distances, your ship is sometimes only as good as others

read you to be (or hear you to be on the radio). As the OPS, ensuring that communications are structured, formal, well-articulated, and produced according to policies and guidelines will amplify your ship's and crew's professional reputation.

Drive the Ship's Schedule

Own the Schedule—and Guard It
No verb more accurately describes this singular responsibility: the OPS owns the schedule. Of all the department heads, only the OPS—empowered with the authority granted by the captain—can make operational commitments for the ship. This includes the day-to-day, weekly, and long-range calendars. Be extremely careful to whom you grant "editable" or "write" access to the calendar, thereby enabling them to make changes. Practice saying "no." Hold weekly meetings among the ship's leadership and key stakeholders to review the schedule minute by minute over the ensuing few weeks to validate its executability. Nothing should appear on the calendar without you first knowing about it; only then can you guarantee that satisfactory planning, synchronization, and deconfliction have taken place.

Understand Your Authorities and Boundaries
You will represent your ship and captain at myriad planning meetings, conferences, wargames, and professional gatherings. Sometimes, you may be expected to make commitments about your ship's availability to participate in certain events; for example, at the numbered fleet's quarterly scheduling conference, ships are expected to volunteer for at-sea testing events, exercises, port visits, or distinguished visitor embarkation visits. Find time to sit down with your captain before you commit the ship to any tasking, which will become your captain's responsibility.

Be Able to Access the Schedule at All Times
The OPS is the person to whom the XO, CO, or other off-ship planning nodes will turn if questions arise about the ship's or crew's movements. As a result, consider carrying a copy of the ship's short- and long-term schedules on you or in your notebook at all times. If traveling to a meeting off the ship, ensure you have consulted with your security manager and are following all courier protocols, since the long-range schedule is typically classified.

Establish a Working Battle Rhythm but Be Flexible
Create a template for an "ideal" schedule that includes all anticipated limitations, such as recurring meetings, councils, or boards; physical training

sessions; cleaning, drilling, or maintenance periods; and quarters or all-hands calls. This can serve as a starting point from which to insert other situational requirements (e.g., exercises, inspections, drills, special events, ceremonies) as they arise.

The schedule is a starting point, but nothing is as constant as change. Anticipate changes as best you can. Communicate up, down, and across the chain of command with other key stakeholders; devise courses of action; deliver potential solutions (not more problems) to the XO and CO; and never let a perfect plan be the enemy of a good one.

Inside the Ship's Lifelines

Review All Message Traffic—Inbound and Outbound
Just as you should take an active role in off-ship communications, so too should you review all message traffic (and admittedly, there will be a large amount of it) that arrives or is prepared for transmission. Specifically, scan each message for tasking or other items that could affect the ship and be mindful that some messages include a requirement to formally acknowledge receipt and produce a reply (e.g., the marking "ACK//Y" that may appear at the end of the message). Establishing a professional working relationship with the information systems technicians who work in the ship's radio space will empower them to alert you to important communications developments.

Educate Key Watchstanders—and Even Your XO and CO—on Reporting Requirements
Given your expected familiarity with operational references, you should be involved personally in training duty section leaders—command duty officers and the duty OPS watchstanders—so that they meet expected standards of preparation and intent regarding execution. Invite your CO and XO to these sessions as well—the training can serve as an important refresher and provide a forum to communicate changes in protocols.

Involve the Navigator and Training Officer in Your Planning
Building an effective schedule requires understanding your planning constraints (things you must do) and restraints (things you must not do). In this respect, the navigator (NAV) and the training officer (TRAINO) are important partners. As you develop the plans that govern the ship's movements, the NAV can help with voyage planning, validate time-speed-distance calculations, verify fueling and movement reporting requirements, and ensure the ship is positioned optimally to achieve its tasking. Similarly, integrate the TRAINO

10-1. In addition to crafting and executing the ship's daily and long-term schedules, operations officers in cruiser or destroyer units oversee deck and shiphandling special evolutions.
U.S. Navy photo by Mass Communication Specialist 2nd Class Sean Rinner/Released

into the ship's operational plans and battle rhythms. The TRAINO will track qualifications, schools, drills, and certifications and should pass that information to you to ensure it is integrated into the schedule before these events are projected to lapse or expire.

Participate in Special Evolutions Even If You Are Not on the Watchbill
Nearly every special evolution—entering or leaving port, underway replenishments, mooring to a buoy, towing, flight operations, and man overboard and abandon ship drills—involves either a bridge or deck safety component. The OPS should be involved and positioned—likely in the pilothouse or as a deck safety officer—to observe, coach, or provide seasoned oversight.

Review the Draft Plan of the Day Prior to Publication
Depending on your ship's battle rhythm, the administrative team or one of your DIVOs may generate a draft plan of the day (POD) modeled after the ship's schedule for your review. The OPS must nevertheless review the draft prior to routing to the XO to verify there were no errors or omissions in transposing the schedule and to incorporate any last-minute planning guidance of

which you may be aware. This is necessary for accurate scheduling and precise execution. Consider publishing two days in the POD—the day of execution and the following day—in order to facilitate crew awareness and planning. Repetition and review are valuable learning tools.

Walk the Weatherdecks Daily and Supervise the Department's Maintenance Responsibilities

The ship's outward appearance—the cleanliness of its topside spaces, the smartness of the mooring lines, the lack of visible rust—is a direct reflection on the captain and crew. This responsibility falls to the OPS department (principally, deck division). Walking about the ship (and along the pier when in port) provides an opportunity for the OPS to lend a critical perspective to current or emerging problems that will need to be addressed. Observing the material condition (and recognizing changes to it) is especially important during prolonged periods at sea, in which the saltwater spray can wreak havoc on the steel decks and the equipment atop them. Armed with this knowledge, the OPS can work to schedule maintenance equipment in the ship's next port of call (e.g., man-lifts, barges, or "paint punts" to facilitate topside preservation). Additionally, like any other department, the OPS is responsible for spaces and equipment inside the skin of the ship that must be cleaned, operated, and maintained in order to function properly when needed. An assistant, such as a leading chief or hot-running work center supervisor, can help work out the details, but as the department head, you should remain engaged in tracking and validating maintenance actions and completion. This tracking is especially important when one of the OPS's divisions is scrutinized during the weekly rotational "division in the spotlight" program reviews or when OPS spaces are being checked as part of the ship's zone inspection.

Identify and Monitor Your Personnel Redlines

While all department manning considerations can impact the mission, there are a few specialties—critical naval enlisted classifications—without whom (or enough of whom) the ship cannot sail. The schools to train and certify these specialists are long, especially the search-and-rescue swimmer and tactical air controller courses. Consequently, ensure either you have a plan in place to "grow" one of these niche capabilities from within your ship's roster at an appropriate time in the schedule or that you have identified a Sailor with the required competency detailed to the ship.

OPERATIONS OFFICER

Work to Build Consensus among Your Fellow Department Heads
Despite your pivotal role in orchestrating the ship's schedule, plans, and movements, you will rely on the counsel, inputs, and experience of your fellow department heads. Involve them in your planning, share information, communicate what you know, listen to their concerns, and, where appropriate, support them with the same forceful backup you would expect them to provide to you. Provide feedback; effective communication requires that all parties understand one another.

All in a Day's Work

Arrive Early to Plan Your Day
While every officer's morning routine varies somewhat, perhaps nothing is more important for the OPS than setting a clear course early in the day—before a majority of the crew reports on board (when in port), before one's email inbox is flooded with messages and taskers, and before a scheduled or emergent circumstance changes priorities. This quiet hour gives you time to exercise, check your unclassified and classified email accounts, review and internalize the day's schedule, walk through your spaces, grab some coffee, chat with shipmates, and formulate the "plan of attack" you will pass shortly to your DIVOs and chief petty officers. Morning quarters are arguably the most important fifteen minutes of the day: your chance to issue clear guidance regarding your expectations for what should get done—and for your department leadership to hear it directly from you. If done well, your team will understand your intent and move to implement it. If communicated poorly or with lack of forethought, the day can be lost—and with it, hundreds of man-hours wasted.

Update and Organize Your Thoughts
Maintain a planner, which may include some form of schedule or calendar (e.g., a weekly or monthly appointment book) and/or notepad. Different forms of organization work for different people—a "wheel book" in which you can jot down thoughts or meeting notes to which you can refer later, a piece of graph paper that allows you to create a checklist, and color coding to denote different subjects or divisions are just a few ideas that you may consider. Find what works for you, be diligent about keeping up with it, and refer back to your notes to check your thinking. Doing so will allow you to keep your priorities straight so they do not get lost in the day's "churn."

Optimize Your Email Inbox
The sheer volume of email that will amass in your inbox can become overwhelming; you will receive more than you can possibly read and internalize. Some of this traffic will be notes or taskers from people, but much of it will be record message traffic. While every message transmitted serves a purpose, some are more germane for you and your responsibilities than others. Your ship is likely using the Microsoft Office computer software suite, which includes Outlook for email. Learn the filter and organizational tools inherent in Outlook to funnel messages based on keywords, subject lines, or other identifiers to specially created subfolders within your inbox. This will preserve them for reference but move them out of your inbox, thus allowing you to more efficiently rank, arrange, and comb through key emails and messages.

Identify and Empower a Trusted Deputy and a Cadre of Assistants
The department head's scope, responsibility, and levels of authority can be daunting for even the most impressive junior officer. Time management skills are critical because priorities are really a function of importance and time; there are those things that must be done because they are critical to the mission right now, and there are other items that, while still important, can wait (or at least be done by someone else). Identify a stand-out DIVO, chief, and/or petty officer to delegate what you can (while being careful to still provide necessary oversight) so you can keep your focus on those things that only you can or should be doing. For the OPS, maintenance, the safety program collateral duty, long-range schedule upkeep, training records, and some administration are natural places to seek help and, in the process, empower your teammates.

Learn about Your Sailors
When you are away from home, the crew and your department are work colleagues but are also your Navy family. They have their own lives, ambitions, uncertainties, families, and interests. They are people—usually young people—and you are their leader. Meet them when they report on board to get to know them and their abilities; they will not let you down when you really need their best efforts or support. Just like you, they want to do a good job and succeed.

Address Your Department Regularly
Although gathering your entire department weekly (or maybe even monthly) is not necessary, finding time to bring your entire team together is important.

Not only does it foster a sense of esprit de corps among the divisions that comprise your department, it also offers a valuable chance to communicate your guidance and expectations directly. Finally, few things induce anxiety in a crew more than uncertainty about the schedule, and you are the individual who knows more about the schedule than perhaps anyone on board. Use that time to assuage any potential concerns your Sailors may have by communicating what you can (with the recognition that it may not be all that you know).

Recognize Your Team's Accomplishments
Find ways to spotlight your teammates' achievements. Ask your leadership for their inputs. If you intend to recognize some of your Sailors during a part of your department head call, consider inviting the CO, XO, or command master chief for that portion. Awards, coins, plaques, certificates, days of liberty, "late sleepers," or "early chow"—anything within the scope of your authority—are small but important ways to convey your thanks for a job well done and make your Sailors, chiefs, and officers feel that their work and contributions are valued. Everyone likes to be appreciated and made to feel they are doing important work.

At Day's End, Reflect on What You and Your Team Accomplished
Just as it is important to arrive early, so too is it necessary to reflect at the end of a long day. When the ship is in port and most of the crew has departed, the line outside your door will steadily shrink, messages will stop accruing in your email inbox, and you will find yourself with time (and the quiet) to think. Be introspective: what did your team accomplish today? What still must be done before you depart? What are tomorrow's goals and priorities, and how will we accomplish them given the POD's projected scheduled events? Use this time to go through the email and administrative tasks that piled up through the course of the day, make lists, draft follow-up notes, read, and prepare to effectively communicate your guidance to your Sailors.

Conclusion

The commanding officer's direct representative for all coordination, planning, scheduling, and tactical execution, the ship's operations officer is critical to the unit's success. With responsibilities that lie both within the ship's lifelines and with external commands and organizations, the OPS must be organized, articulate, efficient, and firm. It goes without saying that the OPS is an authority figure whose authority is rooted in not only their rank but also

CHAPTER 10

their character and demeanor. Competence is expected and demanded, but treating people fairly and with respect sets an example that is the hallmark of true leadership and that gives a team cohesion and purpose. A successful operations department is vital to a ship's proficiency and performance. Although the job may seem daunting, with preparation and thoroughness of execution, it can be one of the most rewarding experiences of your time in uniform and something you can reflect on with pride when your Navy career concludes.

CDR Doug Robb is a surface warfare officer who has served four tours in operations departments in USS *Halsey* (DDG 97), USS *Kidd* (DDG 100), and on the staff of commander, Destroyer Squadron SEVEN, where he earned the Navy League's Stephen Decatur Award for Operational Competence. Ashore, he served as a liaison to the U.S. House of Representatives at the Navy's Office of Legislative Affairs, in the surface warfare division on the Navy Staff (OPNAV N96), and as speechwriter for the Chief of Naval Operations. He currently serves as executive officer in USS *Spruance* (DDG 111).

CHAPTER 11
Staff Operations Officer
CDR James Hagerty, USN

*Luck can be attributed to a well-conceived plan
carried out by a well-trained and indoctrinated task group.*
—Fleet Admiral Chester W. Nimitz

Being "the N3"

THERE IS SIMPLY NO JOB on board a ship or afloat staff that has as much potential for impact as squadron N3 or staff operations officer (the two titles will be used interchangeably in this chapter). The N3 has the potential to literally run an entire strike group or task force—placing air, surface, and subsurface assets in the best position to execute the commander's tasking. Conversely, the N3 can also set up the same units for complete failure or, worse, catastrophic loss of life or equipment.

A good N3 runs an effective team that can simultaneously execute current operations and plan future operations. A good N3 ensures that the staff and assigned units are well trained. A good N3 constantly thinks ahead and communicates—both internally and externally—to ensure subordinates carry out commander's intent. Finally, a good N3 identifies problems before they arise and solves them at the staff level or, if necessary, presents well-thought-out courses of action to the commodore for decision.

Chapter 10 described the immense responsibility that comes with being a shipboard operations officer (OPS). In this chapter, we will move up one echelon, expand our scope, and discuss the job of an operations officer on an afloat staff. The chapter will focus primarily on the jobs of the N3 in a destroyer squadron (DESRON) or amphibious squadron (PHIBRON), with some applications for other squadrons, including naval surface squadrons (SURFRONs), littoral combat ship squadrons (LCSRONs), and surface development squadrons (SURFDEVRONs).

CHAPTER 11

Organizational Roles and Responsibilities

The previous chapter covered the roles and responsibilities of the OPS in the *Standard Organization and Regulations of the U.S. Navy* (SORM, OPNAV-INST 3120.32 [series]). There is no special section of the SORM for the staff operations officer, but the instruction clearly states the guidelines are for the head of the operations department for any unit—including an afloat staff. Thus, it is worth reemphasizing the key OPS functions outlined in the SORM that you are likely to execute as the staff operations officer.

The operations officer is "responsible for *all operational aspects of the assigned mission*, such as maintaining *operational readiness in support of battle plans* or other instructions as may be directed by higher authority." Specific functions include:

- ▶ the conduct of surface and air search
- ▶ the execution of anti-air warfare, antisurface warfare, antisubmarine warfare, electronic warfare, strike warfare, and intelligence and/or cryptologic operations as directed
- ▶ the control of assigned aircraft when airborne
- ▶ the preparation of operational plans, orders, and other reports and directives
- ▶ the collection, interpretation, display, and dissemination of meteorological and oceanographic information
- ▶ the collection and transmission of requests for operational and logistic services required by the command in support of operations
- ▶ the preparation and issuing of training schedules
- ▶ the maintenance and dissemination of the ship or unit's operating schedule.

Distinct Roles of the N3 in the Operational and Administrative Chains of Command

There are a variety of surface ship squadrons across the Navy. At their most basic level, DESRON and PHIBRON staffs are tasked to perform two distinct functions: act as immediate superior in command (ISIC) for a group of ships in the administrative (i.e., man/train/equip) chain of command (CoC), and employ naval forces—typically a task group or a task force—in the operational CoC. This operational command function can take several forms, including task force commander in a numbered fleet, sea combat commander in a carrier strike group (CSG), or composite warfare commander in an amphibious ready group (ARG). The operational command function often requires significant interaction with a strike group staff and ultimately with the numbered fleet staff. The ISIC role in the administrative CoC requires more interaction with the type commander staff (commander, Naval Surface Forces Atlantic or Pacific).

One primary difference between the operational and administrative command function is the designed length of the command relationship. The role of an ISIC is meant to be somewhat enduring in order to provide continuity in leadership for manning, training, and equipping—particularly as ships move through the training cycle and prepare for deployment. The operational command function, however, is meant to take advantage of the Navy's flexible command and control structure that allows assets to move rapidly in and out of task forces for predetermined periods of time based on operational tasking. Through this lens, the ISIC relationship is grounded in long-term stability, while the operational commander relationship can turn into a pickup game—with various assets changing operational control between task forces for differing lengths of time.

The operational and administrative command functions each require a different focus, and your specific duties as N3 will vary greatly depending on your assigned squadron. This chapter will concentrate primarily on operational command, but the N3 also plays a significant role in the man/train/equip function, particularly in scheduling and managing risk across a squadron.

Varied Squadrons across the Fleet

Before we dive deeper into specifics of the N3 job, let us take a snapshot of some of the various surface ship squadrons across the fleet and see how they fit into the operational and administrative chains of command.

Continental U.S. Squadrons: Both Operational and Man/Train/Equip Responsibilities
Continental U.S. (CONUS)–based DESRONs and PHIBRONs homeported on the East and West coasts perform both operational and man/train/equip functions, acting as ISIC for a squadron of ships while also deploying with their respective CSG or ARG. These squadrons must balance both operational and administrative functions with limited manpower and resources. To mitigate this challenge, squadrons often prioritize their efforts based on their relative progress through the optimized fleet response plan cycle. For

example, if the aircraft carrier (CVN) and most of the surface combatants in a strike group are in the maintenance phase and planning for the basic phase, you will likely see much of the squadron's effort focused on man/train/equip responsibilities. Conversely, in the integrated phase just prior to deployment, you will see a noticeable shift in focus to upcoming operations.

Forward-Deployed Squadrons: Heavy Operational Focus

- DESRON 7, forward-deployed in Singapore, has operational control of deployed littoral combat ships (LCSs) and plays a significant role in 7th Fleet operations in Southeast Asia. DESRON 7 also oversees the deployed sustainment of LCSs given the ship's special maintenance requirements while deployed. Additionally, DESRON 7 maintains the capability to serve as sea combat commander for the forward-deployed expeditionary strike group.

- PHIBRON 11, in Forward-Deployed Naval Forces Japan, in Sasebo, performs both operational and man/train/equip functions and acts as the ISIC for forward-deployed amphibious ships. PHIBRON 11 is permanently embarked on a forward-deployed big deck amphibious ship.

- DESRON 15, in Forward-Deployed Naval Forces Japan, is the sea combat commander for the forward-deployed carrier strike group and is also the principal surface force for Battle Force 7th Fleet.

- DESRON 40, homeported in Mayport, Florida, is a primarily operationally focused squadron that supports naval operations in the U.S. 4th Fleet/Southern Command area of responsibility.

- DESRON 50, forward-deployed in Bahrain, is primarily operationally focused and has limited man/train/equip responsibilities. DESRON 50 has operational control of forward-deployed patrol coastal ships as well as any other ships that are deployed to 5th Fleet and assigned to commander, Task Force 55.

- DESRON 60, in Forward-Deployed Naval Forces Europe, is located in Rota, Spain. The commodore is dual-hatted as the operational commander, Task Force 65. Taken together, this command is responsible for man/train/equip responsibilities of the destroyers homeported in Rota and has operational command of these ships and all CRUDES deployed from CONUS in the Sixth Fleet area of responsibility that are not part of a CSG.

11-1. **Ships assigned to Destroyer Squadron 23 transit the Pacific Ocean.**
U.S. Navy photo by Mass Communication Specialist 3rd Class Erik A. Parsons/Released

Readiness Squadrons

- LCSRON 1, homeported in San Diego, and LCSRON 2, homeported in Mayport, oversee man/train/equip functions for littoral combat ships. LCSRON 1 has *Independence*-class ships, while LCSRON 2 is composed of *Freedom*-class ships. Additionally, as the LCS program grows, LCS divisions are forming on both coasts. These divisions will comprise four LCSs, each with a common mission package variant.

- SURFDEVRON 1 in San Diego acts as ISIC for the guided missile destroyer (DDG) 1000 class and will oversee experimentation with new platforms, including *Zumwalt*-class destroyers, and unmanned vessels, including the Sea Hunter unmanned surface vehicle.

- SURFRON 14, homeported in Mayport, is also man/train/equip–focused, serving as ISIC and providing readiness support to Mayport-based surface ships. In a similar fashion, SURFRON 5, homeported in Bahrain, has man/train/equip responsibilities for patrol coastal and mine countermeasure ships.

- DESRON 31, homeported in Hawaii, is an example of a squadron that has considerable man/train/equip responsibilities, acting as ISIC for several Hawaii-based DDGs. While they are not permanently assigned to a carrier strike group, they retain the ability to act in an operational capacity for international exercises (including Pacific Partnership) and any other tasking assigned by the fleet commander.

In summary, although the missions of surface squadrons vary depending on their roles in the operational and administrative chains of command, essentially squadrons execute two basic functions—manning/training/equipping ships and operationally employing ships. Even if your squadron is inherently focused on one of those missions, you would be wise to not completely ignore the other.

Practical Advice for a Successful Tour

The following information includes some helpful tips for those currently serving, or seeking assignment, as a squadron N3.

For All Squadrons

Represent the Commodore
Any time you talk, send an email, release a message, or initiate any other form of communication, it is assumed that you are speaking for the commodore, so be sure to keep your correspondence professional and courteous. Also, like any other OPS/commanding officer (CO) relationship, take the time to understand the commodore's vision and learn your left and right limits. This will allow you to understand when you can speak for the boss, need to seek additional guidance, or need to elevate an issue to the O-6 level.

Additionally, just like the relationship between a shipboard OPS and executive officer (XO), take the time to run key issues through the deputy commodore (or back-brief if the operational situation does not allow time). As a post command and major command–screened officer, the deputy commodore can provide valuable insight and may also be a useful sounding board prior to bringing key issues to the commodore.

Respect the Authority of the Ship's CO
This might seem obvious, but any former N3 can tell you it is possible to get into a bad habit of believing the chain of command runs from the commodore to you to the ship's operations officer. It is important to ensure that the authority of the individual ship's commanding officer is well respected and that COs are provided with ample opportunity to provide feedback and communicate concerns. No one knows a ship better than the commanding officer,

and their input should not be minimized. When appropriate, do not hesitate to communicate directly with the individual ship COs or XOs. Often, they will appreciate the opportunity to use you as a sounding board for their own communications with the commodore.

Develop a Good Working Relationship with Operations Officers
Take the time to meet the OPS of each individual ship in your squadron or deployed task force/task group—in person, if possible. If deployed schedules make an in-person visit impractical, a video teleconference or even a personal email might be the next best option. Effective two-way communication with each OPS is the best way to understand the challenges of each ship, which can be especially helpful if a ship is under your commodore's operational control for a short period of time. Additionally, one of the benefits of the N3 position is the opportunity to mentor first tour operations officers in your squadron.

Effectively Utilize Your OPS Team
Most squadron staffs are quite small—often fewer than thirty officers and enlisted personnel. Despite the small size, as staff operations officer, you will very likely have the preponderance of this team working directly for you, so it is important to employ them effectively.

You will typically have at least one division officer working as your principal assistant. These officers usually assist the N3 with planning and scheduling, and they should also be prepared to represent you at meetings you are unavailable to attend. There are also several operations specialists, usually a chief and one or more senior petty officers, on the staff. These Sailors should be heavily involved in daily efforts, as they are typically very experienced and have expertise in key areas such as air control and antisubmarine warfare.

Additionally, this may be the first time in your career that you will have officers of a different designator working directly for you. Most DESRONs have an assigned aviator, usually a helicopter pilot, serving as air operations officer and a submariner assigned as the submarine operations officer. These officers are crucial to any sea combat commander team since they are fluent in the languages of the other unrestricted line communities. They will be extremely helpful when you have air and undersea assets either directly assigned to or working in support of your task force. Lastly, do not feel obligated to only assign these officers taskings based on their designators. With the limited size of your staff, it is important to use these talented officers in other roles, including planning and administrative tasks.

Share the Burden with Your Fellow "N-Heads"

The N3 often shoulders the most significant operational responsibilities on an afloat staff. Many squadrons have mitigated this imbalance by spreading "OPS-like" responsibilities to other N-codes. Some squadrons have created an N5 or similar position that separates long-term planning and short-term execution. Others have created an N7 or similar position that focuses specifically on exercises, training, or scheduling. Embrace any effort to more evenly distribute the workload across the staff—even if you feel like you can manage most of it inside of the N3. Your fellow N-heads are some of the most experienced officers on the staff, and they should play key roles in the primary lines of effort of the squadron.

For Operationally Focused Squadrons

Thoroughly Plan Prior to Execution

Experienced operations officers will tell you that this chapter's epigraph by Admiral Nimitz rings true—you make your own luck through diligent planning and effective training. The success of any major exercise or operation is "baked" weeks or months in advance by the quality of planning conducted by the staff. When planning, take the time to think through all elements of the Navy planning process. Double-check things such as time/distance calculations and logistics concerns (such as anticipated fuel percentages) and pay close attention to safety items, including weather and airspace and waterspace management. Ensure that individual unit guidance is clear and easily accessible via official message traffic, collaboration at sea site, or other official means. Finally, make sure you are assisting the commodore by effectively echoing the commander's intent to all individual units. As the N3, you have the luxury of face-to-face interaction with the boss every day. Individual ships will only understand what you effectively communicate.

Additionally, as a DESRON or PHIBRON N3, you may lead or assist in exercise planning. Whether the exercise is a large-scale multinational exercise with complex events or a small-scale bilateral exercise with simple events, below are a few tips to help with the planning process.

> ▶ Make the planning conferences count. The planning conference may be the only time that most of the key players in an exercise are physically in the same room together. Take advantage of this time and attempt to eliminate all uncertainty before the conference is over. No one should leave a planning conference with any

unanswered questions about the overall schedule of events or any individual event. Questions are inevitably easier to answer in person rather than by email.

- ▶ Share planning documents early with individual units. As N3, you are typically planning events that will ultimately be executed by multiple ships, aircraft squadrons, and other units. These individual units may or may not be heavily involved in planning, but in either situation, they should be provided with draft planning documents as early as possible. This will allow individual units to provide constructive feedback and identify anything that might have been overlooked in the planning process.

- ▶ Focus on relationship development (particularly for international exercises). Depending on the proficiency and culture of the foreign navy involved, international exercises can be challenging. Remember that many bilateral or multilateral exercises are primarily about building partnerships rather than developing tactical excellence. If a partner nation requests to do something differently than is typically seen in the U.S. Navy, it is often best to try and accommodate that request. In other words, unless there is a safety issue, it is often wise to prioritize relationship development over tactical-level concerns. (This is not meant to take away from the tactical rigor of some of the high-end exercises conducted with treaty allies such as the North Atlantic Treaty Organization, Japan, and the Republic of Korea.)

Study and Understand Doctrine

For many surface warfare officers, the tactical action officer (TAO) course in department head school is the last time they thoroughly studied doctrine, specifically joint publications and the Naval Warfare Publication series. It is vital that you and your staff take the time to refresh tactically and become well versed in doctrine—particularly those publications involving surface warfare and antisubmarine warfare. Additionally, most operational squadrons now have the benefit of an assigned weapons and tactics instructor. Lean heavily on this officer to improve the tactical prowess of the staff, and utilize their expertise when developing concepts of operations (CONOPS).

Thrive in the Strike Group Environment

One of the most challenging aspects of the N3 job is operating in a strike group environment. For a DESRON, this typically means acting as the sea combat commander of a CSG, and for a PHIBRON, this could mean acting as composite warfare commander of an ARG. This can be daunting for a small, relatively junior staff. Below are a few tips for you and your staff when operating in this complex environment.

- ► Develop a daily battle rhythm. As N3, you will have significant responsibilities to attend strike group daily battle rhythm meetings. While much of the staff will spend a significant amount of time on watch, your focus will be on battle rhythm meetings, developing CONOPS, and publishing daily intentions messages. Despite this, make sure you stay connected with the watchfloor and communicate the results of the meetings you attend to not only the commodore but also the other key members of the staff.
- ► Work effectively with your fellow warfare commanders. When a DESRON commodore is acting as sea combat commander for a carrier strike group, they are just one of several O-6 warfare commanders working for the strike group commander. These warfare commanders include the carrier air wing commander (CAG) acting as the strike warfare commander and the commanding officer of the cruiser acting as air and missile defense commander. Be sure to develop an effective working relationship with the operations officers of the other warfare commanders in the strike group, since most key issues will be worked at your level.

For PHIBRONs, this dynamic may be slightly different, as your boss is often the senior officer afloat (except in 7th Fleet, where the forward-deployed expeditionary strike group commander is often afloat). In both situations, it is important to understand where your boss sits in the strike group hierarchy and comprehend the limits of their authority.

- ► Work effectively with the strike group staff. A small, highly specialized afloat staff that directly supports the strike group commander, your direct counterpart on the staff is the N3—a post O-5 command officer who might be an aviator or a surface warfare officer. Most strike group staffs rely heavily on their DESRON or PHIBRON, particularly for CONOPS development and readiness management. This reliance should be viewed as a compliment, and like any other senior staff, your goal should be to make their life easier by delivering quality products in a timely manner.

- Communicate asset requirements clearly, but be flexible. Ensure you understand the asset allocation process inside of the strike group—particularly with aircraft. Make your asset requirements known to the strike group N3 and clearly communicate the risk if your requests are not met. Learn to work closely with the strike OPS and CAG OPS in the air planning process. At the end of the process, you may have to operate with fewer assets than requested, but it is your responsibility to work with the assets provided to accomplish required tasking.
- Work effectively with the flag ship. For workups and deployment with a strike group, a DESRON staff will embark the CVN while a PHIBRON staff will typically embark a big deck amphibious ship (landing helicopter assault [LHA] or landing helicopter dock [LHD]). It is vital that your staff understands and learns how to operate in these new environments. In the case of the CVN, the ship is commanded by a senior aviator, and key positions such as the operations officer and navigator are filled by post O-5 command aviators. Carrier Sailors speak a different language than surface warfare officers primarily because of their laser focus on executing daily flight operations, which may or may not agree with the priorities of the sea combat commander. In the case of an LHD or LHA, embarking a ship commanded by another senior O-6 and integrating with Navy and Marine Corps aviation assets can present some special challenges. Below are a few helpful tips to remember:
    1. You are guests in their house. Simple acts like paying mess bills on time, keeping your embarked spaces clean, and accommodating shipboard events in the plan of the day go a long way toward being good tenants.
    2. Develop an intimate understanding of daily flight operations. Take time to closely observe cyclic flight operations, and learn how to read and understand the daily air plan. You simply will not be able to operate effectively in the strike group environment until you understand how the CVN plans and executes flight operations.
    3. Remember that the DESRON does not directly control the movement of the aircraft carrier! It is vital that you work with the ship's TAO (for short-term tactical movements) and the navigator (for longer transits) when you need the carrier to maneuver in a

certain way. Maneuvering a high-value unit for antisubmarine warfare may not directly support the wind requirements for cyclic flight operations. Most of the time, these issues can be worked out, but early communication is key.

For Readiness Squadrons

Approach Scheduling with Operational Execution in Mind
The importance of scheduling cannot be overstated, particularly in the basic phase. Ships succeed because they developed a well-thought-out and executable schedule. Conversely, when ships fail major inspections, it is rarely because they had insufficient talent or resources. Often, the failure is a result of a schedule that did not provide the crew with enough opportunity to prepare. Admittedly, condensed schedules are not uncommon in the fleet today, and sometimes ships are simply put in difficult situations and must make the best use of limited time available. As the N3, your organization might be overseeing a schedule written by an individual ship or authoring large parts of an operational schedule for a deployed asset. In either case, take the time to think through all elements of a schedule and ensure the ship is set up for success. If needed, seek help or guidance from external organizations, and communicate challenges up the chain of command early. Leadership should be allowed time to help with scheduling challenges rather than be surprised by bad news when failure strikes.

Expand Your Waterfront Network
Just as ships' operations officers should build a waterfront network, so should the N3. The ships in your squadron will need your help to advocate on their behalf. This situation can occur when there is a complex problem that requires ISIC intervention or if a ship is at sea and needs the staff to help with face-to-face interaction with waterfront stakeholders. These stakeholders include the port operations officer, afloat training group, strike group staff, type commander staff, fleet commander staff, and the waterfront maintenance community. Take the time to learn the individuals in these organizations by name and meet them in person, preferably before problems arise.

Manage Risk across the Squadron
A good squadron is a team. Friendly competition is to be expected between individual ships, but everyone should have the same goal: a combat-ready squadron. Oftentimes, abrupt changes in operational tasking or unexpected maintenance challenges will present a situation where one ship must make

a sacrifice for the overall benefit of the squadron. Ships might need to swap inspection dates, cross-deck Sailors, transfer parts, or simply be ready to provide resources to a sister ship when asked. As the N3, you should understand the challenges of each individual ship so you can weigh all options with your fellow N-heads (particularly the N4), then make informed recommendations to the commodore.

Do Not Be Afraid to Ask for Help

The planning and execution of complex naval operations can be daunting. As an N3, it is common to feel overwhelmed or even unqualified for the task at hand. Do not hesitate to seek help from individual ships, other squadrons, more experienced officers from other staffs, waterfront training organizations, or any other organization with the requisite experience. You will find that most organizations are willing to help, and if they do not have the answers organically, they may be able to point you in the right direction. Remember that most of what you are doing has been done before. Seek help early when needed.

Conclusion

The staff operations officer job provides a comparatively junior officer with the opportunity for tremendous impact across an entire task force. It provides the chance to work daily with senior leaders, plan and execute complex naval operations across multiple domains, and gain valuable insight into how our Navy operates globally as a member of the joint force. Although the job is exceedingly challenging, by planning diligently, communicating effectively, and efficiently utilizing your team, you can become what the N3 ultimately should be—the most valuable player of an afloat staff.

CDR James Hagerty is a 2003 United States Naval Academy graduate and a native of Baldwin, NY. At sea, he served four afloat tours in operations department, including division officer assignments in USS *Shiloh* (CG 67) and USS *Chancellorsville* (CG 62), and department head tours as operations officer in USS *Higgins* (DDG 76) and N3 in Destroyer Squadron SEVEN. He also served as flag lieutenant to the commander, *Theodore Roosevelt* carrier strike group. Ashore, he served two tours in OPNAV N96 and one tour on the Joint Staff as deputy legislative assistant, Office of the Chairman of the Joint Chiefs of Staff. He currently serves as executive officer in USS *Bainbridge* (DDG 96).

CHAPTER 12

Weapons Officer

LCDR Dylan Ross, USN

Warrior Ethos

CONGRATULATIONS, AND WELCOME to the weapons officer (WEPS) job. You are now the embodiment of the ship's fighting spirit. All guns, from the 5-inch lightweight gun system on the bow (and on the stern for cruisers) down to the 9-millimeter service pistol on the quarterdeck, are under your charge. More importantly, the quick and proper lethal response of the ship and its crew is directly related to your training, maintenance, and qualification programs. In other words, your warship's ability to employ prompt, accurate, and lethal fires is a direct reflection of your leadership.

It is important to note that the WEPS billet as a department head position is particular to cruisers and destroyers (CRUDES). In all other classes of ships, functions of the WEPS job are folded into the responsibilities of another department, typically assigned to a division officer in the combat systems department. This chapter speaks to the requirements of department heads assigned to a WEPS tour on CRUDES ships.

The WEPS job is tangible: point the barrel, pull the trigger, and receive immediate feedback on your effectiveness. Use this quality to your advantage by tying your department's efforts to the ship's lethality. Remind your department that the difference between a ship and a warship is the destructive fires your department delivers. This is a ready-made advantage of the WEPS billet—the purpose of your organization is clear, and assessment on the performance of your duties is swift. Officers who find satisfaction in honing the lethal effects of warrior teams will find the WEPS job deeply satisfying.

Organizational Roles and Responsibilities

The *Standard Organization and Regulations of the U.S. Navy* (SORM, OPNAVINST 3120.32 [series]) outlines the functions, duties, authorities,

12-1. A weapons officer takes inventory of 5-inch ammunition.
U.S. Navy photo by Petty Officer 1st Class Theron J. Godbold/Released

and organizational relationships of both naval unit leadership positions and shipboard billets. Acknowledging that the responsibilities of the WEPS range from collateral duty to department head dependent upon the class of ship, the SORM's definition is necessarily broad. It states that "they [WEPS] are responsible for supervising the employment of ordnance equipment." Where necessary, the *Surface Force Training and Readiness Manual* (COMNAVSURFPAC/COMNAVSURFLANTINST 3502.7) and other similar guidance is leveraged to tailor SORM responsibilities to the functions of a CRUDES WEPS. Below are the WEPS's functions and collateral duties:

- supervising the operation, care, maintenance, and inspection of the unit's armament and fire control equipment, ranging from all caliber of guns, to missiles, to antisubmarine warfare (ASW) systems
- the execution of strike warfare (STW) to include naval surface fire support (NSFS), ASW, antiterrorism force protection (ATFP), and visit, board, search, and seizure (VBSS)
- supervising the explosive safety (EXPSAF), the arms, ammunition, and explosives, and the Navy personnel conventional ammunition and explosives handling qualification and certification (QUAL/CERT) programs

- the procurement, care, handling, testing, stowage, accounting for, issue, and use of explosives, including ammunition, ammunition components, propellants, and pyrotechnics
- the operation, maintenance, and repair of electronic equipment, ASW systems and associated sonar systems, and mine warfare systems assigned to the weapons department
- maintaining the physical security and integrity of magazines and ready-service locker storage spaces; conducting periodic inspection of magazines and testing of sprinkler systems
- ensuring the external physical security of the unit, in coordination with the security officer who prepares the command physical security plan. The WEPS is responsible for executing the security plan.

Practical Advice for a Successful Tour

Below are some insights gathered over the course of a WEPS tour that might be helpful to others serving in the job or seeking a WEPS billet.

Above All Else, Instill a Formal Process

Create a Repeatable, Logical Sequence for Your Teams

Many weapons department evolutions have no formalized processes unless they are developed internally by ship's doctrine. Evolutions such as a gun range day, conducting ATFP qualifications under way, and some live fire events do not have a template of actions and permissions. Scour your command's instruction records for guidance in these matters. If no predecessor has prescribed a sequence of steps for a significant evolution, charge the ship's subject matter expert with drafting such guidance. Avoid overly wordy instructions and seek to call out key aspects of the references, the goal of the evolution, the expected hazards, and the right sequence of events in as few words as possible. Include a checklist as an appendix whenever practicable, since this is the easiest way for your team to translate your guidance into the appropriate series of permissions and actions.

Become Familiar with the Essential References

It is no secret that knowing the publication is a large part of the battle. The weapons department is guided by several instructions that are specific to ammunition handling and storage, meaning that other elements of the ship's crew are often unfamiliar with their content. It is essential that you and your weapons leadership team possess an intimate grasp of ammunition governances. The references you may turn to the most are:

- *Ammunition and Explosive Safety Afloat* (NAVSEA OP-4)
- *Naval Ordnance Safety Precautions* (NAVSEA OP-3347)
- *Safety Process for Navy Gun and Ammunition Systems* (NAVSEA SW300-BC-SAF-010 [series])
- *The Office of the Chief of Naval Operations Navy Personnel Conventional Ammunition and Explosives Handling Qualification and Certification* (OPNAVINST 8023.24 [series])
- *Small Arms Training and Qualification* (OPNAVINST 3591 [series]).

Develop a Brief or Follow a Checklist for Significant Evolutions
You and your team may want to expand the evolutions you consider significant beyond those explicitly called out in standing orders or elsewhere. A recommended threshold is:

- live fire events
- transferring ordnance
- uploading or downloading weapons
- deploying or retrieving the towed array
- energizing the sonar dome
- magazine sprinkler checks—an evolution where inserting the wrong automatic control valve (no two are identical) can flood a magazine
- emptying, entering, or filling the sonar dome—evolutions that have long-lead medical requirements and qualifications and that pose the potential of damage to the sonar dome, which could result in dry docking for repairs
- vertical launch system (VLS) testing while missiles are present—an evolution that presents a risk of inadvertent missile ignition or missile deluge
- ATFP, VBSS, detainee, or prize crew training—due to real-world constraints, these evolutions often intersperse loaded weapons throughout the training environment
- ATFP, VBSS, detainee, or prize crew operations—evolutions that are physically strenuous and mortally perilous and that require a large number of personnel to execute.

When developing a brief or a checklist for a significant evolution, review the warfighting improvement program message series for insights into your event, and always follow combat system operational sequencing systems, maintenance requirement cards, and technical manuals when applicable. Also, consider the geographic area for factors such as protective measures assessment protocol and sunrise and sunset (since daylight might impose constraints). Ensure that the operations department is cognizant of these geographic requirements as well so that they can build the transit plan and coordinate the operational areas accordingly. Developing the brief or checklist with the evolution team and then presenting it to the ship's senior leadership prior to the evolution are essential parts of the critical thinking that can avoid foreseeable pitfalls. In the weapons department, a misstep may mean the destruction of a multi-million-dollar missile, a negligent discharge, or the loss of life. Methodical planning and briefing should not be viewed as an aspiration, but rather as a redline.

Have the Brief or Checklist on Station

During the event execution, it will be important for team members to have ready reference to green range criteria, communications channels, start and finish times, the watchbill, the person overall in charge, and resource providers. Walk the stations before and during an evolution, and check to see that guidance materials are on hand. Remember that you set the tone in regard to the effectiveness of planning, briefing, and then executing. Your management and follow-up of this critical thinking cycle are the bedrock to success. Strive to conduct a post-evolution debrief in order to further refine your team's procedures. This is a powerful way to tighten up the methodology by which you and your department execute evolutions.

Clearly State Who Is in Charge of the Evolution

You will not be present at every event. Place the senior qualified person in charge of the evolution and clearly delineate this on the brief, checklist, or watchbill. Your representative on site should have authority to make decisions on your behalf, but clearly discuss which permissions you retain and require your explicit permission. As an example, a good system to practice is having the range safety officer (RSO) contact you when the range day checklist is complete and request your permission to "go hot," or permit participants to fire their weapons. This level of formality keeps the proper sequence of events in the forefront of your team's mind and reinforces the RSO's responsibility for the safe conduct of the live fire event while allowing you to keep a pulse on your team's progress from afar.

Excel in Long-Term Planning

Know Where You Can Qualify Your Team and Where You Can Reload

Take time to learn where every small arms range, crew-serve weapons range, ATFP schoolhouse, at-sea live fire area, and the like is within your geographic region. Meet with your local base ammunition supply team and learn which piers can receive which types of ammunition. Your plans will be subject to the constraints and restraints of the supporting resource providers. Knowing their availabilities and limitations will serve you well not only when it comes time to create the plan but especially when it comes time to adapt the plan. Additionally, know how to verify that the ammo you received is ready for service. For example, some missiles require a satisfactory built-in test after loading into the VLS. Ensure you have allocated enough time to conduct ammo inspections prior to leaving the pier. Simply put, not allotting sufficient time could result in the ship needing to return to port to swap out ammo, causing significant delays to your ship's schedule.

Work Closely with the Operations Officer

As the WEPS, you are in a constant struggle to reset the clock on your qualifications and to replenish ammunition spent by the ship and her crew. You will lose this battle if you wait until large clusters of qualifications expire or magazines go empty before you take action. Review the ship's schedule out to eighteen months, establish a good working relationship with the operations officer (OPS), and book events such as range days and ammo replenishment evolutions at least six to twelve months in advance. Once ammo handling days have been scheduled, create a plan with the OPS and the port OPS for a berth shift and pier closures, if necessary, to support the ammo replenishment.

Capitalize on PB4T

Planning board for training (PB4T) is also an opportune time to remind cross-departmental leadership that an approaching range event means that roughly a quarter of the crew will be absent on any given day. Provide them a list of the shooters by day so other departments can plan appropriately. Know how far in advance small arms ranges can be reserved, and then seek to book them the day that they become available. This is the best way to translate your calendar laid out at PB4T into a reality. The alternative is like fighting a constant brush fire when coordinating command-wide impacting events with only days' notice. If your lack of foresight is a continuous nuisance to the port, ammunition providers, range schedulers, and your shipmates, your struggle will increase considerably as you face the added friction of their resistance.

Take the better path and manage everyone's expectations and participation months in advance. Your long-term planning skills will be a source of confidence for you and your team and will serve you well in follow-on billets.

Establish Personal Connections to Resource Providers
At the outset of your tour, establish relationships with the folks who run the ranges and schoolhouses, provide ammunition, and certify your teams. Make every effort to do this in person, but if you cannot, at a minimum make a phone call. People are more inclined to be gracious with their time and resources when you have established a personal connection with them first. Expressing genuine interest in them and listening to their feedback and lessons learned may reveal hidden nuances of the WEPS job. It might also provide insight on how to execute a good working relationship with this resource provider. You are more likely to receive support from resource providers if you have developed a rapport with them than if you did not. This is especially true if you have a short notice request.

Identify Critical Skill Losses and Build Bench Depth
Navy enlistment classification (NEC) management is something that either you drive or it drives you. Identify those NECs that have long courses, such as sonar supervisor, or are low in numbers but key to your operations, such as the small arms marksmanship instructor and the antiterrorism training supervisor (AT TRASUP), and develop a replacement plan. Where possible, increase the number of Sailors who possess these critical skills on board, because having only one Sailor fill a critical NEC can leave your team vulnerable. This is especially true for any Sailors that are outside of your department, such as the command master at arms (CMAA), who is typically billeted as your AT TRASUP. Even though the CMAA is the AT TRASUP, he or she is also expected to focus on any legal investigations that arise on board. Seek to create critical skills wholly within the weapons department so that you can resource your own training. Also, identify periods within the ship schedule that allow you to send Sailors off to schoolhouses, especially the ones that are several months in length. Additionally, bear in mind the impact that personnel loss may have on warfare certifications. For example, STW and NSFS typically certify a specific watch team on board a ship. In these circumstances, the loss of a specified number of individuals from those codified watch teams will revoke the warfare certification and require recertification with a new team.

Grow Experts

Sharpen Yourself and Your Team through Verification
The weapons department is entrenched in legal documentation for ordnance custody, gun qualifications, and QUAL/CERT. Deep-dive into these key programs, making adjustments until you are satisfied that they are being well maintained. Challenge yourself to understand the intricacies of these programs and their management tools, such as the ordnance information system. Strongly consider placing your most capable leaders in positions of oversight of these programs and keep to a tight cycle of personally verifying these programs' records.

Task and Organize Individuals along a Trajectory of Mastery
When opportunities arise, send your team to waterfront town halls and training. Though it can be difficult to lose personnel for a few days, they will return with a higher level of knowledge. Their increased understanding is a force multiplier and generally pays off in the ship's readiness and assessment results.

A good place to look for these opportunities is on the Naval Ordnance Safety and Security Activity website, which lists explosive safety waterfront trainings. Additionally, the Naval Surface Warfare Center in Crane, Indiana, which manages all small arms for the Navy, also conducts waterfront training for weapons maintenance. In fact, they will conduct a courtesy shipboard inspection of small arms and mounts if requested. These hands-on training sessions and nonattributional inspections pay large dividends.

Additionally, for your own development, you should strive to own the tactical action officer chair for all STW, ASW, and live fire events. Challenge yourself to be the ship's strongest watchstander for your department's warfare areas. This will deepen your tactical skills and strengthen credibility with your Sailors, and it is an essential aspect of being an expert in weapons department affairs.

Create a Culture of Teamwork, Feedback, and Good Sense

Cultivate a Team of United Department Heads
The ship's main function is not to serve as a field examination of your individual competency as a naval officer. It is to conduct prompt and sustained combat operations at sea. Your ship's success in this mission is predicated upon you and your fellow department heads translating a chorus of actions into a unified goal. A successful tour, mission accomplishment, and even joy are the byproducts of a unified department head team. Support one another. Listen to the most trusted department head and take their advice. Enlist a

fellow department head to give you candid feedback on your individual performance and critical thinking so as to reveal and correct your own blind spots. Challenge yourself to someday be that senior department head ready to support the newly arriving junior department heads.

Listen, Learn, Help, Then Lead
One of the most serious and intricate events for the weapons department is a large-scale ammunition onload or offload. If you do not have previous weapons department experience, it can be difficult to grasp the complexities of your role, requirements, systems, and processes. Some of these considerations are:

- nuances of pier capacity
- ordnance handling gear limitations
- QUAL/CERT watchbill implications
- situational maintenance checks
- fire party requirements
- 5-inch ammunition loading sequence
- VLS gas management
- harpoon preparations
- missile book inspections
- weapons station contractor support constraints
- weather
- hazardous electro-magnetic radiation to ordnance configurations.

A successful offload or onload requires a keen understanding of how to interlace these aspects across a multidepartment, multiday event. Adopt a listen-and-learn attitude when approaching important events such as this for the first time. Poll your departmental leadership team for their insights, near-misses, and recommendations. Ask them to build a plan, and then gather your leaders in a room to review it out loud, expressing that you want to hear their thoughts, concerns, and limitations so that you can learn. Once the weapons department leadership group is satisfied, take the plan and review it with the most seasoned WEPS available on the waterfront or with your combat systems officer if they are a former WEPS. When it comes time to execute a major event such as an offload or onload, look for opportunities when you are not on the watchbill and share in the manual labor. Revel in this time to demonstrate your desire to help your department, to join in their hardships, and to converse with your Sailors. The listen-learn-help approach to first-time experiences strengthens the team bond, expands your knowledge, and deepens your ability and credibility to lead the next time the event occurs.

Use "We" and Minimize "They"
Though it is standard to arrange the ship into divisions and work centers, this structure strives to group personnel by arenas of expertise more than it seeks to create internal divides. Whether or not a "one ship, one fight" mentality pervades all departments, it must be alive and well within the weapons department. Set the tone at departmental quarters by using "us" and "we" when talking about any department effort and guide your divisional leadership to do the same. Work with your departmental leading chief petty officer to establish fair rules for cross-divisional support, to include lead times for notification, so that no one work center becomes a tiger team for the department as a whole. Overcome concepts of rating fiefdoms by orchestrating cross-training in watchstations and routine cross-checking of programs. The agility and willingness to mutually support efforts within the weapons department is often the key factor for success for programs such as EXPSAF and ATFP, which demand innumerable hours to achieve satisfactory marks.

Harness the Power of Debriefing
Planning and briefing critical evolutions are a must for the weapons department. However, the most powerful element of a proper cycle of operations is the post-execution analysis of planned outcomes versus actual performance. Such analysis elevates the team or individual toward optimal performance. Without this feedback, performance is likely to stagnate, as participants may not be aware of how to improve. When offering feedback, avoid trite expressions such as "Communications could be better." Debriefing points should be constructive, critical yet respectful, and actionable. Typical obstacles to debriefing are a fear of bruising egos or the perception that there is insufficient time. The surest way to counter this resistance is to lead by example and have the team critique your performance. Your willingness to accept and absorb constructive feedback will positively influence others to do the same. In regard to finding time to debrief, you write the schedule. Build it into the cycle of operations. Also, do not let perfect be the enemy of good. That is to say, do not forego a quick but effective debrief because you do not have time for a longer, perfect one.

Always Know Where the Safe Fire Bearing Is
There is a key saying in the weapons employment world: "Gun lay sat." Before firing any major caliber gun topside, the officer of the deck, executive officer

(XO), or commanding officer (CO) is required to visually confirm that the gun barrel is pointed in the intended direction and that that direction is visually clear of any nontarget contacts. This is akin to the concept RSOs express to Sailors at the gun range: "Never point the weapon at something you do not intend to shoot." Expand this style of thinking into every weapons evolution. If you can avoid placing something at risk, do so. If you must incur a risk, such as chambering a round, think about ways to mitigate that risk. For instance, if you are in formation one for a 5-inch shoot and a round gets stuck inside the barrel, do not return the mount to normal stow, which points the loaded weapon at the ship directly off of the bow. Rather, always know the safest bearing to point the gun, and keep the barrel aimed in that direction. This response is good sense. Find time with your teams to ask "what if" questions in order to increase everyone's good sense. Should a negligent discharge occur or if a weapon were to malfunction, you will be happy that your team reduced the impact of such an event and knew how to expeditiously get to the safest state possible.

General Advice

Transforming a Good Team into a Great One Starts with You

A department head cannot singlehandedly ensure the readiness and success of all areas under their charge. You must grow a team capable of translating your vision into mission success. A team generally flourishes when its leader is humble, credible, and approachable. Regardless of your own level of expertise, exude humility by letting your juniors know that you rely upon them having a deeper knowledge of their respective fields than you. Where applicable, seek to defer to their judgments, which deepens their ownership and increases mutual trust. Encourage your team to think aloud whenever possible so that their ideas receive the benefit of cross-checking while building a shared mental model among the group. Be credible by spending time digging through the reference material so that your knowledge foundation elevates the department's decision-making prowess. Finally, taking time to listen and respond to juniors with care, incorporating the team's input into the plan, and praising the deserving in public while correcting the errant in private can make you a more approachable leader.

Communicate the Desired End-State and the "Why" to the Team

Describing the desired end-state and why it is important to the ship's mission is an essential element in creating teams that are capable and driven. In crafting your "why" statements, take time to denote how the ship's readiness is enhanced by the intended effort and always align it to your CO's vision or philosophy. After giving the "why" and the objective, allow the junior leader and their supporting element a measured amount of autonomy to formulate how to achieve it. Your job is then to review their "how" for conformity to guidance and the ship's schedule and to verify the availability of resources. Seek to review these plans with your evolution leader at the 10, 50, and 90 percent completion milestones. The first review at 10 percent serves as a sanity check of the objective, means, and timeline of the plan—in other words, whether they have a solid idea of what they need to do and how to go about it. The 50 percent review examines the glideslope of the project and verifies that resources are confirmed (e.g., is the gun range booked, and will the right ammo be on hand?). The 90 percent review is your chance to go over the briefing materials with the event leader before they are formally presented to the watch team and the ship's senior leadership. You will find that this measured amount of autonomy for your team gives them the satisfaction of owning their process while also avoiding rework that comes from insufficient department head involvement.

Develop Your Subordinates and Their Ability to Make Sound Decisions
Assuming their actions were not illegal, unethical, or immoral, standing by subordinates only when the outcomes are positive erodes their ownership and initiative, leaving you to make all the decisions. Avoid the easy trap of judging subordinate leaders by outcome alone. In the event that a junior Sailor falls short, assess whether the shortcoming was earnest or the product of being disinterested. An earnest mistake can be characterized by a subordinate not recognizing or communicating obstacles to the mission or moving at a speed that outpaces formal adherence to procedure. Consider an honest shortcoming as a tuition to the junior Sailor's school of leadership—a tuition that is only effective when you take the time to conduct a constructive post mortem with the individual. Furthermore, do not hold back from distributing proper and fair punishment when deserved. In the rare event that you find a junior leader who is genuinely disinterested in their job and/or the outcomes of their team, discuss this immediately with the XO and CO, and place them in the most inconsequential role possible. You and your team cannot afford leaders who do not or will not give a full measure of their effort to the handling and employment of the ship's weapons.

CHAPTER 12

Conclusion

The warship's lethality is inextricably linked to the efforts of the WEPS. The ship and her crew will reflect the warrior ethos exemplified by you, and your effectiveness is reflected in the prompt and accurate employment of the unit's fire power. Importantly, weapons department evolutions are inherently dangerous, requiring an effective planning, briefing, executing, and debriefing cycle. Additionally, foresightedness in resource management and scheduling is foundational to a successful tour. Although challenging, the WEPS role can be deeply satisfying, as the responsibility of producing combat readiness for a commissioned warship is something you can recall with pride long after your tour.

LCDR Dylan Ross is a surface warfare officer who served as the weapons officer in USS *Carney* (DDG 64), where he led a team that earned the USS *Arizona* Memorial Trophy, achieving the fleet's greatest combat readiness in strike warfare, surface fire support, and antisurface warfare. Ashore, he qualified as an integrated air and missile defense warfare tactics instructor and served as the lead tactics developer for surface warfare employment of directed energy and integrated fire control.

CHAPTER 13
Combat Systems Officer
LCDR Carleigh Gregory, USN

Being "the CSO"

THE COMBAT SYSTEMS OFFICER (CSO) is a unique and challenging position on board any ship. You are responsible for some of the most complex equipment in every space on the ship, from after steering to the top of the mast. The personnel who work for you will have the most technical training and expertise on weapons systems, interior and exterior communications circuits, computer networks, air and surface search radars, and all manner of electronics. You also have the most experienced senior enlisted and limited duty officers (LDOs) keeping the gears spinning and the day-to-day department operations running smoothly. To put it simply, your equipment and the personnel responsible for maintaining and operating it are the primary reason the ship is a national asset capable of combat operations, representing the power and prestige of the surface Navy. Get excited! If you fleeted up to CSO from weapons officer, you will be expected to leverage your previous experience on board to ensure the whole ship is successful, not just your department. If you are a second tour department head reporting from another ship, your previous experience and your fresh set of eyes will be key to maintaining or attaining superior performance in the pursuit of mission accomplishment.

Organizational Roles and Responsibilities

Chapter 3 in the *Standard Organization and Regulations of the U.S. Navy* (SORM, OPNAVINST 3120.32 [series]) outlines the duties and responsibilities of the CSO. As the CSO, you are "responsible for all the functions prescribed for the Weapons Officer" and are charged with "supervising the maintenance of the unit's combat systems including armament, associated appurtenance, magazine spaces, search and detection equipment, command and control equipment, and fire control equipment." In general, the CSO will be in charge of communications equipment, radars, and a collection of weapons systems or portions thereof. With the advent of the plans and tactics (PT) department, divisions assigned to the weapons, combat systems, and PT departments (any division starting with the letter C) will vary from ship to ship. As an inbound department head, establishing early communication with your predecessor will help you understand the scope of your responsibilities, the personnel assigned to you, and the status of programs and equipment.

Relationships

On-Ship Relationships
As a second tour department head, you will be one of the more senior officers in the wardroom. Besides the executive officer fleeting up to be the commanding officer or the LDOs, you may also have the most time on board if you fleeted up to CSO. Leverage your past experience on board to ensure the crew and leadership repeat not mistakes but rather successes. Do not hesitate to provide feedback from the last time an infrequent evolution or certification was conducted.

Core Departmental Team
There are three critical personnel assigned to your department who are tasked to keep the complex network of systems under your purview maintained, integrated, and available.

The system test officer (STO) is responsible for maintaining "maximum combat system material readiness" and "directs and functionally integrates combat systems/subsystems to achieve the optimum combat system material readiness status." Part of this is configuration management, including maintaining the smooth log and coordinating all updates and upgrades to combat systems equipment.

The electronics material officer is "responsible for the readiness of all assigned electronic equipment" and "provides for the correct use, maintenance, and repair of assigned electronic repair equipment." This officer will generally be in charge of electronics technicians and, on some ships, interior communications specialists. These personnel will own equipment in every space from the top of the mast to the after steering. The electronics material officer may also own the test equipment program, fall protection program, and microminiature electronics repair (2M) program.

The combat systems maintenance manager (CSMM) is the senior enlisted subject matter expert for weapons and combat systems equipment. Depending on the number of chiefs in your department, their level of experience, and leadership capability, the CSMM may also be your department leading chief petty officer. This will add administrative tasking to their workload, so be cognizant of what you need them focused on and make personnel changes as necessary.

Weapons Officer
Of all the department head relationships on board, this one can be the most difficult to navigate. If you fleeted up from weapons officer (WEPS), you are in the unique position of remaining on board with your relief. Depending on the WEPS's proficiency and leadership style, as well as the rapport you established with personnel in the weapons department when you were WEPS, Sailors from the department may still seek your guidance when you are CSO. It is very important that lanes in the road are established between you and the WEPS but that you leverage the knowledge, skill sets, and experience of your core department team to ensure that both departments are successful.

Chief Engineer
This key relationship with the chief engineer ensures not only that you have air, power, and water but also that daily operations and maintenance are completed efficiently and with proper coordination. One effective way to maintain this relationship is ensuring engineering department representation at ship's electronics readiness team (SERT) weekly meetings. Another is ensuring that counterparts such as STO and the main propulsion assistant, CSMM and top snipe, and you and the chief engineer are on the same page and regularly communicate in person and not just by email.

Plans and Tactics Officer
On ships with a plans and tactics officer (PTO), you have a unique opportunity to share some responsibility that traditionally falls to the CSO. Battle order revisions and the combat systems training team (CSTT) are two examples of where the PTO and CSO can share responsibilities. For example, the PTO could take lead for CSTT tactical and the CSO take lead for CSTT technical. Team composition and ownership will vary from ship to ship based on individuals' areas of expertise, so talk it over with your personnel and the chain of command, and do what works for your ship.

Off-Ship Relationships
There are a number of key people on the waterfront you should introduce yourself to prior to or shortly after becoming the CSO. Face-to-face introductions

are preferred, but email or phone calls are also appropriate if the personnel are geographically located elsewhere. Take time to have a quick discussion about upcoming events and equipment installs/upgrades with them. Keeping their contact information will help you navigate a variety of shipboard challenges.

Immediate Superior in Command
As CSO, you will primarily engage with your squadron N6 and/or N8 for combat systems issues, but you should also introduce yourself to N3, N4, and N7 personnel for operations, material readiness, and training, respectively.

Department Heads on the Waterfront
At a minimum, you should engage with the other CSOs across the waterfront, whether you're moored pierside or in an extensive maintenance period in a shipyard. It is also helpful to establish relationships with department heads on the other ships within your squadron. Establishing a network with other department heads around you will go a long way, whether it's with parts support, help with troubleshooting and fixing equipment, or requesting personnel support if you have personnel temporarily assigned for training.

Maintenance Team
The combat systems port engineer, the ship's port engineer, and the project manager make up the core shoreside maintenance team that will keep your ship in the fight. The combat systems port engineer will be instrumental in tracking all repair and modernization efforts for all of your equipment. The regional maintenance center is also staffed with technicians available to help troubleshoot and repair equipment. It would be useful to swing through your local code 200 building and meet some of the technicians that your personnel will contact for help.

Training and Certification Organizations
The afloat training group and the numerous readiness assist teams in each concentration should also be on your meet and greet list. Readiness assist teams are another entity available to ensure your equipment works properly by giving you a "look" before certification events.

Practical Advice

As CSO, you will spend a good amount of time explaining how your equipment operates, the overall impact to your operational effectiveness when it is degraded or out of commission, and what support you need in order to correct equipment degradations.

Ask questions, and communicate at the right level. When your technicians identify an equipment issue, asking a few key questions can help bound the problem and formulate a plan for correction:

- What system is degraded/out of commission?
- What is the operational impact of the casualty?
- What symptom(s) are you seeing?
- What troubleshooting steps have been completed so far?
- What component(s) failed? Can the item(s) be 2M screened?
- Do we have replacement parts on board? If not, where are parts available?
- Is there a redundant system or signal path? This will help determine if it is a major or minor impact to a warfare area based on redundancy.
- What outside help has been engaged, and what further assistance is needed?
- Have we had this issue before? If so, what was the fix action?
- What is the estimated time to repair? If your personnel have not isolated the issue, establish an update time (one hour, the next day) to keep the chain of command informed on progress.

Once you have a good understanding of the issue, communicate at the right level. Balancing the level of detail to explain the degradation without quoting chapter and verse of the technical manual will take practice.

Have a Ready Reference of System Diagrams

Simple diagrams with major system components and critical information on air, power, and water make life easier when articulating system degradation. Even if they consist of just boxes and lines with nomenclature, these simple diagrams can assist in succinctly understanding the problem, impact, status of troubleshooting, plan for repair, and what outside help you need. With that said, you should not use these simpler diagrams in lieu of more complex and thorough diagrams for a tag-out or troubleshooting or in place of combat systems operational sequencing systems.

Keep a Log

Good technicians keep records of equipment issues and the corrective actions taken. Once you have been in the job a little while, you will be able to do this too. You can also use this method to track trends, which can decrease troubleshooting time as well as provide information to off-ship entities for quality control and potential change in maintenance procedures or repair parts availability. A log can also help you keep track of personnel accomplishments and scores on certifications, which in turn makes evaluations, fitness reports, and unit and personal awards easier to write.

Understand Signal Paths

For communications gear, walk through each system by frequency, and understand the name of each major component in the signal path and which antennas each system uses to transmit and receive. If you're on a ship with SPY radar, walk the signal path end to end. Put your eyes on all the cabinets so when your Sailors present you with issues, you have a starting point for discussion on corrective action. This also gives your personnel an opportunity to show off what they know about their equipment, and you get quality time with them in small groups or one on one.

Take a Tour of the Mast

Whether for a spot-check, part of your turnover, or just professional curiosity, make time to go up and take a look. It is also a really nice view—if you are not afraid of heights. You will gain a better appreciation for what it takes to maintain equipment that is constantly exposed to the elements, have a chance to assess the integrity of antenna mounts and waveguides (which tend to generate several jobs for the current ship's maintenance project), conduct a program review on fall protection, and evaluate how well your harnesses are maintained. If there is time during a maintenance availability, always request scaffolding and mast preservation be included in the maintenance package.

Make the 2M Program Effective and Efficient

The combat electronics division will own the program and, more often than not, be the only qualified technicians on board. There is a series of courses that your Sailors must take to make them fully qualified 2M technicians. The first element of the two-part 2M program is screening a circuit card for faulty components, and the second is repairing the circuit card with piece parts rather than replacing the entire circuit card. This process is tedious and takes time to do properly. Instead of relying on a select handful of Sailors in the combat systems department to screen and fix circuit cards, request that Sailors from other departments also become 2M qualified. Some suggested rates include gas turbine systems technicians, electrical, fire controlmen, and cryptologic technicians. This will help them screen their own components and possibly repair them too. This will decrease repair time, support buy-in across the ship for the importance of the program, and save the Navy money.

SERT Is Critical

This meeting is only as good as the level of participation. A representative from each division that begins with a C, cryptologic technicians, operations specialists, and an electrician's mate from the engineering department should all attend SERT. It would be helpful to have the top snipe attend as well. Publish the SERT plan early and make it editable so that the meeting is used to review and deconflict the plan, not to build it from scratch. Schedule SERT each week following the planning board for training (PB4T) meeting, so any fine adjustments can be made with the most current plan of the week. The STO or CSMM will run the meeting. Your personal level of participation will depend on how effective the meeting is and how often you need to change the maintenance plan.

Know System Configurations for Training Evolutions

At SERT, discuss system configuration for training or certification events, and know which events can occur simultaneously. For example, you can conduct a ballistic missile defense scenario and a strike scenario at the same time, but both weapons systems cannot use the vertical launch system launchers at the

13-1. **A combat systems officer reviews a training scenario during a combat systems training team drill.**

U.S. Navy photo by Mass Communication Specialist 1st Class Fred Gray IV/Released

same time. By having system knowledge prior to PB4T and SERT, you and your team can avoid many scheduling conflicts. Knowing which scenarios require georepositioning is also important. This will ensure that your team is not scheduled for an off-ship scenario during a special sea and anchor or a straits transit. Planning ahead will help to avoid a lot of miscommunication and headaches. Include systems set-up in the SERT plan and, once approved by the commanding officer, you should be on station with your combat systems watchstander and in the combat information center.

Combine Eight O'Clock Reports

Depending on how equipment and divisions are distributed on board, the STO and CSMM will need to have oversight of the combat systems, weapons, and possibly plans and tactics departments. Instead of having them search through or try to track material issues across multiple departments with multiple documents, one suggestion is to combine eight o'clock reports. While the document will be much longer, it will be a consolidated report that they can review in order to provide oversight and expertise. This will help them leverage their experience across the ship without additional administrative burdens.

Be Smart on Communications Security Management

If the communications officer works for you, they may be responsible for "the vault," where electronic key material is stored and managed. This program is critically important and requires oversight. Vault inventory should be part of your turnover, and the program should be spot-checked monthly. Know the difference in reporting requirements when issues arise. Vaults are better maintained when the electronic key management system (EKMS)/key management infrastructure (KMI) manager is not a collateral duty. In fact, some ships have information professional officers for this reason. If you have the bandwidth to have a dedicated information technician in the vault besides the manager, do it. If you can, avoid making your KMI manager a first tour division officer. It is a heavy responsibility for someone very new to the Navy. There are many references associated with this program, but the *Communications Security Management for Commanding Officers Handbook* (8 May 2017) gives a good overview of the program and provides spot-check forms. The more extensive (six-hundred-plus pages) instruction is the EKMS-1 series.

Combat Systems Officer of the Watch

The combat systems officer of the watch (CSOOW) represents you and the department. If they are not prepared for the watch or lack the requisite level of knowledge to stand the watch, combat readiness will be negatively affected, and equipment damage can occur. Holding a high standard is important. This is another program that the STO and CSMM will own. The CSOOW needs to be able to think quickly, prioritize information, and communicate effectively over multiple circuits. They are a critical node in your ship's command and control structure, from daily operations to casualty control. Make sure they are up to the task. As the CSO, you should also establish reporting criteria, similar to standing orders, for equipment issues from the CSOOW. What should they call you for? How often?

Balance Transparency with Reality within Your Department
If you have a difficult few weeks ahead preparing for a certification event, clearly define your expectations and metrics for success. Do not just say, "We need to be successful"—explain how. Be specific about what equipment needs to be fixed and discuss a number of training scenarios that need to be completed successfully before the event. When your department is successful, celebrate it. Recognition on the SPY honor roll, radar maintenance excellence, clearing a number of casualty reports, or receiving a final score on a certification event are all examples of "shout outs" you can bring to department quarters.

Conclusion

As the CSO, you are responsible for the equipment and personnel that make a ship a warship. It is a heavy burden, but with the right personnel around you, good management techniques, and the right attitude, you will be successful. Knowing your resources, establishing good relationships, and maintaining your equipment to peak performance will ensure you are ready to execute the mission when called.

LCDR Carleigh Gregory is a surface warfare officer who served as weapons and combat systems officer in USS *Ross* (DDG 71) and as a division officer in USS *Decatur* (DDG 73) and USS *Coronado* (LCS 4). Ashore, she served as a seamanship and navigation instructor at the United States Naval Academy. She most recently served as the material readiness officer for Destroyer Squadron 22 in Norfolk, Virginia.

CHAPTER 14
Engineer Officer
CDR Sam O'Neil, USN

Being "the CHENG"

NO OTHER DEPARTMENT HEAD TITLE carries quite the same punch as the chief engineer (CHENG). Also known as engineer officer or the engineer, the CHENG is often considered the most grueling and dynamic department head billet on board any ship. What the job lacks in glamour, it makes up for in reward. The scope of your responsibility is far-reaching and intertwined with every other department on the ship. A strong engineering department is the backbone of all shipboard operations, as the ship cannot get to the fight without main propulsion, electrical, and auxiliary support and cannot survive the fight without expert damage control.

The engineering course at department head school provides you a baseline level of knowledge encompassing engineering principles, plant and program management, and exposure to resources and organizations charged to assist you, and culminates with a comprehensive assessment including engineering operations casualty control (EOCC) response procedures. This immersive course exposes you to all facets of engineering and equips you with best practices and lessons learned, providing you a solid foundation for a successful tour as the CHENG.

The information within this chapter is not all-encompassing and is not a replacement for any reference or instruction. Rather, use the information in conjunction with what you learned in school, along with other chapters of this book, to help you prepare for your tour as the CHENG.

Organizational Roles and Responsibilities

The *Standard Organization and Regulations of the U.S. Navy* (SORM, OPNAVINST 3120.32 [series]) and the *Engineering Department Organization and Regulations Manual* (EDORM, COMNAVSURFPAC/COMNAVSURFLANT Instruction 3540.3A [series]) offer you a starting point for understanding the range of your responsibilities.

The SORM provides a broad and basic overview of your duties. It states that the CHENG is responsible for "the operation, care, and maintenance of all machinery, piping systems, and electrical and electronic devices not specifically assigned to another department, damage control, repairs of the hull and its appurtenances, furnishing of power, light, ventilation, heat, refrigeration, compressed air, and water and the operation, care and maintenance of associated equipment." Additionally, the SORM states the CHENG is responsible for the following:

- the operation, care, and maintenance of boat machinery
- the maintenance of the engineering log and the engineer's bell book
- the maintenance of interior communications equipment
- the coordination of all shipyard work and correspondence or communications relating to alterations or repairs to the hull and installed equipment
- the safe handling of hazardous materials
- the maintenance and repair of all equipment associated with the degaussing system, and acting as degaussing officer
- establishing an organization of qualified personnel to monitor progress and inspect work performed on engineering department equipment
- the personal inspection of boilers, main engine, and generator reduction gears, the main and auxiliary condensers, main engine lube oil sumps, and the main engine internals before closure to ensure proper reassembly.

Expanding on the roles and responsibilities defined in the SORM, the EDORM is more prescriptive and outlines in specific detail your and your team's individual billet and watchstanding responsibilities. The EDORM's specific functions inherent within the CHENG position include:

- serving as damage control officer for firefighting and damage control functions
- serving as plant control officer upon getting under way, proceeding to anchorage, arriving pierside and at other times when extra care is required, and personally supervising the engineering officer of the watch (EOOW)

- ensuring that the organization, training, and qualification of the engineering and damage control training teams are current and effective
- acting as the final personnel qualification standards qualifying authority for all engineering watchstanders except the EOOW
- personally inspecting major pieces of equipment and specific spaces before and prior to closure
- supervising the departmental training program and its effectiveness
- operating ship's equipment in the most fuel-efficient manner as directed by the commanding officer (CO)
- preventing unauthorized discharge of pollutants to the air or sea
- verifying valve line-up prior to fueling/defueling operations
- developing and promulgating a recall procedure in the event of an emergency under way
- developing local operating procedures, ship-specific EDORM, engineering officer's standing orders, restricted maneuvering doctrine, emergency steering doctrine, special operating orders, or temporary standing orders for approval by the CO
- reviewing, signing, and dating the engineering log, department logs, and operating logs and records.

Practical Advice for a Successful Tour

Your assignment as the CHENG will be demanding and complex. As such, you must be organized and thorough in your planning to effectively lead personnel and expertly manage programs and equipment.

Show Up Ready

Review Shipboard Documents

While you are still a student, correspond with the person you are relieving. At a minimum, request copies of your ship's EDORM, CHENG's standing orders, and eight o'clock reports. You will find the CO's restricted maneuvering doctrine embedded in the EDORM, and all temporary standing orders, departure from specifications (DFS), and casualty reports (CASREPs) listed in eight o'clock reports. These documents will provide you a snapshot of the engineering department. Reading these documents in advance also gives you ample time to ask questions.

Familiarize Yourself with Key Instructions

The EDORM is the most important instruction that you will rely on and refer to as the CHENG. Successful CHENGs know the EDORM inside and out and enforce the standards prescribed within it. Tab A of the EDORM provides a comprehensive list of references specific to each engineering program.

With the exception of memorizing EOCC casualty response procedures verbatim, you are not expected to memorize every detail within every instruction. Instead, have the most updated references accessible and have a general idea of what information each instruction contains. Expect your team to cross-check information in instructions so that you can make decisions in accordance with the current guidance.

In addition to the EDORM, it is also important to familiarize yourself with the following instructions:

- *Engineering Operational Sequencing System User's Guide*
- *Tag-Out User's Manual* (NAVSEA S0400-AD-URM-010)
- *Surface Force Training and Readiness Manual* (SFTRM) (COMNAVSURFPAC/COMNAVSURFLANT Instruction 3502.7)
- *Watchstander's Guide* (COMNAVSURFORINST 3500.5 [series])
- *Redlines* (COMNAVSURFPAC/COMNAVSURFLANTINST 3504.1 [series])
- *Mobility-Engineering* (ATGLANT/ATGPACINST 3502.3 Appendix P)
- *Naval Ships' Technical Manuals* (NSTMs) 241 (*Propulsion Reduction Gears, Couplings, Clutches, and Associated Components*), 300 (*Electric Plant–General*), 541 (*F76 Fuel System*), 555 V1(*Surface Ship Firefighting*).

Conduct a Thorough Turnover

No single reference exists that details which CHENG-specific items and information shall be included in turnover. However, best practices inform you of items that, at a minimum, should be addressed during your turnover.

Inventory the following items:

- keys to all locked equipment and spaces, including main reduction gear (MRG) keys

- maintenance assist modules
- test equipment
- special tools.

Receive the safe combination. Located in the logroom or in your stateroom, the safe should contain keys to the MRG and any other keys or equipment for which you want to maintain control. Practice opening and closing the safe to validate that you can open it with ease. Also, discuss and identify individuals whom you trust to share the safe combination.

If operationally possible, open and inspect the MRG. Consult applicable planned maintenance system and NSTM 241 prior to conducting the evolution. The inspection requires thoughtful planning and should not be rushed. Document all findings in the engineering log and include them in your turnover letter. Take pictures of the gears and nozzle spray patterns for future comparisons.

Take Charge

Plan Your Day

If in port, arrive on board early enough to check your email, review message traffic, and, most importantly, walk your spaces. Early morning often is the quietest part of your day, and it provides you an opportunity to allocate tasking and identify any last-minute conflicts to address. If under way or on deployment, do your best to create a routine just like you would in port.

Look the Part

Just as your Sailors do, wear engineering coveralls and carry a rag, hearing protection, red and black pens, and grease pencils. Also invest in a quality flashlight, inspection mirror, and magnetic pickup tool. These tools will empower you to take a closer and deeper look at your spaces and equipment, especially when you are crawling around under your engines or in the bilges or assessing small spaces. Your department should already have these items, but having your own set readily available to you will help you assess your spaces and equipment more independently.

Walk Your Spaces with a Critical Eye

Walk your spaces through a safe-to-operate and safe-to-train lens using afloat training group (ATG) checksheets as your guide. Are there any fuel leaks or lube oil leaks? Are hazardous materials stowed properly? Is the space clean and free of debris? Are your spaces and equipment in compliance with the tag-out and electrical safety programs? Remember to also take time to assess damage control equipment. As you become more familiar with your spaces, you can detect when something is out of place or when a piece of equipment does not sound like it is operating correctly. Similarly, trust your instincts if you see something in your space that does not look right.

Closely Monitor Operating Logs
When thoroughly reviewed daily, proper log-keeping will help you identify equipment operating trends. In some cases, you and your team will be able to anticipate when additional maintenance will be required or when pieces of equipment require replacement. If a reading is out of parameter or specification, ensure a job sequencing number is created and appropriate action is taken to address the issue. Develop a plan to correct the discrepancy, and, once corrected, ensure the job is closed. Just as it is important to create a job sequencing number, it is equally important that your team properly account for the hours they spent fixing the discrepancy, as that will influence your manning.

Review Other Departments' Eight O'Clock Reports
Your department's eight o'clock report should complement other departments' reports. It takes coordination and cooperation to ensure that departments are on the same page and that there are no communication gaps between them. Occasionally you may find other departments reporting equipment discrepancies that your team can fix but were either unaware of or did not understand their priority (most often the case).

Think Critically
Your CO will expect you to communicate the impacts and limitations of equipment degradations and will look to you to provide recommendations on how to mitigate and fix the issue. Understanding system interoperability will help you recognize the second-, third-, and fourth-order consequences of these degradations and assist you in providing recommended courses of action to the CO. It is your responsibility to ensure your CO has a clear understanding and full picture of the issue as well as its follow-on effects. When briefing the CO about casualties to major pieces of equipment, it is appropriate to bring your main propulsion assistant (MPA) or top snipe with you to answer any follow-on questions. This is especially true if you have recently reported on board.

CHAPTER 14

Prepare for Inspections
To start, a plan of action and milestone (POA&M) will provide your team with a roadmap to prepare for an upcoming certification. While a POA&M offers a framework, there are additional actions you can take to get ready for a certification. Begin by reviewing past inspection reports. At the very least, you do not want the same discrepancies identified again. Assessment organizations such as the Board of Inspection and Survey and the Safety Center also publish information about common discrepancies. Similarly, if another ship has an upcoming inspection, ask the ship if you and a member of your team can observe the event. If you have this opportunity, capture lessons learned on what worked well and what did not work well; note how the other ship prepared for the assessment, and observe how the other ship orchestrated the assessment. Where did the ship set up central communications? How were division officers employed? How were discrepancies identified and tracked? Did they have a small team of Sailors on standby to correct discrepancies? Be respectful and not critical of another team's shortcomings, as your team will also experience struggles during an inspection. Assessments are not meant to highlight what a team does well but rather to point out areas for improvement. You can also ask your N4 organization at your immediate superior in command (ISIC) for assistance. Your N4 will have had the benefit of observing inspections on board many other ships and can draw your attention to specific items. With your CO's concurrence, you can also request a courtesy space walk-through or program review conducted by your ISIC or ATG to give you unofficial feedback. Take all the feedback on board as actionable items for you and your team.

Cultivate Ship-Wide Interest in Program Effectiveness
While many programs are specific to the engineering department, strict adherence to all safety and occupational health (SOH) programs is a command-wide requirement. Sailors in every department must know and follow all heat stress, hearing conservation, electrical safety, and tag-out guidance. Program effectiveness consists of two parts: administrative organization and deckplate compliance. Empower and equip your chiefs and division officers to effectively manage SOH, critical, and other engineering programs. Routine reviews of your programs will help your program managers stay organized; while walking your ship, observing Sailors perform routine maintenance and demonstrating evolutions and drills will provide you a snapshot of each program's actual effectiveness. If your chiefs and division officers are not receiving

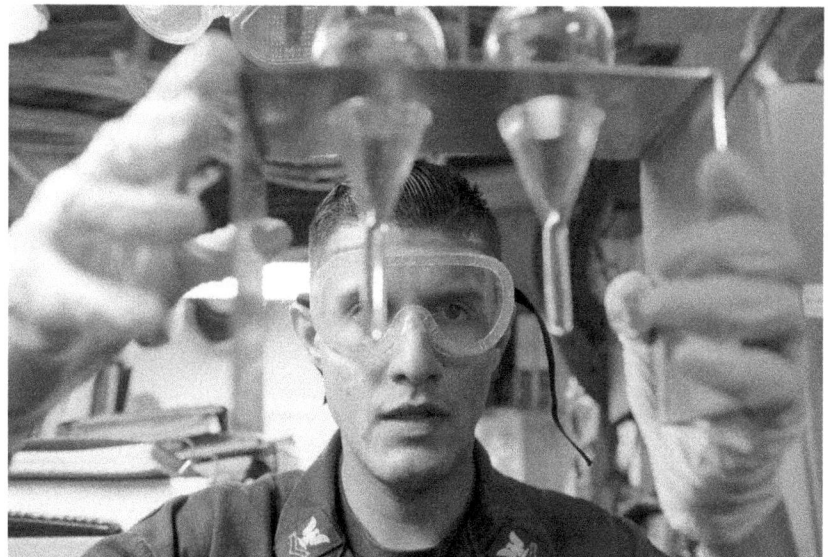

14-1. An assistant oil king inspects fuel oil samples. A key tenet of effective engineering program management is to ensure programs are properly implemented and administered on a daily basis.

U.S. Navy photo by Mass Communication Specialist 3rd Class Paul Kelly

support from other departments or you notice Sailors not following proper procedures, especially for any SOH program, then elevate your concerns to other department heads and the executive officer. Address any inconsistencies with your team, and make a plan for how to address program noncompliance.

Know Final Approval Requirements
The EDORM specifically states CO and chief engineer approval requirements. It is critical that not only you, but also your team—even at the most junior levels—strictly adhere to the guidance. Risk decisions must be made at the appropriate level, and that can only happen if your department understands the requirements. If there is ever a doubt, ask questions.

Keep Your Team Focused in the Shipyard
Although a necessary part of a ship's lifecycle, the shipyard is the most stressful and exhausting time for an engineering department. Your team's focus will shift away from underway operations to laying up equipment and supporting contractor maintenance. No matter how long your ship is in the yards, your team must prepare for end of shipyard assessments, such as damage control material condition assessment, light off assessment, and main space fire drill.

CHAPTER 14

Your team may be tempted to relinquish ownership of their spaces to contractors, but it is imperative that they maintain a presence in all their spaces. This will prove even more challenging as Sailors attend schools and your team is split, working from various locations, and while normal communication methods are degraded. Similarly, as opportunities to meet with your whole department are reduced, you will still need to coordinate and plan training, which often occurs outside normal working hours to accommodate shipyard work. This is particularly true when rehearsing all-hands evolutions such as main space fire drills. In spite of these challenges and competing priorities, you must continue to motivate your department to maintain a steady strain to training and managing programs with the end-state of exiting the shipyards and returning to sea as your primary goal.

Show Your Divisions Equal Attention
You may find yourself focused on one division more than others for a variety of reasons. Regardless of the reasons, do not neglect your other divisions and work centers, such as the repair division. While much of your time as the CHENG is focused on your main engine rooms and auxiliary spaces, your damage control team and your temporarily assigned damage control petty officers are equally important members of your engineering department.

Lead with an Even-Keeled Temperament
You will experience the full range of emotions as the CHENG, all heightened during stressful certification periods. You might breathe a sigh of relief after passing light off assessment, feel elated following a successful full-power run, or, worse, feel defeated when you inform your CO that your ship will "fail to sail" or when one of your critical engineering programs is assessed "not effective." It is easy to let the highs and lows of your job dictate your emotions, but take each event in stride. Keep your team focused and provide unconditional encouragement even after a setback. How you respond to your team's successes and failures will set your department's tone and influence their attitudes moving forward.

Build Your Network

Lean on Your Departmental Triad
As you do with the command triad, build a cohesive and trusting triad with your MPA and top snipe. Get to know each other's professional strengths and learn about each other's families and hobbies. These professional bonds will help strengthen and reinforce your engineering triad and reverberate

throughout the department. As a first tour CHENG, your MPA and top snipe will provide invaluable training and forceful backup for you. Over time, their experience and technical expertise will complement your own leadership and managerial skill sets.

Work with Your Shipboard Team
Your department's success, like that of your equipment, is intertwined with personnel outside of your department. Whether you are coordinating with the operations officer identifying underway replenishment requirements, the supply department for replacement parts, the combat systems team to schedule switchboard cleaning, or the maintenance material management coordinator for scheduled maintenance, supporting each other and clearly communicating and identifying areas where your team can assist will contribute to your ship's overall success. Cross-departmental coordination should occur at every level and not be limited to one specific pay grade.

Establish a Relationship with Your ISIC N4
Use your introduction to your N4 as an opportunity to learn about your ISIC's priorities, reporting requirements, and expectations of you. Keeping your N4 informed and clearly stating what type of assistance (if any) you need from them will equip your N4 to advocate on your ship's behalf.

Meet the Program Managers at Your Type Commander
Introduce yourself to the N4 organization at your type commander, specifically the DFS, CASREP, and class managers. If possible, meet individual members in person; otherwise, an email introduction will suffice. Knowing who you can reach out to with questions or concerns before an issue arises on your ship will help you make informed decisions.

Know the Experts in Your Maintenance Organization
Expect to work closely with your port engineer and project manager while you are the CHENG. As experts who have been assigned to your ship for a long period of time, your port engineer and project manager will know the ins and outs of major pieces of equipment. Maintain open lines of communication with them, especially when a new equipment casualty occurs or if your team corrects a casualty that initially required outside assistance. Similarly, develop a rapport with key personnel at the regional maintenance centers. For example, knowing supporting personnel in the gauge calibration shop, gas turbine shop, or the damage control warehouses will be vital when you have a special request or need extra assistance.

CHAPTER 14

Develop a Strong Network with CHENGs on Other Ships
Invest time to meet CHENGs from within your squadron first and then across the waterfront. From inspection preparation to parts assistance to personnel management, a strong network of people experiencing the same hardship will help you as the CHENG.

Focus on Professional Development

Embrace Quality Training
Training just to complete a requirement is not quality training. Tackle training topics in small, consistent doses and encourage your khaki leadership to attend departmental training. Training is not just for junior Sailors, but rather for your whole team. Attendance and participation from all khaki leadership not only improve overall level of knowledge, but also emphasize training importance. Training can be conducted both in port and under way in a classroom form, walk-through and talk-through of evolutions and drills, as well as execution of actual evolutions and drills. There will be times when quality training seems untenable, especially during a shipyard environment, but your team must continue to provide it. Taking a consistent and uncompromising approach to training will pay off in the long run.

Make Engineering Understandable and Exciting
Engineering operations and management can be intimidating, especially to individuals outside of engineering rates. To be effective watchstanders and effective damage control repair locker members, it is imperative that Sailors and junior officers know where key pieces of engineering equipment are located throughout the ship and the impacts of engineering equipment casualties. Encourage your crew to walk the engineering plant, ask questions, and get involved. Your enthusiasm and support will encourage your crew to learn beyond the engineering basics and extend into ship-wide evolutions such as main space fire drills.

Identify Opportunities to Drive the Ship
The EDORM permits the MPA to be designated as the plant control officer. Use that watchstation flexibility as an opportunity to assume officer of the deck responsibilities for routine underway operations as well as special evolutions. Your shipdriving skills can quickly atrophy if you only spend your time standing watch as the plant control officer and tactical action officer, and it is easy to be consumed by all things engineering. If in port, allocate time to

get to the ship simulators. Remember, being comfortable driving the ship is a critical aspect of command at sea.

Recognize Your Team and Have Fun

Snipe of the Month
Many engineering departments recognize an exceptional engineer every month. Often this recognition includes displaying a picture of the Sailor and perhaps a twenty-four-hour liberty or other creative incentive. This type of recognition also helps make your Sailors more competitive for shipboard Sailor of the quarter.

Spot Awards
Take time to recognize Sailors with specific achievement awards such as Navy and Marine Corps achievement medals, flag letters of commendation, or letters of appreciation. Command policy varies ship to ship, and submitting an award, even if not approved, draws positive attention to your Sailor and your team's accomplishments.

Create Friendly Competitions
Find opportunities to build your department's cohesion on and off ship. Plan a friendly bowling or softball competition between divisions or create competitions between drilling watch teams. This will encourage camaraderie and motivate your teams to perform at higher levels.

Recognize Your Off-Ship Supporting Teams
One way to offer recognition to outside entities is to publicly recognize specific individuals in official bravo zulu messages. Copy their parent organization and your chain of command on the message. Your CO can also present them a letter of appreciation.

Create Your Own CHENG or Department Challenge Coin
Another thoughtful way of recognizing your teams on and off ship is to present a ship-specific CHENG or engineering department challenge coin, which they can proudly display.

Conclusion

Being "the CHENG" is an unglamorous but incredibly rewarding experience. The chief engineer position requires a strong work ethic, superior organizational skills, attentiveness to detail, and a firm understanding of

CHAPTER 14

the interconnectedness of both the ship's systems and crew relationships. Although the job may seem overwhelming at times, you can rest assured that your team will work hard alongside you. When the job is done, you will no doubt reflect on your time as the CHENG as one of the most gratifying jobs you will ever have in the Navy.

CDR Samantha A. O'Neil served as chief engineer in USS *Preble* (DDG 88) and USS *Cowpens* (CG 63), where she was the recipient of the Navy and Marine Corps Association Leadership Award. Ashore, she served in the Commander's Action Group at Commander, Naval Surface Forces Pacific.

CHAPTER 15
Staff Readiness Officer
CDR Rob Keller, USN

Being "the N4"

COMPLETING A SUCCESSFUL TOUR as the engineering officer (CHENG) is no small task. The daily grind of the job is nearly all-consuming yet incredibly rewarding. It is undoubtedly a job that teaches you teamwork and advanced management skills and that pushes you through the full spectrum of emotions. You may never see a bigger smile than when the CHENG has a great full-power run during an inspection or certification event. That same smile quickly gives way to slumped shoulders and a look of defeat when the CHENG takes the long walk from the central control station to the bridge to inform the captain the ship will "fail to sail." These experiences, both high and low, will influence and prepare you for your next assignment as the staff readiness officer in a destroyer or amphibious squadron.

Your assignment as the staff readiness officer, or N4, will challenge you in different ways from when you were the CHENG. Your role as N4 is dynamic; you will be expected to integrate readiness and logistics into the operational planning process while ensuring the ships in your squadron maintain the highest level of readiness. Leverage your experiences as the CHENG and transform them into opportunities for you to make a larger impact on the larger Navy and Marine Corps team. You may recall the elation of certifying a major mission area or passing an inspection as the CHENG, but as the N4, you must quickly refocus your attention toward another ship's next major event. You must be integrated into the progression of milestones toward key events across *all* of your squadron ships simultaneously. Therefore, since you will not have a lot of time to reflect on each event, gather your lessons learned, disseminate them to your other ships and within your staff, and prepare for the next event! Unlike when you were the CHENG, managing your squadron ships' readiness and certification requirements will deter you from dwelling on the emotional highs and lows that come from the stress of approaching and completing every major milestone.

As the N4, you will also find that your problem-solving methods expand rapidly as you liaise with additional outside staffs in the readiness and maintenance communities to help each of your squadron ships meet certification requirements. While you will not have as many middle-of-the-night phone calls as you did as a CHENG, you will still play a vital role in your squadron's success. You will have freed up capacity that you previously did not have as a CHENG and, consequently, will be able to add great value to the engineers and supply officers in your squadron. You become their advocate to help remedy their greatest challenges—and you will find a tremendous amount of pride in knowing your effort "behind the curtain" helped them accomplish their mission. You will take away a wealth of knowledge from serving on the staff, and at times you will wish you had had that perspective as the CHENG. Be agile, be flexible, and always be looking over the horizon for your ships—this assignment will require you to balance several important events for each of your ships.

Practical Advice for a Successful Tour

Finding Your Footing: Defining the Undefined Role
You have read the *Standard Organization and Regulations of the U.S. Navy* (SORM, OPNAVINST 3120.32 [series]) many times throughout your career by this point, and it is a great reference for understanding your roles and responsibilities. As the CHENG, you referenced the *Engineering Department Organization and Regulations Manual* (EDORM, COMNAVSURFPAC/COMNAVSURFLANT Instruction 3540.3A [series]), which precisely detailed what you needed to accomplish daily and what your job responsibilities were. You will not find a reference that explicitly defines the roles and responsibilities of the staff readiness officer. However, the SORM provides a great initial reference to understand what your ships are responsible for and how you can ensure they can succeed.

One way to think about the N4 position is to think of yourself as an individual tasked with removing barriers to success for your ships' department heads. You are not the "Super CHENG," but rather a key staff officer expected and empowered to keep a watchful eye on all the departments in all of the ships in the squadron to ensure maximum combat readiness. Recall how busy and, at times, overwhelmed you felt as the CHENG; now envision someone with the authority, legitimacy, and time, showing up to ask how they could help. *That* is your role as the N4 in the simplest of terms. Use your time to be a second set of eyes for an engineering plant walk-through to check for safety issues, assist in deconflicting outside maintenance, and help review training plans with the afloat training group.

Being an Extension of the Commodore

Communicate with Caution

You may not be accustomed to working on an afloat staff, but your external communications must be carefully managed since you will represent your commander in ways you may not have had to do when you were a department head serving on a ship. You work for the commodore and, because of that, represent them in totality. Common failures stem from individuals who think they carry the same power as the commodore or those who do not recognize the context of what they say. When you communicate with a ship, it can become quickly misunderstood as "the commodore wants." Be cautious with every email you type and everyone with whom you speak, and ensure that if you do say, "The commodore wants," they did authorize you to speak on their behalf. Do not abuse the power entrusted to you by using the commodore's name in order to get what you want.

Be a Trusted Agent

You will gain a wealth of information working on an afloat staff and will acquire a greater understanding of how leaders at higher levels make decisions. With this comes privileged access, be it words spoken directly by the commodore or information in an email forwarded to you. Avoid following the trail to gossip; recognize that your peek behind the curtain comes from implicit trust and that violating that trust will render you ineffective nearly instantaneously. It is inappropriate to share the raw and emotional comments you may hear from your commodore with the leadership of your assigned ships. Sometimes predecisional discussions occur and are not meant to leave the small group setting. You may be privy to decisions about future operations, individual and unit awards, follow-on assignments, and evaluation rankings. It is vital to know when information is to be protected. While this information is not solely for the N4, it is important to help make you a respected staff officer.

Tell the Commodore What They Need To Know

You had a robust set of eight o'clock reports as the CHENG. Now, multiply those reports by the number of ships you have assigned, and suddenly you are tracking a lot of information! The commodore does not need to be apprised of everything. As the N4, it is your responsibility to synthesize that data into meaningful information. For a baseline assumption, enter with the belief that your commodore has a squadron of fully mission-capable ships. If there is anything that prevents a ship from being able to execute a potential tasking, you need to ensure they understand that limitation. You will not impress the commodore with how much you know, but you will make their job easier by providing them with the information necessary to make informed decisions that will impact squadron operations and missions. At a minimum, they need to understand the source of the impact, the repair and mitigation plan in effect, and an estimated time the casualty will be restored. Depending on the scope of the casualty, you may need to provide follow-on reports with increased fidelity as the situation develops.

Become the Subject Matter Expert
Your squadron will comprise different ship platforms or ship configurations. Whether they are assigned to you permanently or just during the duration of an operation, you must quickly learn each ship's capabilities and current limitations. Along with this understanding, you must be the expert in standing instructions that apply across the spectrum. You should keep a personal copy of the *Surface Force Training and Readiness Manual* and the EDORM. Additional documents that you must stay current on include Navy ships' technical manuals, maintenance and material management program instructions, and guidance promulgated by the type commander (TYCOM) and the training organizations. You can help arm your commodore, and the ships in your squadron, by knowing the references and ensuring they are operating in accordance with present requirements.

Know When the Appropriate Authority Makes Decisions
Your commodore expects you to execute your tasking with a certain level of autonomy. You will be required to work at or above your level to facilitate the commodore's priorities. On occasion, staff friction will result. You may be told, "No, we cannot support that." You may find that whomever you are coordinating with may not have the authority to approve what you need. However, there are occasions, not through negligence, that senior leadership within that organization supports your request. It is far better to tell the commodore, "My action officer at the TYCOM does not believe they can support our request" than "the TYCOM said no."

Add Value to Your Ships

Leave Your Office and Tour the Waterfront

You will learn exponentially more about your ships, their challenges, and what is going on when you leave the headquarters. Visiting your ships can be challenging because you may be geographically separated. Regardless, when able, it is always best to conduct visits and to do so even when you do not need anything. Frequent visits will help you learn the culture of your ships and will knock down any perceived tension between the staff and the crew. It is comfortable to sit behind the computer and task via email, but building strong relationships is far more effective if you are present on board the ship. You will find that the communication channels open quickly when the staff comes over not because they "need" something but rather to have a cup of coffee and ask what you can do to help a ship. Remember, when you were a CHENG, you carried a great amount of pride and were hesitant to give up the reins on anything. As the N4, work to build solid relationships with your squadron CHENGs and supply officers, and they will be much more open

15-1. **Engineering department conducts operations around the clock on every ship. Assisting them in routine inspections offers a great opportunity to demonstrate your interest in what they do for the ship.**

U.S. Navy photo by Mass Communications Specialist 1st Class Toni Burton/Released

to accepting the help you are offering. If you only come around the ships to deliver taskings, expect to have a much harder time to get the ships to want to work with you.

Be a Helping Hand, Not a Nuisance
Through your frequent visits, you will learn about what your ships need. They may require assistance with parts support, which provides you an opportunity to deliver a simple win. Perhaps they would just like a second set of eyes on a safety walk-through. You can also learn a great deal of information by reading their off-ship reports. You are an addressee on casualty reports and operational reports for a reason—if they are unclear, you can request clarification. Still, few things are as frustrating as when ships must provide information repeatedly through several different channels. Additionally, you can help share lessons learned from the other ships in the squadron as they progress through shipyard availabilities, training cycles, or other issues that you can help another ship avoid.

Coordinate with the Maintenance Team
You can help all departments on a ship by integrating with the maintenance team. Get to know the port engineer and project manager for each of your ships so you can help advocate for critical repairs. Additionally, attending routine maintenance updates (e.g., planning board for maintenance, weekly meetings with the regional maintenance center, or milestone conferences at the shipyard) will help show a united effort and keep you informed. You can help inform your commodore of the status of events, which creates an additional opportunity for them to elevate issues your ships may be having.

Build Relationships with the Training and Certification Teams
Training and certifying commands exist to help ships, and it is best to start building a connection before the start of the training cycle rather than trying to debate the finer points of a disagreement during an inspection. These organizations want ships to succeed, and you can help establish and build those relationships so that your ships step off on the right foot. Connecting early with their training and certifying teams can help you identify common shortcomings well before they are unrecoverable. When you have built a solid rapport with these teams, you will find that inspections and certifications tend to run much more smoothly due to the frequency of communication leading up to the events.

Establish a Plan

Divide and Conquer

As the N4, your department is much smaller than it was when you were a department head on the ship. Your scope of responsibility to oversee ships in your squadron requires methodical task delegation to meet the demands. You may only have a team of four to six people. Between your small department of division officers and chief petty officers, find a way to collaborate efforts on a consolidated tracker. Remember, though, these individuals are experts in their fields, so employ them effectively. They are not to conduct administrative duties solely. They need to be on the deckplates of your ships as well!

Be Humble

Welcome to a role that will force you to operate well outside of your comfort zone. You are now the supply officer for the squadron and thus cannot excel on a division officer level of understanding on how repair parts get to your ships. Additionally, you will be overseeing at least one engineering plant that you are not familiar with. You will not survive if you attempt to fake your knowledge; use your resources, find the references to build the foundation, and ask many questions. It is okay to feel a little overwhelmed at first, but through the course of your tour, your professional knowledge will increase tenfold. Within your staff, and on each of your ships, Sailors are filled with pride in their jobs and will gladly teach you what you need to know about your new role as the N4.

Look over the Horizon

Your management skills will be put to the test serving on an afloat staff. It will be common to have ships in separate regions of the world and in different parts of their life cycles. Success will depend upon your ability to step back from what is directly in front of you and consider the needs of other ships in your squadron. You cannot think only in linear terms. You have to conduct routine assessments of each ship and apply the lessons learned from one to prevent the same challenges from replicating elsewhere. As is true of every department head, having a tracker with milestones assigned will prevent you from being lost in the daily grind and will ensure your ships will be fit to fight.

Conclusion

Not unlike your previous assignment as the CHENG, your role as the squadron readiness officer is dynamic and fast-paced. However, as the N4, you are expected to become an expert in the material readiness and operational capabilities of all your assigned forces and are responsible for integrating with the staff on the coordination, planning, scheduling, and oversight of squadron operations. You must also foresee potential barriers and help remove them to ensure your squadron ships maintain the highest level of combat readiness to conduct the full spectrum of missions. Your time as the N4 will not only help you gain a greater understanding of naval operations above the department head level, it will also help you when you become an executive officer and commanding officer. Ultimately, you should find tremendous satisfaction that your direct efforts helped each of your squadron ships accomplish its mission.

CDR Rob Keller is a surface warfare officer who has served across multiple platforms and departments. His department head tours were as chief engineer in USS *Stockdale* (DDG 106) and as the staff readiness officer with commander, Amphibious Squadron THREE (CPR-3). He is a recipient of the Navy and Marine Corps Association Leadership Award as well as the Carrier Strike Group ONE Tactician of the Year. Ashore, he has served as a company officer at the United States Naval Academy, assistant director, surface warfare officer assignments (PERS 41), surface enlisted community manager (BUPERS-3), and was most recently assigned to U.S. Northern Command and North American Aerospace Defense Command. He is slated to take command of USS *Jason Dunham* (DDG 109).

CHAPTER 16

Shipboard Plans and Tactics Officer

LCDR Ashley O'Keefe, USN

Being "the PTO"

THE PLANS AND TACTICS OFFICER (PTO) job represents the most rewarding opportunity available for a second tour department head. The PTO integrates all long-range planning, tactics, and training. If the operations officer (OPS) is the choreographer, making the day-to-day plan work, the PTO is the director—you take the long view, developing the long-range schedule and turning it into reality. The PTO is the senior watch officer (SWO), senior tactician, and planning expert. As a senior department head, you collaborate with your fellow department heads to ensure that you are all aligned to a common vision and are properly trained, resourced, and manned to achieve it. This cross-departmental approach is vital to ship success and represents the missing link that the PTO role was developed to fill.

As the PTO, you may have a variety of duties as you carry out your integrative functions. *Plans and Tactics Officer Roles and Responsibilities* (COMNAVSURFORINST 3120.2) states that the PTO's responsibilities include ensuring alignment of long-range planning and tactical training with present and future ship operations, developing briefing processes and applying lessons learned, and directly supervising the training officer and independent duty intelligence specialist. A person who will find joy in exploring opportunity, providing valuable training, and closing operational seams will be happily employed in the PTO position. This job is for an integrator, a people person, who unites the combined departments of a ship into a cohesive whole and toward safe mission accomplishment.

As a ship's operational tempo, current phase, tasking, and operating procedures may vary, so will your job as PTO. Maintaining ship alignment across departments and planning cycles is essential; therefore, there is inherent flexibility to the job description, allowing the PTO to adjust their role with the ship's life cycle phase. For example, you may be tasked with leading the sonar technicians and the cryptologic technicians—a tactical sensing team—in addition to your duties as the lead tactician and planner. Perhaps you will take over the command, control, communications, and intelligence divisions. Or, to ensure effective alignment and integration across the ship you may assume the duties of a set of previous collaterals, now elevated to equal stature—perhaps safety, training, and administration. These together can make a crew happy and productive or, if poorly executed, ill-trained and ineffective.

Depending on your ship's timing within the training cycle, you may have added duties that include significant watchstanding responsibilities, cross-deck training during fleet-level exercises, and coordination of warfighting experimentation on board your ship. No matter the moment in time or location that you arrive on board your ship as PTO, there are plenty of best practices that you can apply for an effective tour.

Because differences exist between PTOs serving on board cruisers and destroyers and amphibious ships, your expected operational and tactical competencies are different as well. Ultimately, most PTOs are bound to find similarities in their roles as tactician and lead planner, and the flexibility provided the PTO is designed so that they are able to work with the commanding officer (CO) and executive officer to evaluate and identify the highest priority areas of focus and ensure alignment across them. In any case, a sense of comfort with ambiguity and a self-starting nature will be key to doing the PTO job well.

Organizational Roles and Responsibilities

The general duties assigned to the PTO in COMNAVSURFORINST 3120.2 are to "lead, direct, and synchronize warship plans," "plan for the long-range employment of a task unit and the tactical training of all watchstanders," and "serve as the lead tactical trainer for the unit." In addition, specific functions include:

- ▶ planning future operations, generally mid- to long-range scheduling, exercises and operations, as well as the synchronization of mission planning
- ▶ holding a deep knowledge of the applicable tactics associated with the sea control and power projection missions the unit executes, including serving as primary liaison with the Surface and Mine Warfighting Development Center (SMWDC)

- providing feedback on doctrine and tactics, techniques, and procedures' (TTP) effectiveness and usability
- understanding how these tactics contribute to the overall employment of the ship
- training of all tactical watchstanders, including serving as the integrated training team coordinator and combat systems training team (CSTT) (tactical) leader
- building competency of the unit's tactical action officers
- ensuring the plan-practice-perform-progress-promulgate cycle is integrated in all unit events
- in conjunction with the OPS, ensuring execution of the preparation of operational plans, orders and reports, and training schedules
- serving as exercise support for fleet-level exercises to build a higher degree of understanding of the most recent tactical employment trends
- coordinating subject matter expert support for the unit
- coordinating requests for capability assessments, experimentation, and future requirements that require ship support and execution.

As with the rest of the department heads, you will report directly to the CO. Your performance is measured not numerically but by the perceived effectiveness of your actions. Have you built a successful team? Provided value as a tactician? Increased the competency of the ship's watchstanders and passed training cycle inspections? If so, you are likely on the right path.

Practical Advice for a Successful Tour

The following information describes some helpful tips for those currently serving, or seeking assignment, as a ship's plans and tactics officer.

Close the Seams

Find the Gaps

As the senior department head, you have been around the block a bit. Now is the time to apply those skills and hard-earned knowledge for the benefit of the ship. Are you planning an exercise that will require extra speed and thus increased fuel expenditure? Make sure the chief engineer is in the planning loop. Do you notice holes in bridge watchstanders' antisubmarine warfare

(ASW) knowledge? Set up wardroom training with the ASW officer. As PTO, you are going to be part of a wide variety of conversations and planning cells on board. Look for places where the ship can be better, and close those gaps. A person who is internally motivated to start hard conversations and find zones for improvement will be a natural in the PTO role. If you are not that person, you will develop these skills as PTO.

Be the Integrator
The PTO leads the integrated training team on board, but there is more to the "integration" of the ship than just being the training team lead. As the long-range planner, the PTO often will be the first to recognize points of friction. As the senior watch officer, the PTO often will notice gaps in knowledge or poor training before the rest of the department heads. If the PTO position on your ship is not already serving as the senior watch officer, advocate for it. You are best placed to help out the team and to bring people together. Planning boards are a great place for this integration to happen, in addition to having an open door and a friendly attitude. Do not allow others to miss things that you are seeing, and invite them to participate in planning for and fixing the discrepancies you may find.

Lead Your Fellow Department Heads
This might be the hardest thing to do as PTO. You are only about eighteen months senior to them. There is no real rank structure. But it is your responsibility to help keep the team together. You are responsible for a lot less maintenance and fewer people, so there is time for the big thoughts. Think them, and execute! Build up your teammates, get them to the top of their game tactically, and use your long-range planning prowess to make the team hum. Once the department heads are looking out a quarter or more and working closely with one another, the ship's operations and planning cycle will feel a great deal smoother to the junior Sailor on the deckplates.

Think about Crew Resource Management
The PTO should be looking beyond just the bridge teams and surface warfare officers to ensure that the whole ship is involved in an evolution or operation. This competency is critical in Condition IV steaming, when not many SWOs are on the watchbill. As the SWO, with a cross-departmental mandate, the PTO can use the watchbill and personnel qualification standards to make something that may seem taxing (such as ship's nautical or otherwise photographic interpretation and exploitation teams) into a means to get all hands contributing to the fight. Additionally, as the SWO, the PTO can ensure

that the ship enacts circadian rhythm best practices, which are critical to top performance.

Planning Competencies

Know Who Your Bosses Are

Although this might seem simple, it is not, but it is absolutely essential to anticipating the ship's needs and to success in driving readiness. Knowing both your operational and administrative chains of command at all times is vital, especially when they seem, or are in fact, opaque. This knowledge matters for tasking—who can write your schedule—and tactics—whose operational tasking orders are in effect. You and the OPS should work closely together. Consider briefing daily at the operations/intelligence meeting who your operational commanders are, and make and brief a line diagram when they change. On deployment, associated support, tactical control, and direct support lines might all point to a different commander. For example, you might work for commander, Task Force 55, but be assigned associated support to a counterpiracy task force and also be operating under tactical control of a senior ship when conducting a specific operation. It can be confusing. Break out your joint publications (Joint Publication-1, *Doctrine for the Armed Forces of the United States*, to start) and explain to your wardroom what these terms mean. Teach your combat information center (CIC) team why they matter and how to find the relevant publications.

Have a Questioning Attitude

Plans are written by people like you, not by some all-knowing source. Try to understand the planners' perspective as they were writing the document. What demands were they responding to? What was their frame of reference? Unstated assumptions about capabilities, intent, and the adversary's reaction always will be present. When you read plans, think through the second- and third-order effects. Does being on station at a given time mean that you will need permission to stop doing something else earlier than planned? Do the aircraft listed in the plan have the same understanding of TTP as your team does? Call them. Reach out and confirm. Never assume that a schedule, concept of operations, or execution brief can in fact be executed as-is. Think about how you will get it done, find the seams, and work with your fellow department heads to make sure that they understand the plan too.

Participate in the Evolutions You Plan

Just as the OPS should be on the forecastle during an underway replenishment, the PTO should be in the CIC for a missile shoot or strait transit. The more time you spend with your tactical watchstanders as they execute the operations that you planned, the better off you will be. The team will see you as involved and invested in them. This presence has a positive effect on junior and senior Sailors alike, in addition to the tactical benefit of helping you evaluate the next actions for improved training and alignment. Perhaps next time you choose to focus on communications structure and frequencies more, plan an extra rehearsal, or add a second helicopter to your overhead coverage scheme. Running a hot wash or debrief is one thing; personally participating in events is quite another. You may be busy, but the value in being on-scene cannot be overstated.

Operationalize Administration

Your ideas and improvements are great. But will they stick around? Your plan, brief, execute, debrief (PBED) processes and the lessons that you learn are only as good as the administrative necessities that codify and promulgate them. On USS *Lassen*, navigation councils were a critical enabler of this process. Each week, as a team—from CO to junior quartermaster—we sat down and reviewed a single standing order. What had we learned recently that might make the standing order better? Was there an improvement to a checklist, or had we updated the optimal radar settings? These changes were debated and then approved by the captain. Each week after the council, the updated standing order was "yeomanized" and then sent out as a change to the standing orders, which we had bound with a change page for each bridge watchstander. This quick cycle from "lesson learned" to "adminized" increased shipwide buy-in to the efficacy of the lessons learned process. Watchstanders could see that their suggestions were being implemented quickly and that their voice mattered. Most importantly, it ensured that the best practices and lessons learned would be adhered to and utilized well into the future, ensuring the safety and success of the next generation of watchstanders.

Meet the Right People and Stay in Touch

The Navy is full of organizations that are trying to improve surface warfare lethality and tactics. Located in Dahlgren, Virginia, Carderock and Indian Head, Maryland, and Point Loma, California, these other warfighting development centers are also valuable resources for you to utilize as PTO. The training carrier strike groups—Four and Fifteen—and SMWDC have lots of resources for you. When they come on board your ship, engage with them. Ask questions, give feedback, and participate in the work that they are doing. When the opportunity arises to attend a planning conference, a tactical symposium, or a training event, go! Your ship will be better connected and resourced to meet the challenges of the operational environment when you attend these events and follow through on the connections that you make.

Be Fluid

You might think "be flexible," but more movement than that is involved. Sometimes we have to go with the flow, and sometimes we can control the flow, but it is all going to keep moving. Just like the sage advice given to any prospective OPS, do not fall in love with the plan. Ships break, plans change, people leave—it will be okay. Build your plans to account for depth on the bench, a few extra hours of transit time, and a healthy dose of reality.

Training Is Key

Live the Standard

Develop skills and maintain a training mindset. Do you see your watchstanders not paying attention? Neglecting check prints? As the senior tactical watchstander, it is the PTO's responsibility to hold the line. Model good behavior when you are on watch and ensure that others do the same. If watchstanders need practice, get the sets and repetitions in through CSTT scenarios and empower your training team to stop and correct personnel who are not getting it right. In the training cycle, if the training team catches a mistake and briefs it later, afloat training group (ATG) assessors will look favorably on that point in the gradesheet. Build your teams to look for and fix mistakes before the off-ship assessors find them or before they have real tactical impact. But remember, it is not just about the assessors. We are warfighters. Life might go kinetic quickly, and ATG assessors will not be there with you. Be ready.

Consider Safety

Safety does not just mean keeping a hand on the ladder rail at all times. As part of your planning process, think through the ways that a tactical scenario might impact operations or watchstanders not in the CSTT organization. For example, does your gyro data change on the bridge if you reposition the ship for a scenario? Will the gun mount move or be stationary in your current configuration? What other ships are around you when you bring down radars for technical training? Safety is central to the PTO's portfolio of responsibilities.

PBED Helps

As PTO, you are the process owner for the PBED cycle. Make it your own and build the processes that will enable your bridge and CIC teams to execute

CHAPTER 16

automatically. Consider reviewing and using the naval aviation community's concept of threat and error management; it makes tangible the more opaque aspects of "operational risk management." As you build a Condition III PBED process, consider how watch team turnovers are set up, and work with the OPS to ensure the plan of the day enables thorough debriefs. Enforce use of logs during formal debriefs. Create a repetitive, repeatable process. A team that instinctively wants to brief and debrief their actions is more effective, and safer, than one in the habit of action only.

Build a Learning Organization

Ultimately, your job as PTO revolves around building an organization that is prepared for the challenges it might face and flexible enough to learn from its mistakes. This starts with the culture needed to enable such behavior. Build an environment in which admitting failure is acceptable. This can be hard. Life on a ship can be stressful, and the old "SWO culture" might still raise its head. Work to tamp this impulse down and to allow for innovative solutions. On USS *Lassen*, in place of the typical debrief or critique, the PTO facilitated Sailor-centered collaborative workshops focused on getting to root causes in a way that invited collaboration, rather than threatening

16-1. **Plans and tactics officers work with warfare tactics instructors to provide combat mentorship and tactical guidance in ships across the fleet.**

U.S. Navy Photo by Mass Communication Specialist Seaman Bill M. Sanders/Released

punishment. This methodology enabled the collection of invaluable input from those closest to the source—the Sailors. Sticky notes and an open communications path allowed everyone from a fireman to the executive officer to compile their observations and describe how the event might have gone differently. These were voyages of discovery that taught all echelons of leadership and operators on board how to look past the result and to evaluate decision-making processes. And they were cool! Sailors were motivated and empowered to improve their ship. Ultimately, be creative and encourage learning behaviors.

Own the Fight

Tactical Training Is Yours

You have the opportunity and the writ to focus on training; do it! In certain periods of the ship's life, training and staying sharp can be difficult. Look far enough ahead and you may be able to schedule tactical trainers on shore for your ship's use, or pull portions of the training cycle forward. The PTO should be present and running the combat systems training team from the CIC. When complete, make sure that you and the team are doing a full debrief and that you are in fact applying the lessons you learn from one day to the next. This may mean that you personally go find the log that the air watchstander said they did not have, or make the slide on the tactic that the tactical action officer missed to brief the following day. Have ownership, and make the ship better.

Write the Battle Orders

The Commanding Officer's Battle Orders direct the fight on board your ship. They are equivalent to a CO's bridge standing orders, but likely of more breadth and detail. Commander, Naval Surface Forces has promulgated a baseline set that will help you get started, but you and the combat systems officer owe the captain a tailored, high-fidelity document with which the crew will train during the basic phase and execute on deployment. Get personally involved with writing this document, and if you have a warfare tactics instructor on board, be sure that they are deeply invested too. As you work to build the battle orders, warfare leads on board should be closely consulted to ensure they have buy-in on the results. If not, the first time you set weapons posture one on deployment, you may be disappointed to learn that your system configuration is not only suboptimal but also unsafe.

CHAPTER 16

Run War Councils

Get war councils onto the schedule monthly—and more frequently on deployment. These councils are a venue for warfare leads and tactical watchstanders to engage with the CO about their direction for the tactical employment of the ship. Consider going over a chapter of the battle orders for edit and review, having a warfare lead present on new TTPs, or briefing a new threat region. In addition to keeping the tactical part of the brain sharp during a long yard period, war councils allow watchstanders to understand the CO's risk tolerance and talk through scenarios with them, long before the pressure of any live situation exists.

Ask to Participate in TTP Testing, or Test It Yourself

Keep a sharp eye out for cutting-edge tactics and try them out whenever feasible. Participating as opposing forces in another strike group's certification event is a terrific time to get the whole crew into the game. As the PTO, you should be present at most of the early planning conferences for large-scale events. Find the SMWDC representative or the warfare leads and ask what is new this time around. Scan the Navy Doctrine Library system before you go, and ask if anyone is implementing the newest tactical memorandum. The Navy has built some amazingly capable ships; explore the limits of their performance and the ways in which your systems can be manipulated to achieve tactical effects. We tend to train to the mean—we infrequently utilize the full potential of the systems at our disposal. It is your job to make sure that we do.

Share Your Lessons Learned

Of course, SMWDC is looking for your feedback as they build out the newest doctrine and apply new technology to write new TTPs. Give this feedback to them, as much as you can. But on the ship, some of your biggest impacts can come from the work you do with your fellow department heads in the strike group or amphibious readiness group. Talk with them about particular tactical configurations or employment that you have tried. Share when you get new insight about the purpose of an exercise or maneuver. Have a great training plan? Push it out. The PTO can be a great integrator and closer of seams at the operational level, not just on board. Use what you learned to make the team better.

Conclusion

The plans and tactics officer is a highly rewarding job because the PTO has the opportunity to make a good warship a terrific one. By building the connectivity—on- and off-ship—that deeply weaves a ship into the fabric of operational forces, the PTO enables tactical competence and sharp, safe operational execution. In the learning organization that is today's Navy, the PTO is the right job at the right time. Our Navy will be better served by the skill sets the PTO cultivates, the increased flexibility of the shipboard leadership team, and the enhanced support for creative solutions to the complex world around us.

LCDR Ashley O'Keefe is a surface warfare officer who served as combat systems officer and plans and tactics officer in USS *Lassen* (DDG 82). Previously, she served as weapons officer in USS *Gettysburg* (CG 64) and as a division officer in USS *Farragut* (DDG 99). Ashore, she completed her master's degree in public policy at Harvard University's John F. Kennedy School of Government. She has served as flag aide to the superintendent of the United States Naval Academy and as speechwriter for the Chief of Naval Operations.

CHAPTER 17

First Lieutenant

LCDR Audrey Herrington, USN

So You Want to Be a First Lieutenant

WELCOME TO ONE of the fastest-paced, most rewarding tours of your career. As a department head first lieutenant (1LT), you will command deck department on an amphibious ship. Deck department is the heart and soul of an amphibious warship, and the 1LT is the glue that holds the department together. Deck department has a role to play in every evolution that occurs on an amphibious ship, so it is imperative that the 1LT is assertive and flexible and can communicate effectively at all levels.

Amphibious ships are the only platforms that have a department head filling the 1LT billet. What the billet lacks in platform choices, however, it makes up for in the myriad programs and evolutions that fall under the 1LT's purview. The 1LT has their hands in every evolution that takes place on board—from getting the ship under way to mooring her safely back in port. Compared to other departments, deck department has the widest range of leadership experience, from the newest seaman recruit to the saltiest boatswain mate. As members of deck department, the newest and most inexperienced Sailors' perception of the Navy is directly influenced by the way they are treated and the example that deck leadership, including the 1LT, provide for them.

If you enjoy leading and mentoring Sailors, maintaining long-kept traditions, engaging in hands-on training, and seeing the results of your labor, 1LT is the billet you should seek. The time and effort you put into your department and your Sailors will produce results that you will find hugely rewarding.

Duties and Responsibilities

The *Standard Organization and Regulations of the U.S. Navy* (SORM, OPNAVINST 3120.32 [series]) lays out the duties of the first lieutenant and delineates the role as "supervising the employment of equipment associated with deck seamanship." Specific responsibilities within the role of 1LT are as follows:

- preservation and cleanliness of the exterior of the ship
- supervision of the paint, sail, and boatswains' lockers
- the operation, care, and maintenance of the ground tackle, mooring lines, and related equipment
- the operation, care, and maintenance of the ship's boats, the life rafts, and other life-saving equipment
- the operation, care, and maintenance of the ship's booms and winches associated with amphibious operations, replenishment, and salvage
- the operation, care, and maintenance of the towing gear and equipment, rigging, gangways, fueling and provisioning at-sea gear, and other deck appurtenances
- the planning and execution of all matters related to deck seamanship, including anchoring, mooring, fueling, and replenishment at sea, loading, unloading operations, and stowage of cargo
- in ships not having an air department, the operation, care, and maintenance of the ship's flight deck, hangar, and all other prescribed flight deck equipment
- the abandon ship personnel assignment list for the ship, including temporarily embarked personnel; providing the current assignments to each officer and petty officer in charge of abandon ship stations.

Preparing for First Lieutenant

Before You Check On Board

Know and Understand Your References
There is no specific 1LT course in the Surface Warfare Officers School curriculum. You will attend the operations officer course with two weeks set aside for 1LT-particular functions. Be prepared to give yourself an independent crash course in the time you have before you report to your command. While you will gain most of your knowledge through on-the-job training, you should familiarize yourself with the following references before checking on board:

- *Navy Tactics, Techniques, and Procedures—Underway Replenishment* (NTTP 4-01.4)
- *Wet Well Operations Manual* (COMNAVSURFLANT/PACINST 3340.3)
- *Naval Ships' Technical Manual* (NSTM) Chapter 583—"Boats and Small Craft"
- NSTM 571, 581–589
- *Surface Force Training and Readiness Manual*

Also familiarize yourself with standard operating procedures. Focus your attention on the risks of each evolution, go and no-go criteria, and mitigations that can be put in place to manage risks. As the 1LT, you will help the commanding officer (CO) make informed decisions on whether to conduct an evolution based on risk factors such as equipment casualties, weather, and personnel qualifications. You will find this information is imperative when briefing the CO, regardless of the evolution.

Familiarize Yourself with Your Collateral Duties

As the 1LT, there are several collateral duties that you will assume once you check on board. One of the largest of these duties is the search and rescue (SAR) program. Although there will be a designated SAR officer, as the 1LT you remain responsible for all of the life-saving equipment; thus, you will be accountable for a large portion of that program. Deck department owns the rigid-hull inflatable boats or rigid inflatable boats (RIBs), which are vital components of the SAR program. You are responsible for making sure that the RIBs are outfitted with the correct life-saving equipment in accordance with the search and rescue manual. Along with the RIBs, the 1LT also owns the life rings, life preservers, lifeboats, and other safety equipment. The SAR swimmers' personal gear also falls under your purview and must be maintained in accordance with the Board of Inspection and Survey deck checklist. It is always a good idea to verify that the SAR swimmers are conducting the proper maintenance on their personal gear after every use. For ships that do not have a designated safety officer, the 1LT often assumes that role as well. Even if you are not identified as the safety officer, you will own the respirator protection program, the fall prevention program, the crane program, and, on dock landing ships (LSDs), the aviation safety officer program. For ships that have a paint locker separate from hazardous material issuance, the 1LT will have ownership of that as well.

Understand Who Will Be Working for You
On an LSD, you will have a limited duty officer (LDO) boatswain and boatswain's mate chief petty officer (BMC). On an LHD, you will have an LDO or chief warrant officer (CWO) boatswain and an LDO/CWO assistant first lieutenant (AFL). These individuals will be your go-to subject matter experts for every evolution of which you are in charge. Use every chance you get to learn from your boatswain, AFL, and BMCs. No matter how many times you have read the instructions, there will always be something that your boatswain/AFL/BMC can teach you.

The majority of Sailors working for you are boatswain mates (BMs). You will learn very quickly that BM is a very proud rate, filled with tradition. BMs chose their rate because they want to work hard, and they value a hands-on job where they can see the product of their efforts. Undesignated seamen make up the next largest part of your department. It is beneficial to understand that not all the undesignated seamen in deck department want to be BMs. Most of them are trying to strike other rates and move into other departments. It is essential to remember that they may be motivated differently than your BMs.

Establish Your Presence

Take Charge of Your Post
While the age-old adage "if it's not broken, don't fix it" holds merit, try not to follow it as if it is law. Just because a process or procedure is not broken does not mean that it cannot be improved upon or made more efficient. You do not have to be content with a department that is merely functional. You, like all leaders, want your department to excel. It often takes three Sailors to make one watchstander. Be proactive and predict shortfalls. Do not let your department have single points of failure. From the moment you accept the reins, you may find it useful to review your department's training and qualification process and insert yourself into it. You do not have to sit every board for every watchstation, but spot-checking the boards occasionally will ensure that standards aren't slipping. As 1LT, you are in charge of the Sailors that are driving the ship. These Sailors get more face time with the CO than most other rates. Instill formality in your Sailors daily, and it will show through their watchstanding.

Stay Ahead of Schedule
It's your department, and you own the schedule—to a certain extent. A good way to set up a battle rhythm is to make it reasonable yet as all-encompassing

as possible. Bouncing it off of the command calendar before you promulgate it to your department is a good way to ensure you have not double-booked your Sailors with things such as cleaning stations, all-hands training, and drills. Of course, there will always be last-minute changes, but for the most part, you want to know what significant items are coming down the pipeline. Certain events require months of planning and preparation. Failure to plan for a certification can devastate your department's morale and potentially impact your ship's ability to meet operational tasking.

Maintain Professional Working Relationships with Your Fellow Department Heads
As a 1LT, you depend heavily on other departments. You work hand in hand with the operations officer and training officer while scheduling your evolutions and certifications through the basic phase. The supply officer will be one of your go-to department heads in terms of ordering the parts and equipment necessary for a successful deployment cycle. You will work side by side with the navigator while planning and working out the intricate details of your amphibious operations. While your relationship with all fellow department heads is important, your relationship with the chief engineer (CHENG) is critical. You can start building this relationship as soon as you check on board. The CHENG has ownership of the mechanical portion of most of your equipment. This relationship will drive the success of your 1LT tour just as much as your hard work.

Cultivate Relationships Outside the Ship

- Port operations/Naval Facilities Engineering Command (NAVFAC). You will eventually find yourself on a first-name basis with port operations as you schedule line handlers for pulling into port, placement and removal of the oil boom, and pierside small boat operations. You will also find yourself working heavily with NAVFAC to schedule crane services to place/remove the brow/ramps.
- Maintenance team. During maintenance availabilities, you will see your ship's port engineer more frequently. A good relationship with the port engineer is important to ensuring your equipment is getting the care and attention it needs from outside activities. The port engineer will be your go-to point of contact for all of your maintenance jobs during the availability, so keep their contact information close at hand. Be open to visits from the corrosion control assist team; it is one of the few times that you have an excess

of working tools on board and experts to train your Sailors on how to conduct preservation properly.
- ▶ Board of Inspection and Survey preparation. When preparing for Board of Inspection and Survey, contact their deck team as early as possible. A good rule of thumb is to schedule a deck self-assessment groom training visit prior to the inspection. This carefully chosen team of deck experts will help guide you in conducting a self-assessment, identify your trouble areas, and point you in the right direction to get the assistance you need to repair your equipment.
- ▶ Basic phase preparation. During the basic phase, afloat training group should be your number one point of contact, followed by your assault craft unit, naval beach group, and beach master unit. Lastly, do not forget to reach out to your network of waterfront 1LTs. They will have advice and lessons learned that will help you and your team prepare for inspections.

Be the Leader the Deck Department Needs

Know Your Sailors, and Take Care of Them

Getting to know your Sailors is arguably one of the most important things you can do as a department head. Having a good idea of your Sailors' "normal operating mode" will allow you to determine if that Sailor is acting out of character. This is crucial in deck department. Remember that not everyone who is assigned to deck department is a BM, and many Sailors did not choose to be in deck department. This, coupled with a fast-paced environment of manual labor and often long hours, leaves deck department ripe for quality-of-life issues. Sailors can become quickly overwhelmed with the pace and not know how to handle the stress in a responsible manner. Being aware of these types of situations early is key to stopping an incident before it occurs.

Be Present and Available

While every ship does things differently in regard to departmental quarters, you may find it beneficial to attend quarters for each of your divisions. The more you attend your departmental/divisional quarters, the more quickly you can gauge things such as departmental morale, culture, and communication. Deck department usually will have two divisions (in some cases, three divisions). This makes it reasonably easy to have departmental quarters versus divisional. There is no set guidance for how frequently this needs to occur; usually, it is accomplished in conjunction with an awards presentation or departmental safety stand-down. This is your time to ensure that the things you disseminate during your khaki quarters are getting passed down to your Sailors. Lastly, while an open-door policy is a useful tool for letting your Sailors know that you are available, remember that it can easily get out of hand. You do not want to completely cut out of the communications loop your leading petty officers (LPOs), chief petty officers (CPOs), and division officers (DIVOs).

Be the Expert

Know Your Real Estate

As the 1LT, you own more than 50 percent of the ship's real estate. Regardless of the ship class, you own the hull—from the life-rails to the waterline. The 1LT is also in charge of the well deck, upper and lower vehicle stowage, the boat deck, the forecastle, the underway replenishment stations, the mooring stations, and the fantail. On LSDs, the 1LT also owns the flight deck and all associated gear and equipment. These are just the "big" areas—there will be several internal spaces and weather decks of which you are also in charge. Know your spaces, and walk them regularly. The first and most prevalent way to instill space ownership in your Sailors is to demonstrate that sense of ownership yourself. The easiest way to lose the trust and confidence of your Sailors is by having to ask where your own space is. That is not to say that when you first check on board, you should know everything, but once you have been on board for a few months, walking your spaces should be second nature. Knowing your real estate is only the first part of the battle; you also need to know the evolutions that take place in the space, the problem areas of each space, which division owns the space, and what gear is supposed to be stored there. It sounds like a lot—and it is. The bigger the ship class, the more time you will need to invest in truly knowing your real estate.

Be Familiar with Your Equipment and Understand Your Evolutions

To understand the complexity of deck department evolutions, it is vital that you understand what equipment you own and have a basic understanding of how it operates. You must be able to speak to the material degradations of your equipment and any impacts that it will have on your evolutions and the ship's missions. A brief look at deck gear can be broken down into a few major pieces of equipment:

- ▸ life-saving equipment: boat davits, small boats, and life rafts
- ▸ cargo and stowage: winches, capstans, cranes, and lashing gear

- replenishment: fueling at sea, replenishment at sea stations, and associated gear
- mooring: mooring lines, accommodation ladders, ramps, and brows
- ground tackle: anchors, chains, stoppers, and windlasses.

Have your senior enlisted leadership walk you through the evolutions and familiarize you with the equipment before the ship conducts the evolution. This way, you will have a better idea of what to expect. Read the manuals and look at the blueprints beforehand, but do not rely on written documents to replace being on deck. From getting under way to mooring, anchoring, underway replenishment, small boat operations, towing, and amphibious operations, deck department is at the center of all the action. If your CO expresses the desire to have you in the pilothouse for all evolutions, make sure you attempt to get on station for each evolution at least once. Try to view these operations from each station before situating yourself in debark control. This will help you have an excellent idea of the evolutions before you take charge of them as the debark control officer. The information you will learn by physically watching and interacting during the evolution will be invaluable.

Hone Your Writing Skills

Because the 1LT owns so many of the evolutions that take place on board an amphibious ship, you also own myriad instructions that are in constant need of updating. Additionally, with one of the largest departments on board, writing performance evaluations and fitness reports can become cumbersome. The *Department of the Navy Correspondence Manual* (SECNAV Manual 5216.5 [series]), the *Navy Performance Evaluation System* (BUPERSINST 1610.10 [series]), and the *Navy and Marine Corps Awards Manual* (SECNAVINST 1650.1 [series]), as well as the selection board precepts found on the Navy Personnel Command website, are tools designed to help you write about your Sailors' performance. Proper administration is not only about keeping things organized and up to date; it is also the time to take care of your Sailors and show them that you are paying attention to the work they are doing. You may find it extremely beneficial to keep an evolution tracker. When it is time to write evaluations and awards, having a tracker with all of the evolutions the ship has conducted can save you time, and it can keep your correspondence accurate.

Integrate with Your Marine Corps Counterparts

As the 1LT, you will work hand in hand with Marine Corps counterparts during embarkation and debarkation. The combat cargo officer (CCO)—usually a

CHAPTER 17

17-1. Deck department Sailors conduct amphibious operations, launching U.S. Marine Corps combat rubber raiding craft.
U.S. Navy Photo by Mass Communication Specialist Seaman Sabyn L. Marrs

Marine officer assigned to the ship—will be your go-to point of contact for most functions that involve embarkation/debarkation of Marine troops. Some specific items you will receive from the CCO include:

- ship's loading characteristic pamphlet
- detailed loading and off-loading plan identified by space requirements or equipment priorities
- current inventory of Marine Corps equipment, vehicles, and personnel
- a record of landing craft, boats, and helicopter requirements necessary to complete loading/unloading.

These items will help you plan and execute the embarkation and debarkation of Marine troops. The CCO, along with the combat cargo team, also supervises the loading and off-loading of all landing force personnel, supplies, and equipment. During operations, the combat cargo team works with the 1LT and deck department to prepare realistic timelines for ship-to-shore movements and also supervises the situating of all equipment, gear, and personnel that will be debarking during the operation.

General Advice for a Successful Tour

Understand Your Limitations

You cannot do this on your own. While it may be tempting to micromanage everything in your department, you can be quickly overwhelmed. Delegation and time management are two of your best tools for maintaining your composure and your sanity. Keeping track of your day-to-day routine is a good way to determine your mental and emotional limits. Understanding your limitations will not only provide you peace of mind and quality of life, it will also allow you to create reasonable deadlines for your team. Remember that everyone needs time throughout the day to regroup and reflect, everyone needs to eat, and everyone should have time for personal growth—even you.

Recognize Your Team's Accomplishments

The workload of deck department can be daunting and oftentimes overlooked in the daily hustle and bustle. Recognizing your team's accomplishments regularly is a good tool for congratulating them on a job well done; sometimes that's all it takes to make a difference in departmental morale. Some great ways to recognize your Sailors are special awards, added notes in their fitness reports and evaluations that highlight their specific achievements, time off/liberty, and implementing a "Sailor of the week" program. Departmental get-togethers are also an excellent way to let your Sailors know that you recognize their efforts and appreciate their hard work.

Be an Adaptable Leader

Being a leader encompasses more than knowing when and how to delegate and being able to influence people. A big part of leading is about teaching and mentoring. Remember that not everyone learns the same way, and not everyone responds to one leadership style. Adjusting your message delivery or your leadership approach will ensure your message reaches the largest number of personnel. Try different approaches and figure out what works best.

Get Organized—Mentally and Physically

Because of the size of deck department, you may find publishing a departmental philosophy extremely helpful. A departmental philosophy can be a simple one-page document that lists your priorities. Once you have a solid philosophy, it will be much easier to communicate your priorities to your department, and communication is a critical component to any organization.

Other ways to help you stay organized include keeping a calendar and sharing it with your DIVOs, CPOs, and LPOs, filtering message traffic, and creating multiple Outlook personal storage data files (PSTs). While having one PST is fine, it can quickly become a rather large file and be easily corrupted. If you create multiple PSTs, you can keep the file size much smaller and still have access to all of your correspondence.

Lastly, you may find it helpful to have a notebook *and* a planner. A good trick is to scribble your notes down in the notebook and then pick out the important things and transfer them neatly into your planner later. This way, you can order items based on priority and keep the events in chronological order. However you decide to keep organized is up to you; the key is to have a plan on how you want to stay organized.

Conclusion

You might feel that you embody many roles as first lieutenant. You have to emotionally invest in your evolutions and your Sailors. You have to be able to shift between the rough and tough figurehead the boatswain's mates are accustomed to dealing with and the softer-voiced, more easygoing leader that your undesignated seamen need. At the end of the day, you can start to feel like you have more than one personality crammed inside of your head, but because your department has a wide range of leadership and naval experience, it requires flexibility in your leadership style. Constantly adjusting your leadership style can leave you exhausted, and that is not counting the workload. Often the work will seem endless, and there will never be enough time in the day to finish all of the tasks, but the respect, pride, and effort your Sailors put into their work will leave a lasting impression on you. When you look back on a completed department head tour, you will understand that you could not have chosen a more rewarding billet than the ship's first lieutenant.

LCDR Audrey Herrington is a surface warfare officer who has served two tours as first lieutenant in USS *Pearl Harbor* (LSD 52) and USS *Essex* (LHD 2). Ashore, she served as squadron navigator at Littoral Combat Ship Squadron One, legislative affairs officer for Navy Recruiting Command, and flag secretary to Commander, Expeditionary Strike Group SEVEN.

CHAPTER 18

Air Department

CDR Jonathan "Shank" Lushenko, USN

The Ship-Air Team

THE COMPLEXITY OF MODERN NAVAL OPERATIONS requires knowledge and awareness of warfare communities outside your own. Integrated operations with traditional naval warfare communities—surface, subsurface, and aviation—across the full spectrum of conflict routinely occur as a means to maintain maritime superiority and battlespace dominance. As a surface warfare officer (SWO), you will undoubtedly work with embarked aviation units at some point in your career. Developing a solid understanding and appreciation of ship-air interoperability will enhance your tactical and operational competency as a department head and beyond, and it will equip you with professional military knowledge necessary to successfully interface with your aviation counterparts in support of various forms of naval operations.

The topics presented in this chapter are meant to serve as a quick reference and should not replace fundamental guidance found in publications such as the *Aircraft Operating Procedures for Air-Capable Ships NATOPS* [Naval Air Training and Operating Procedures Standardization] *Manual*. Establishing mutually beneficial relationships with air department members is an important way to expand ship-air team knowledge. Seeking information and clarification from air department members further expands your knowledge and develops cross-community relationships that could one day prove critical to achieve victory in war at sea.

Types of Aviation-Capable Ships

Embarked aviation units operate from three different classes of ships: aviation ships, amphibious assault aviation ships, and air-capable ships. Aviation ships consist primarily of nuclear-powered aircraft carriers, while amphibious assault aviation ships include landing helicopter assault ships and landing helicopter dock ships. Air-capable ships include guided missile cruisers, guided missile destroyers, and littoral combat ships. Like the surface warfare community, naval aviation is built upon foundational principles of operation that remain consistent regardless of aircraft model and class of ship. However, the broad scope of naval aviation warrants focused discussion of an air department most illustrative of ship-air interoperability that a large majority of SWOs will experience as part of normal career progression: cruiser-destroyer (CRUDES) helicopter air departments.

Nearly 70 percent of all SWO department heads eligible for command have experience serving on CRUDES units. However, the relative absence of open-source literature pertaining to CRUDES air departments should compel you to thoughtfully consider how your SWO duties and responsibilities intersect, support, and enhance the ship-air team. Similarly, your aviation counterparts will also work hard to understand the many unique and broad tactical and operational surface warfare considerations that impact ship-air team interoperability.

Air Department Organization

Composition
CRUDES air departments are self-sustaining units of approximately thirty maintainers and aircrew that are sourced from expeditionary or carrier air wing (CVW) helicopter maritime strike (HSM) squadrons to support training and operational deployments. While expeditionary and CVW HSM air departments are nearly identical in composition, CVW HSM-sourced CRUDES air departments are generally referred to as a combat element (CEL), while expeditionary-sourced CRUDES air departments are referred to as a detachment. CVW-based HSM squadrons will typically provide between one and three CELs depending on carrier strike group (CSG) CRUDES composition, while expeditionary HSM squadrons are capable of providing a total number of detachments commensurate with squadron required operational capabilities/projected operational environment (ROC/POE) guidelines. Except for rare circumstances, detachments and CELs will deploy with two MH-60R helicopters to support composite warfare commander operational taskings when attached to a CSG or during single-ship operations, such as a ballistic missile defense.

Manning
Regardless of operational tasking and force structure, air department manning consists of a specific collection of approximately twenty enlisted aviation

maintenance professionals and approximately ten officer and enlisted aircrew. Air department enlisted aviation maintenance professionals are identified by general ratings divided into distinct occupational categories that are described in *The Bluejacket's Manual*:

- aviation machinist's mate
- aviation electrician's mate
- aviation structural mechanic
- aviation ordnanceman
- aviation electronics technician
- aviation maintenance administrationman
- aircrew survival equipmentman.

Similarly, air department enlisted aircrew are identified by the naval aircrewman general occupational rating that is further subdivided into the aircrewman tactical helicopter service rating within the HSM community.

While pilot manning may fluctuate based upon unique training and career progression needs of individuals, you can expect a standard mix of approximately six pilots that range in rank from lieutenant (LT) junior grade (LTJG) to lieutenant commander (LCDR) with specific jobs that correspond with rank and experience:

- officer in charge (OIC): LCDR
- detachment maintenance officer (DETMO): LT
- operations officer (OPS): LT
- training officer: LT/LTJG
- communications officer (COMMO): LT/LTJG
- administrative officer: LT/LTJG.

Department Leadership

The air department is led by an OIC who is a squadron department head and the most senior aviator assigned to the department. The OIC is closely advised by the DETMO and OPS, who are both helicopter aircraft commanders, and a leading chief petty officer (LCPO), the most senior enlisted maintenance professional among all department enlisted personnel. The OIC, DETMO, OPS, and LCPO plan and execute all facets of aviation operations, maintenance, and training. They interface with shipboard counterparts on all operational, maintenance, and supply issues as well as squadron and external support staff assigned to the CVW, destroyer squadron, CSG, and type wing, the aviation equivalent to the surface community type commander.

The Air Boss

Affectionately referred to as "the air boss" or simply "boss," the air department OIC is responsible for all aspects of air department operations, including safety, training, maintenance, and operational employment of assigned aircraft. Like SWO department heads, the air boss is a department head who has been selected in a competitive statutory and administrative screening process to serve in an operationally demanding role for a thirty-month period. Deploying as a CRUDES OIC is generally considered the highlight of an HSM department head tour since it requires the employment of skills and knowledge acquired in roughly ten years of aviation and Navy experience preceding an OIC tour. While the path to becoming an HSM OIC may differ from one HSM department head to the next, every air boss has been certified through a crucible of operational and staff tours that equip them to direct all facets of air department operations.

While the air boss is responsible for all detachment operations, he or she is not the reporting custodian for assigned detachment aircraft. Rather, the air boss is the head of a separate embarked unit fully accountable to the squadron commanding officer (CO). It is the responsibility of the air boss to ensure that squadron leadership is informed about all pertinent factors impacting detachment operations and warfighting capability, as well as ensuring that shipboard leadership understands air department manning, qualifications, activity manning document specifications, and ROC/POE guidelines. For instance, unlike CVW HSM squadrons, the expeditionary HSM squadron activity manning document does not include billets authorized for food service attendants. This difference is particularly important to understand when deploying with a new air department.

It is also important to remember that the ship CO maintains direct operational control of embarked aviation assets. This final authority and responsibility make it even more important for the CO and the air boss not only to develop a sense for each other's risk assessments but also to align and reinforce each other's assessments. Lack of understanding and miscommunication have unfortunately resulted in aviation-related accidents at sea. For a detailed description of air department responsibilities, see chapter 6 of the *Aircraft Operating Procedures for Air-Capable Ships NATOPS Manual*, which highlights open lines of communications between the OIC and ship and squadron COs as a fundamental component of ship-air team success.

Key Relationships

Throughout your career, you have undoubtedly learned the importance of positive working relationships in complex organizations. Your time as a SWO department head will further reinforce this principle, especially as it relates to ship-air team interface. Establishing solid two-way working relationships built upon trust with your aviation counterparts is critical to mitigate operational friction, support common goals, and achieve peak ship-air team performance.

It is important to understand that while the air boss maintains responsibility of air department operations and maintenance, air department OPS and DETMO are empowered to conduct all planning to reduce administrative burden and task saturation. Although both air department OPS and DETMO are lieutenants filling division officer roles, SWO department heads should not shy away from working directly with them. Both the air department OPS and DETMO are designated helicopter aircraft commanders whose responsibility imbues them with positional authority. This does not circumvent the need for air boss and SWO department heads to routinely interact, but this coordination helps streamline the complex range of planning factors inherent in naval operations. There are several other critical relationships to consider.

Engineering Department and DETMO

The main propulsion assistant, or on some ships the assistant chief engineer, will interact heavily with the DETMO and their team. Working together will ensure that the engineering department is ready to support refueling operations and address any equipment casualties to the horizon reference system, the helicopter doors, or the recovery, assist, secure, and traverse (RAST) system. Typically, the ship RAST technician, an electrician, and a member of the auxiliaries division will also be ready to troubleshoot any issues that arise during flight operations.

Ship COMMO and Air Department COMMO

The air department COMMO will work closely with ship's radio and information systems technicians to ensure reliable communication during all phases of flight operations and with external support assets and the home squadron.

CHAPTER 18

Ship OPS and Air OPS

A close relationship between both ship OPS and air OPS will set the stage to support safe and efficient flight operations. Deck department, including the first lieutenant and "boats," will be expected to work intimately together to help ensure procedurally compliant flight operations and emergency response, while also seeking mutually beneficial training opportunities.

Trusting relationships between all air department and ship enlisted and officer personnel are critical to develop common understanding and alignment of effort. Take every opportunity to remove barriers preventing teamwork through social engagements and team-building activities. Ice cream socials, flight deck movie nights, and steel beach picnics are proven ways to build ship-air team cohesion. Likewise, in-port liberty events such as hail and farewells or wardroom dinners can do wonders in building camaraderie.

Flight Operations

Ultimately, ship-air team integration is about supporting the ship's overall mission. During your time as a SWO department head, you will observe a variety of flight operations and events that range from unit-level training to

18-1. An MH-60R conducts practice vertical replenishment during initial ship aviation team training.

U.S. Navy photo by LT B. E. Taylor

coordinated large force employment events with multiple aircraft from multiple squadrons. The inherent danger of shipboard flight operations requires disciplined adherence to time-tested procedures regardless of type and scope of flight operation. For example, taking off and landing on a CRUDES flight deck is a highly complex orchestration of procedures and teamwork that demands best effort each and every time. Seamless communication between dispersed personnel such as bridge watchstanders, the tactical action officer (TAO), and the landing safety officer (LSO) is essential to safely operate aircraft to and from the ship. Having a solid understanding of the special relationships between ship-air team personnel during flight operations will set you on the right course as you work together with the air department to support the ship's mission.

Internal Coordination

Embarked helicopter operations are anything but routine. Broad shipboard aviation requirements contained within the *Air-Capable Ships NATOPS Manual* are amplified by ship helicopter standard operating procedures (SOPs) that contain job-specific guidance required before, during, and after aviation operations. Air detachments should offer—and ship wardrooms should ask—to conduct an air operations integration brief before deployment or during the work-up phase. This will build understanding and strengthen watchstander knowledge from the early stages of this important relationship. Careful review of the helicopter SOP will also ensure you have full awareness of your departmental and other departmental requirements during flight operations.

As the TAO, your ability to critically assess flight operations will be stressed. You will be responsible for communicating any equipment or personnel issues to the CO along with a mitigation plan. Constant and clear communication between the TAO, LSO, bridge watch team, helicopter control officer, and the flight deck team will assist you in assessing overall flight operations. Likewise, your team will also help you in identifying competing priorities, whether it is a shipboard training evolution or balancing operational requirements with aviation requirements. Early identification of any issue will help mitigate risk. Therefore, it is imperative that all personnel share the same mental mindset and awareness when conducting flight operations. This crucial coordination is reinforced prior to flight quarters when the pilots visit the bridge and the combat information center.

Just as importantly, as TAO, you must ensure you have a firm understanding of your CO's philosophy concerning authority for granting flight deck clearance—green deck, yellow deck, and red deck. Some ship COs will delegate green deck authority to the officer of the deck following the first takeoff and landing of each fly day, while other COs retain full authority at all times.

It is also important to take into consideration aviation proficiency and currency requirements that require a certain number of takeoffs and landings in a given period of time. Ship OPS and air OPS should work together to balance ship plans of intended movement with daily flight crew approach and landing requests to the maximum extent practical since it may alleviate deck landing qualification training requests at the end of deployment. Likewise, air boss and detachment leadership will coordinate closely with respective ship counterparts to support and deconflict ship training requirements.

External Coordination

How well you communicate to both deployed and nondeployed staffs during flight operations will set you apart from your peers. Building and maintaining a strong relationship with the air boss and other air department pilots will aid in your ability to transmit critical information in a timely fashion. This information includes aircraft status and degradations, operational impacts and changes, along with a number of other factors you may have never considered.

Chat and email will generally serve as your primary conduits of information to inform the staffs of major warfare commanders about your ship's aircraft operations. However, if necessary, voice communications should be used to provide information in a timelier fashion or to seek clarification. External reporting requirements are no less important if conducting independent operations, but they are generally less frequent and time-sensitive. Nonetheless, your ability to accurately assess the air picture and current flight operations and accurately communicate off ship will demonstrate your team's robust ship-air communication efforts.

Conclusion

The topics presented in this chapter serve as a primer for ship-air operations and should inspire you to learn more about ship-air team integration and interoperability. Highly efficient, integrated naval sea and air operations rely heavily upon close coordination between you, the ship, and the air department. Having a basic understanding of the roles, responsibilities, and composition of the air department is only the starting point. As a SWO department head, you must develop a strong and cohesive relationship with the air department built on mutual respect and understanding. The air department cannot succeed in its mission without you and your team's support and vice versa. A united team, with a common vision, will ensure that your ship properly employs and supports the air department, enhancing your ship's warfighting capability. Like the surface warfare community, the naval aviation enterprise is dedicated to deploying naval aviation forces that win in combat as signified by its motto: "We fly, we fight, we lead. . . . We win!" Your leadership and understanding of air department operations are integral to achieving victory at sea, together.

Recommended References

- A1-H60CA-NFM-900, *H-60 Wind Envelopes*
- Airworthiness website, https://airworthiness.navair.navy.mil
- CNAF M-3710.7, *NATOPS General Flight and Operating Manual*
- MPP-02, vol. 1, *Helicopter Operations from Ships Other than Aircraft Carriers*
- NAEC-ENG-7576, *Shipboard Aviation Facilities Resume*
- NAVAIR 00–80T-105, *CVN NATOPS Manual*
- NAVAIR 00–80T-106, *LHA/LHD NATOPS Manual*
- NAVAIR 00–80T-122, *Aircraft Operating Procedures for Air-Capable Ships NATOPS Manual*
- OPNAVINST 3120.28D, *Certification of the Aviation Capability of Ships Operating Aircraft*
- OPNAVINST 3120.35L, *Requirements for Air-Capable and Amphibious Assault Ships to Operate Aircraft*
- OPNAVINST 3750.6S, *Naval Aviation Safety Management System*
- PERS-43 website, http://www.npc.navy.mil/Officer/Aviation/

CHAPTER 18

CDR Jonathan "Shank" Lushenko is a naval aviator and plankowner of Helicopter Maritime Strike (HSM) Squadron SEVEN ONE, where he participated in the first operational deployment of the MH-60R. He served as the squadron maintenance officer and Detachment THREE officer in charge in the Navy's only forward-deployed HSM Expeditionary squadron, HSM-51, stationed at NAF Atsugi, Japan, where he led HSM-51 Detachment THREE during operational deployments in USS *McCampbell* (DDG 85) and USS *Shiloh* (CG-67); and on the staff of Commander, Destroyer Squadron TWO TWO as the air/future operations department head. Ashore, he served as the fourteenth company officer and executive assistant to the eighty-fourth and eighty-fifth Commandants of Midshipmen at the United States Naval Academy and as an intelligence, surveillance, and reconnaissance capabilities analyst on the OPNAV staff (N810). He holds a master's of professional studies in leadership education and development from the University of Maryland, College Park. He was most recently assigned to the staff of the Chief of Naval Operations, where he served as the deputy executive assistant to the director, integrated warfare (OPNAV N9I).

CHAPTER 19

Preparing for Early Command

CDR Cameron Ingram, USN

Command Early and Command Often

FIRST AND FOREMOST, to be a good commanding officer (CO), you must be a good department head! The experience gained by leading a department is critical in your development toward becoming a good CO. In command, you will find that your experience as a department head earned you an impressive level of knowledge and shaped your leadership style, decision-making ability, and professional competence. Among the leadership qualities that a CO must possess are the ability to drive, fight, and manage a warship, communicate effectively, manage stress, and lead Sailors. You will exercise these skills daily while in command; therefore, you must build and refine them during your department head tours.

Up front, it is imperative to understand that command is the pinnacle of a naval officer's career, and the decision to pursue command should be taken with a great deal of consideration and conversation with family, peers, mentors, and other COs. A great number of references can aid in this decision, including *Command at Sea* by ADM James Stavridis and RDML Robert Girrier for its context and guidance.

While the surface community will always value command at sea, the early command opportunity is not a requirement in your career path. There are multiple points at which an officer can pursue command, starting at the post–division officer level, and again at the post–department head level. You will hear the mantra that "sustained superior performance at sea" is the key to all career milestones, and it holds even truer if you pursue command early in your career. Because early command is not a requirement, officers must make the determination if they are willing and ready to fulfill the duties and responsibilities of a CO at this point in their career.

There are professional gains to be made for those who pursue the early command track. Statistically, officers who successfully complete early command tours select for O-5 command above board average. However, like all CO jobs, early command incurs risk. A bad day in command could plateau your career. The responsibility of commanding a ship can be emotionally, mentally, and even physically exhausting. There is no harm in waiting until your commander (O-5) command board if you are unsure about your ability to execute the role as a CO directly after your division officer or department head tours.

There are few early command ships/units, and most ships are homeported overseas. Once you screen for early command, you remain eligible to slate to any platform or homeport. Most early command COs report after their second department head tour, and a few will report after a shore duty tour. Therefore, when vying for early command, you must be willing to serve an additional sea duty tour overseas. Are you willing to do an executive officer (XO)-CO fleet-up tour (thirty months) on a minesweeper out of Sasebo, Japan, after completing your second department head tour? If the answer is no, then early command may not be a good fit.

Early Command Opportunities

While early command opportunities and platforms will remain in flux as the surface force adapts to emerging threats and aligns with strategic guidance, one thing that will remain constant is that the surface warfare community values command at sea and the ability for SWOs to command at multiple levels throughout their careers. Currently, there are three post–department head and one post–division officer early command opportunities.

Cyclone-*Class Patrol Coastal*

Patrol coastals are designed to support a variety of mission sets, including surface surveillance and control, visit, board, search, and seizure, maritime interdiction operations, counter–illicit trade operations, escort, and coastal patrol duties. They are designed for fast insertion and have a high level of maneuverability, with a crew size of approximately twenty-four to twenty-eight Sailors. The CO reports directly to the position, as there is no fleet-up. They are homeported in Bahrain and Mayport, Florida.

Avenger-*Class Mine Countermeasures*

Mine countermeasures are essential in maintaining open sea lines of communication through their ability to detect, classify, and clear mines from vital chokepoint waterways. The crew is composed of approximately eighty-five Sailors, and the CO will first serve as the XO prior to fleeting up. They are homeported in Sasebo, Bahrain, and San Diego, California.

Mark VI Patrol Boat
Mark VI patrol boats are the primary vessel supporting the coastal riverine force arm of the Navy Expeditionary Combat Command. They are designed to operate in harbors, rivers, and bays across the littorals with a primary mission of maritime security operations and defending high-value assets, critical maritime infrastructure, and ports both inland and on coastal waterways. They are employed by coastal riverine squadrons who report to Coastal Riverine Group (CRG)-1 in San Diego and CRG-2 in Virginia Beach, Virginia. Post–division officers command the Mark VI patrol boats, and post–department heads serve as company commanders for a company of three Mark IV patrol boats.

Where to Start

The most definitive place to begin the process is the PERS-41 website, and the command at sea instruction, "Surface Force Command Requirements" (CNSP-CNSL Inst. 1412.2 [series]). This instruction presents the minimum requirements to become "qualified for command."

Approaching Your CO
Your CO will provide a key endorsement to your application. It is imperative that your CO is aware of and supports your pursuit of the early command program. When engaging your CO on the topic, timing is an important consideration. Focused and determined officers, set on pursuing command from the onset of their careers, may be excited to start the process right away. However, a CO must be allowed time to observe your performance before providing an endorsement. It is recommended that you give yourself six to eight months in your department head role prior to initiating the talk with your CO.

You Have Your CO's Endorsement—Now What?
CNSP-CNSL Inst. 1412.2 (series) lays out the requirements in four categories: at sea, Surface Warfare Officers School, command oral board, and a flag officer's endorsement. Command qualification requirements are periodically refined via Navy messages, and it is your responsibility to ensure you are familiar and comply with the latest guidance and requirements. Your

immediate superior in command (ISIC) will likely have experience with processing early command applications, so the N1 may be a good place to receive guidance.

At Sea
You must be an 111X officer who has qualified officer of the deck–underway, engineering officer of the watch, and tactical action officer. Additionally, a CO must observe you executing several ship handling evolutions (moorings, underway replenishments, man overboard maneuvers, etc.).

Surface Warfare Officers School
You must be a graduate of the department head course and have completed the command qualification assessment (CQA). Of note, officers can apply (and screen) for early command prior to taking the CQA. Those officers must successfully complete the CQA during their training pipeline prior to heading to command.

Command Oral Board
The board comprises three afloat COs, to include one afloat major command CO/commodore to serve as the board chairman. Board questions are typically less technical and more focused on critical thinking skills, temperament, risk management, and leadership style.

Flag Officer's Endorsement
The final step is to have your early command package endorsed by a flag officer in your chain of command, usually the type commander (TYCOM). Successful completion of this process will designate you as "qualified for command," and you are now eligible for consideration at the next early command selection board.

Record Review and Screening Process

Congratulations on becoming "qualified for command"! Every fitness report (FITREP) from this point forward, until you have screened, must annotate that you are qualified for command. At this point, let your detailer know that you are interested in being considered at the next early command screening board, which convenes semiannually in the spring and fall.

While the board process is out of your hands, you must be diligent in reviewing all documents presented to board members. Review your record on the BUPERS Online website and ensure at a minimum that your officer data card, performance summary report, and official photo are all current, complete, and accurate.

Have a mentor or someone familiar with the board process review your record to ensure it is board-ready. There is a difference between a record that is "good" (board-ready) and a "good record" (board-competitive). Your professional record is your responsibility, so give it the proper diligence.

After the screening board adjourns, PERS-41 will notify your CO of your screening status. For those who do not screen, this is not the end of the road. You may apply again for early command at the next board and should have a conversation with your CO and detailer on ways to improve your competitiveness. Again, not screening for early command not does mean that you will not select for O-5 command at sea.

Congratulations, You Screened for Early Command

This is the most selective community board so far in your career, and you should be proud of your accomplishment. Simultaneously, you are still a department head until the day you check out, so there is no taking off the pack. Finish your department head tour strong. Observe your CO and XO, and continue to build your own command style. Study how they weigh various considerations and risks, and put yourself in their shoes as issues arise. This is a golden opportunity to hone your leadership skills and better understand the demands and roles of a CO. Administratively, ensure that every FITREP from this point until you are serving as a CO annotates that you are "screened for early command."

Hey, PERS, Where Am I Going?

You will submit preferences to the early command detailer, who will in turn build the slates. Ensure they are aware of any special considerations (exceptional family member, co-location, dual military, etc.). The inventory of early command units is limited and geographically constrained, so have realistic expectations. For manpower reasons, the community screens more officers than available ships, allowing for flexibility in the detailing process. An effect of this is that not every officer who screens for early command will slate to a ship. There is no negative implication in not getting slated; however, your record could be negatively flagged if you are slated and then decline the opportunity.

Pipeline

The training pipeline is approximately four to six months depending on platform. While the training is platform-specific, everyone will complete the surface commander's course, senior leadership legal course, and naval leadership and ethics center command course, all in Newport, Rhode Island. During this time, you will be in class with fellow prospective early command officers and prospective executive officers heading to O-5 commands. You will be tested on your understanding of various shipboard programs, along with material readiness, warfighting capabilities, and ship driving proficiency. Expect to take a Rules of the Road test, a chart drawing exercise, simulator scenarios, and exams on engineering and combat systems. Other intermediate stops include TYCOM indoctrination and various tactical schools. You will work with your placement officer to build your pipeline as your orders are developed.

Reporting to the Ship

Reporting on board as the prospective CO or XO is a unique experience. You will quickly gain an appreciation for the ship's current readiness and crew morale. Typically, you have the most critical eye of your new command in your first few weeks on board. Utilize your scrutiny to take notes and build your situational awareness. Ask questions and listen to Sailors as you interact with them. Their first impression of you is lasting, so be mindful, as you will be observed more closely than ever before in your career.

If you are reporting as the XO, be prepared to run the change of command (CoC) and work closely with the outgoing CO. If you are reporting as the CO, understand that the CoC ceremony is not about you. The age-old adage for the new CO at the CoC is to "be early, be brief, and be seated;" also, always remember to thank your predecessor and your family.

Assuming Command

The first time a Sailor refers to you as "captain" or rings you on or off the ship can be exhilarating and daunting. For the first time in your career, there is no one standing over your shoulder to help you make decisions. It is all on you now. This is thrilling and sometimes terrifying. Expect your first sea and anchor detail, outside inspection, weapon shoot, or all-hands call to be nerve-racking. This is natural, but in time you will find it extremely fun. Your crew will already have their rhythm, so observe and orient yourself prior to making any major changes. This does not apply to safety or procedural compliance issues, which must be addressed immediately. For most administrative issues, you should get a feel for how the ship operates and make your adjustments accordingly. As a side note, do not be surprised when you answer the phone with, or roger up to, your old title: "Pilot House, OPS. . . . err, I mean, captain." This happens to all of us! Just smile, and keep going.

First Stop: The Commodore

If there is anyone who is as interested in the success of your ship as you are, it is your commodore. You should have an office call with them before you take command, or soon thereafter, to discuss their expectations and priorities. This is not your commodore's first run at command, and they have observed many COs, so take advantage of their experience to continue to build your understanding of your new role. In your first conversation, expect to listen, take notes, and ask questions. Ask your commodore what their preferred method of communication is and become familiar with the frequency and level of detail they desire for reports and updates. Your early reports set the tone for your professional relationship with your commodore.

The deputy commodore is also a great resource and advocate, and most deputies will fleet up to the commodore. They too have prior command experience and are highly invested in the success of your ship. Utilize your deputy to build your communication style and level of knowledge, and you may find value in bouncing ideas off them prior to going to the commodore.

Your Crew

Your expectations of the crew should be communicated early and clearly. This is typically done through an all-hands call or smaller group discussions—whichever is your preference—after your initial conversation with the commodore.

Command Philosophy

You will discover that a command philosophy is just as much for you as it is for the crew, and it should be written well in advance of reporting to the ship (with the ability to tailor it once you have arrived). There are many examples in the fleet, so start there and tailor one toward your approach, desires, and style. The command philosophy will be drawn upon for everything you want to accomplish. It sets the tone for how you command, so ensure you give it due time and consideration. Consider discussing it with your crew, and allow for questions and conversation.

The Triad

You are now part of the command triad. Lean on your XO and senior enlisted advisor to help you understand and work through issues and to show the crew a unity of effort at the top. This is a good group to vent concerns or frustrations to. Their experienced positions lend great insight, so utilize them consistently. Cohesiveness within the triad is imperative in everything the ship does.

Communication

The crew likes to be kept informed and to hear information straight from the captain's mouth, so develop a comfortable style of communicating with them. Whether you gather on the mess decks, topside, or over the one main circuit, you should have a pattern of open communications and have a means for the crew to ask you questions and push ideas up the chain: open-door/email policies, CO suggestion box, all-hands calls, or some combination of these. Effective communication is critical in gaining crew trust and providing guidance on priorities and ownership of the mission. Remember, bad news never gets better with time. Your crew understands this, so be upfront.

Testing the New Guy

Early in my patrol coastal command tour, my father and closest mentor, who previously commanded USS *Doyle* (FFG 39) and USS *Leyte Gulf* (CG 55), advised me, "Your crew will test you. But in the end, they want you to succeed." This held true from day one. These "tests" are not a sign that the crew lacks integrity or is lazy; rather, they are signs that the crew is constrained by time and resources, and they look to you for efficiencies and relief. Your crew wants the reputation of being the best damn ship on the waterfront, and that requires hard work, consistency, and strong camaraderie. Keep an eye out for these tests, and ensure that you remain consistent in your expectations, standards, and values.

Prioritize

When addressing priorities, you may find it helpful to break items into three buckets: hold fast, check, and slack.

Hold fast items are ones on which you never waver. Some are obvious (maintenance and material management, personnel qualification standards, etc.), but others are more personal, such as who can qualify certain watch stations, how you handle new check-ins, or how zone inspections are conducted.

Check items are important but cause no immediate concern if they must be periodically missed—for example, command physical training or holiday routine.

Slack items are ones you wish to delegate. These allow your crew to take charge and gain leadership experience. They can include the menu review board process, topside preservation plan, or morale, welfare, and recreation event planning. Remember, "slack[ed]" lines serve a valuable purpose; they should never be ignored and can always be "check[ed]" when necessary.

Squadron Staff

When communicating with the commodore or deputy, be prepared to provide thorough yet concise notifications and updates on your ship and crew. As the captain, make the decision, and be prepared to brief the commodore on your reasoning and plan. Do not expect that the commodore will make decisions for you. When in command, command! Remember, however, your commodore wants your ship to be successful, and that sometimes may require additional guidance or even overriding a decision you have made. Try to understand their perspective in such circumstances. You do not need to blindly agree, as you have the best observation of the circumstances, so continue the conversation until there is understanding across the board.

Depending on your platform, the ISIC staff may be part of your team. This could be true for supply, maintenance, legal, and/or administrative purposes. While the ISIC staff will be "part of your crew," it may not always feel like it. A well-functioning staff will be completely on board and supportive, but in some circumstances, you will need to finesse these relationships. Work with the staff while maintaining your number one priority: to advocate for your ship and crew. Build relationships with the staff and get buy-in early, as you will not be able to do your job without their support. Ensure your crew understands your expectations for working with the staff (that is, professionalism), and if there are conflicts between you and the staff, bring it up to the deputy and, if need be, the commodore.

Fellow Captains

Your peers on the waterfront are the absolute best allies you will have. Strive to develop strong relationships with the other COs, and learn how they conduct business. As with your department head tours, you will find that most grunt work is done at the ship-to-ship level, so never be afraid to ask for help. Also, extend a helping hand to other ships whenever possible; this will pay dividends later. Lastly, you may find command lonely. Finding connection, support, and camaraderie with the other COs will help you through this arduous tour. The reputation of your ship on the waterfront will depend on how well you work with the other ships, so be a team player both inside and outside the lifelines.

Several Bosses: Who Is Who?
When operational, you will have a multitude of reporting requirements. It is important to always know who is in charge of what. This includes knowing who has administrative control, operational control, and tactical control, who the senior officer present–afloat, screen commander, and warfare commander are, and the list continues. As the captain, you must communicate with all these bosses simultaneously. Email is a great tool, since you can include many players in the "cc" line. Executing the plan and communicating with your bosses will set the reputation for your ship, so communicate frequently and ensure everyone understands your intentions. Your bosses may be less interested in how you get things done than in the fact that you are executing the mission and communicating well. As stated earlier, when in command, command. Make decisions, and communicate your intentions. Do not look to your bosses to do that for you.

Lastly, you may find that some staffs do not have a good understanding of your ship's capabilities and limitations. A great example is sea state limitations, as you will probably be more operationally limited than other platforms in the area. Sea state limitations are a safety issue, so it is important to routinely check the weather from multiple sources and to take action early to avoid inadvertently placing your ship in adverse weather conditions. Communicate your intentions to all your bosses and be prepared to follow up with governing instructions if challenged on the matter.

Helpful Hints for a Successful Command

Risk Management
Safety comes first. However, if safety were the only priority, then ships would never get under way. Shipboard operations are inherently dangerous, and you have spent a good part of your career constructing risk mitigation. Now, you will be making the call on safety issues and determining what is and is not

PREPARING FOR EARLY COMMAND

19-1. USS *Zephyr* (PC 8) conducts a live-firing event. The captain must consider all aspects of operational risk management.
U.S. Navy photo by Mass Communication Specialist 3rd Class Casey J. Hopkins/Released

acceptable. Risk management is an all-hands effort, with the final authority lying with the captain. It is imperative that your ship has a culture where the crew speaks up when they see a safety concern. This culture should be so ingrained that your most junior Sailors feel comfortable speaking up when they see an issue. Ensure there is sufficient qualified and experienced oversight throughout evolutions, and ensure safety measures are implemented at every stage. Expect to spend a great deal of your time and effort thinking about and managing risk.

Deviating from Instructions

This may be the first time that you have the authority to say "no" or deviate from instructions. This license is given to COs to cover unforeseen circumstances. A CO's freedom to deviate from instructions is a tool that must be utilized sparingly and with great caution. For simplicity, default to the instructions and only deviate when absolutely necessary. Ensure your crew understands that deviations from instructions must be approved by the CO and must include a thorough explanation as to why the deviation is necessary and what mitigating factors will be implemented to ensure safety is maximized. Explain to the crew why and how you came to this decision, and confirm their understanding. Make it clear that a deviation from instruction at one point does not authorize a permanent deviation unless explicitly stated so. The CO must weigh in every time a deviation from instructions is necessary. Consider generating a departure from specification or temporary standing order to quality assure and properly document the deviation.

Contact Reports
Contact reports are for you as the CO. When you write your standing orders, practice your contact reports and have a mock report read to you to ensure it paints the right picture. When you get called in the middle of the night, the contact report will be the first (and possibly only) opportunity you will have to weigh in on a potential collision at sea. As the contact report is read, you should have a clear understanding of what is happening with your ship, the contact(s), and the bridge team actions. Therefore, pay particular attention to the format and flow.

FITREPS and Evaluations
As CO, you will establish your reporting senior's cumulative average (RSCA), which will be the average against which all future FITREPS and evals will be compared. You may want to "take care" of one Sailor, but you may unintentionally place yourself in a circumstance where you cannot take care of other Sailors because your RSCA is too high. Instead, decide on an RSCA (for example, a 3.75 for O-3s, or 4.25 for E-7s) and build every summary group around that average, breaking out the top performers while averaging the rest. You can annotate that you are establishing RSCA in the summary block to give better clarification to board members.

Plan Your Day
Depending upon circumstances, you may or may not run the morning routine (khaki call, quarters, etc.). In either case, clearly articulate your priorities and make sure that your leadership understands the day's expectations. Soon after quarters, your team will run off and start the workday. You may find that the middle of the day is a lull for you, as your team is chipping away at their taskers. This lull can be a good time to walk the deckplates. Be aware, however, of the impact of your presence. You will draw a high level of attention as you walk the ship and may even be a distraction from the day's work. If your engineers are working on a maintenance check and you walk through the

space and ask them about another piece of equipment, you can expect that they will stop what they are doing and quickly address your question, in turn delaying the maintenance check. Encourage your team to keep working on their taskers, and bring up your questions later with their leadership. This lull in the day may be a good time for you to catch up on administrative work or get in some physical training.

Trust

Trust is a two-way street. You will need to trust your crew as much as they will need to trust you. Whom you trust with certain situations will differ from Sailor to Sailor. Trust is built through open communication, consistency, and fairness. Do not be afraid to tell a Sailor that, because of their inexperience, they have not yet earned your confidence. This does not mean that you will never trust them; it simply means that you owe them more opportunities to build proficiency. Communicate openly, and your Sailors will understand your expectations and, in turn, will build more trust. In the end, trust is required unless you never plan to sleep or leave the ship. Figure out how you will internally and externally manage your trust, and remain consistent.

Crew Size

Your crew size can be both a benefit and a hindrance. For example, completing all-hands training is quick, while conducting multimission operations or building watchbill depth may be a challenge. The small crew size results in less khaki leadership, and a lot of your support comes remotely from the ISIC staff. Understand this when setting expectations.

"Early Command Is Not Commander Command"

You may hear this, and while there are many differences in varying levels of command, all COs are universally essential to their ships. You must approach this role with the same level of presence as the commander approaches their strike group. The Navy is charging you with the grave responsibility to lead Sailors at sea, and that principle is universal at every level of command.

Conclusion

Command at sea is rewarding, challenging, and truly the zenith of the surface warfare community, as emphasized by former Commander, Naval Surface Forces VADM Rich Brown. All surface warfare officers are encouraged to pursue it early and often. For those who make it to the captain's chair, relish

CHAPTER 19

this opportunity and remain optimistic, for "where goes the captain, there goes the Ship." A ship's performance and reputation are directly correlated to the captain's performance. Hold high standards, focus on mission success, take care of your Sailors, remain positive, and your ship will surely be the finest on the waterfront. Fair winds and following seas!

CDR Cameron Ingram is a surface warfare officer who served as the commanding officer in USS *Zephyr* (PC 8), a three-time Battle-E winner. He also served as the operations officers in USS *Monterey* (CG 61) and USS *Bulkeley* (DDG 84) and served division officer tours in USS *Hopper* (DDG 71) and USS *Mitscher* (DDG 57). Ashore, he served in the surface warfare division on the Navy Staff (OPNAV N96) and at Commander, U.S. Pacific Fleet. He is the recipient of the Surface Navy Association's Admiral Arleigh Burke Award for Operational Excellence and holds a U.S. Coast Guard unlimited tonnage license. He is a graduate of the Eisenhower School at National Defense University and is slated to take command of USS *Thomas Hudner* (DDG 116).

APPENDIX 1
Notional Turnover Schedule

WHETHER YOU ONLY HAVE A FEW DAYS or the luxury of a few weeks, the amount of time you have to complete a turnover will vary from command to command. Similarly, your billet, ship type, and your ship's current mission will influence how much attention you give each turnover item. If you are relieving a solid department head (usually the case), he or she will likely have a turnover schedule developed. Our suggestion is to follow the turnover timeline provided by your predecessor, but you can use this timeline as a framework to ensure that all the essential high points are covered during your turnover period. Items noted with an asterisk may require more time to assess than allotted during your turnover period. If there are turnover items that you could not complete, ensure those items are documented and addressed in your turnover letter.

Day One

- Meet with commanding officer, executive officer, and command master chief and discuss command priorities.
- Review the plan of the day and plan of the week.
- Introduce yourself to other department heads.
- Meet with your department leading chief petty officer and principal assistants/technical assistants.
- Familiarize yourself with the ship by walking your spaces. Use zone inspection discrepancy lists (ZIDLs) as well as past inspection reports as a guide when assessing spaces.*

Day Two

- Conduct required inventories and inspections.
- Review major casualties to equipment (redlines, casualty reports).
- Meet your division officers and chief petty officers.*
- Review current ship's maintenance project (CSMP) with each division officer and discuss plans to correct deficiencies; ensure ZIDL discrepancies are documented in CSMP.*
- Develop a plan to conduct warfare areas/program reviews. Use afloat self-assessment checklists as a guide.*
- Review relevant instructions/notices/checklists.
- Discuss planning board for training, planning board for admin, and planning board for maintenance processes.
- Discuss administrative processes and any admin currently in routing.

Day Three

- Review the short-range and long-range schedules.
- Review your watch team replacement plan and watch quarter station bill.
- Discuss the department training plan/personnel qualification standards.
- Discuss relational administration data management.
- Discuss any pending investigations or legal issues and status of career development boards.
- Review personnel prospective gains and losses, status of critical Navy enlisted classifications, and personnel redlines.
- Discuss status of awards/fitness reports/evaluations.
- Review status of junior officer qualifications.*
- Review programs for any collateral duties you are assuming.*

Day Four

- Route turnover letter. Document turned over items, items that you could not properly assess, and any discrepancies.
- Review division officers' notebooks.
- Discuss lessons learned.
- Review maintenance and material management program; meet with program coordinator to review your department's status.
- Meet with port engineer, combat systems port engineer, and ship's project manager.
- Introduce yourself to your immediate superior in command counterpart.

Day Five

- Conduct a department head call. Acknowledge the work of your predecessor, and convey your excitement to lead the best department on your ship!

APPENDIX 2

"So You Want to Be a Department Head" Revisited

RADM Fred W. Kacher, USN

TRADITIONALLY, MOST SURFACE WARRIORS aspire to command ships, not serve as department heads. Department heads are sometimes viewed as the Navy's classically hapless middle managers, a prejudice that comes with consequences that do not serve the Navy well. First, the job's tough reputation drives some great young leaders to look for challenges beyond the Navy. Second, this attitude undervalues the tour, which provides commanding officers their longest and most substantive at-sea leadership prior to arriving at the ship they will command.

Yet when I talk with department heads who have recently completed their tours, their memories often run counter to the stereotype of the put-upon middle manager. Hard work was a mainstay, to be sure, but so were camaraderie, a sense of accomplishment, and even some fun. From these conversations, some indispensable advice emerged that, though it focuses on aspiring surface warfare department heads, could apply to all professional naval leaders. I hope these tips will help those considering taking the department head leap of faith to not only survive but thrive in this critical at-sea billet.

Strengthen Your Weaknesses Early

In this case, "early" means before you arrive on your ship. Use department head school for what it is, the last "free" opportunity you will enjoy to gain knowledge before reporting to your ship. Your instructors, selected to serve competitively at Surface Warfare Officers School, have been detailed based on their expertise and performance. Don't just play to your strengths—if you are an air warfare pro, stand as much tactical action officer (TAO) in the undersea warfare simulator. Use simulators to flex ship-handling skills that have not been exercised during your shore tour. Think about the things that you did not worry about as a division officer because they were "department head"–level issues. For me, supply and parts management, departmental budgeting, and combat system maintenance programs warranted extra attention.

Be Ready to Sit in the Chair

Because you almost always will be relieving a fully qualified TAO, your ship will be looking for you to step up as soon as you can. Whether or not you gained ample TAO experience during your previous sea tours, the watch team requirements of the training cycle will almost immediately demand your insertion as the TAO of the future. The members of your chain of command will understand that you may not be in midseason form when you arrive to your ship, but neither will they expect you to be clueless. Start preparing now.

Command Your Department

Most department heads will be the leader of more than fifty (and in some cases more than one hundred) officers and Sailors on a U.S. Navy ship. Carry yourself that way. Find opportunities to address your Sailors, set your agenda, and be a leader. I have yet to meet a commanding officer (CO) or executive officer (XO) who wants to go back and do a third department head tour; make sure you leave them no doubt that you are on the job.

Win the Battle of Information Warfare

Do so, and you never will lose the war. Whether you are dealing with afloat training group assessors, ship squadron representatives, or contractors during a yard period, work to "out-learn" and "out-know" the experts. These efforts, which include walking your spaces, visiting technical representatives, and reading the fine print, will help ensure your team drives the program rather than the reverse. Demand from your subordinates concise, honest reports that allow you to solve the problem before it is too late. Honor your CO and XO with the same courtesy.

Extend Your Planning Horizon

A division officer who looks a month in advance might be exceptional; a department head who looks only that far will almost certainly be a failure. Recognize right away that almost every substantial challenge, inspection, or exercise will take at least two months to plan and execute. Consider mapping out a ninety-day campaign, day by day, to meet every broad requirement for the quarter beyond the one you are in. Develop a detailed roadmap of the ship's schedule for the next year as well. In addition, develop an event preparation matrix for every major challenge and warfare challenge and area to ensure your Sailors are set up to succeed. When emerging events disrupt your preparations, these plans provide the foundation to adapt to changing circumstances.

Don't Just Answer the Mail

The routine demands of email, message traffic, reports, evaluations, and awards packages often will be enough to fill the workday. To borrow a phrase from one of my favorite division officers of the past, take time to "dream big" rather than merely being defined by your inbox. Put another way, you cannot merely blindly tackle your inbox (email or otherwise); you must plan, prioritize, and execute as well.

Demand and Deliver All-But-the-Signature Staff Work

Although you do not want to be defined by your inbox, the quality of what leaves that inbox does matter. Like the old adage that a ship is often judged by its communications, a department is often judged by its staff work. Demanding complete work from your subordinates does not mean that you can sign a fitness report, message, or firing plan without reading it, but it establishes a standard that will signal your expectations and prevent you from doing the work your divisional leaders are there to do. In addition, providing your boss the most complete product possible saves time by preventing rewrites. Our "perfect" effort may still fall short under the XO's scrutiny, but imagine how much greater these shortfalls would be had you dedicated only 80 percent of the attention to detail you were capable of giving.

Focus on Warfighting

Remind your folks that everything we do is a means to an end: combat capability. As a nation that has been in conflict since the terrible events of 11 September 2001 and that is now engaged in Great Power competition with China and Russia, we in the Navy must be brilliant in the basics, but department heads must focus on the warfighters in your span of control as well. Seek out opportunities for your department to fight fires, run air defense drills, or hone whatever combat competency is its core responsibility. As the primary scheduling force in your department, put combat drills on the calendar first rather than trying to jam them in as an afterthought.

Manage Your Equipment

During my tenure, I never pretended to be the equipment expert, but I made sure I could competently articulate our equipment management approach. Monitor your technicians, other ships, and shore experts to anticipate high-failure items, order needed parts, and find opportunities to groom your systems. Your job is to not merely bring the CO the bad news of the latest casualty but to provide options for how to fix them. Make sure your eight o'clock reports completely and accurately capture the problem-solving spirit you want your department to be known for. Rest assured that as you rise to command a ship—or even a strike group—command of your organization's material readiness remains an essential skill and directly contributes to combat readiness.

Treat Division Officers as Executive Talent

My number one joy as a department head was leading some of the finest young Americans in our country. By nature of their profession, they are idealists who want to be inspired. Treat your division officers like the potential frontline Fortune 500 executive talent they are (consider all the division officers who are accepted to top-twenty business schools every year). Make sure they understand that, as your frontline leaders and managers, they not only will run a division, but they also will be warfighters and tackle departmental challenges.

If you plan on demanding the best from them, make sure they are afforded the best equipment, loyalty, treatment, and leadership possible; they will not disappoint you. Finally, avoid impressing your division officers with how much harder you work than they do. Let them see you enjoy your job, grab a workout, or laugh during a departmental dinner. If they think you don't enjoy your job on any level, how are you going to convince them to come back to sea and relieve you?

Count on Your Senior Enlisted

You cannot afford to go it alone. As division officers rotate, your more permanent relationships may be with your chiefs. Treat your departmental chief petty officer as the command master chief (CMC) of your department. My department leading chief petty officer made the things that can drive department heads crazy—berthing inspections, enlisted rankings, work parties—"fire and forget" items. Your departmental CMC will do the same for you. Finally, your ship's command master chief can be a tremendous leadership partner and sounding board—providing advice if needed on getting the best out of the chiefs that work for you or even understanding the CO's intent given the conversations they are having with the commanding officer and executive officer.

Never Forget Your Sailors

Every interaction with a Sailor is a leadership opportunity. Seek out the stars in your department and encourage them to apply for every commissioning program available if they are interested. This effort not only demonstrates that you recognize truly noteworthy performances, it also provides your best with an opportunity that represents one of the best aspects of the Navy's incredible upward mobility. A word of advice: don't yell at your Sailors. While there are possible exceptions to every rule (for example, a dire safety or combat situation), the image of a senior manager dressing down a young enlisted Sailor in public is not what our profession is about. Regrettably, for most of us, yelling doesn't make you look tough; it usually makes you look like you've lost your composure. Rest assured that your division officers and chiefs will address whatever transgression you have witnessed after you let them know about it.

Follow Up

I once asked a Marine serving on his first ship the differences in leadership between the Navy and Marine Corps. He answered, "Marines follow up." He explained that Navy leaders, likely based on their faith in their people, often would issue an order and would not check on its progress until just before completion (and many Sailors you will work with will indeed be "fire and forget," but not all of them). "Follow-up" encapsulates what department heads must do best. We check our folks' progress, reassess, provide guidance and correction, and often bear the lion's share of the credit for their labors. As I look back on the adventures—and misadventures—a department head can face, I believe that bumper stickers with the words "Follow Up!" should be attached to every car in fleet parking!

A Job You Will Always Remember

There are many people who view their department head tours as the best of times and the worst of times. The job is hard work; few things worth doing come without it. But these tours can be satisfying as well. There is no better way to describe meeting a real-world Tomahawk tasking on time, watching some of your best being selected as a chief petty officer or limited duty officer, or bringing a whole department home safely after a successful deployment. I deeply hope that these tips might help convince our best and brightest that a successful department head ride is in their future.

INDEX

acronyms and abbreviations, xv–xviii
administration: all-but-signature standards for, 233; duties and paperwork responsibilities, 11–12, 63–64; N3 duties in surface ship squadrons, 126–30; 1LT duties and writing skills for, 199, 201–2; OPS reporting requirements, 116; PTO ideas about and improvements of processes for, 186; references on, 11, 199; reporting requirements, education on, 118; training module on, 18, 23–24; turnover schedule, 227–29
advocacy and ambassador roles, 73
Aegis Training and Readiness Center, 13–14, 24
afloat safety officer course, 18, 21–22
afloat training group (ATG), 164, 166, 187
air boss (officer in charge, OIC), 205–7
air department, 203–12; communications and relationship with ship COMMO, 207, 209; flight operations communications, 210; leadership of, 205–7; organization and manning of, 204–6; references on, 203, 211; relationships important to, 203, 207–8; ship-air team integration to support flight operations, 208–10; ship-air team operations, 203, 211
air warfare commander, 114
aircraft carriers: language spoken by Sailors on, 135; N3 duties in strike group environment on, 133–36; operations officers on, 113. *See also* carrier strike group (CSG)
Aircraft Operating Procedures for Air-Capable Ships NATOPS Manual, 203, 206–7, 209, 211
airworthiness website, 211
ambassador and advocacy roles, 73

ammunition. *See* weapons and ammunition
Ammunition and Explosive Safety Afloat, 141
amphibious ships: billet options on, 10; embarkation/debarkation coordination with Marine Corps, 199–200; first lieutenant billet on, 192; operations officers on, 113
amphibious squadrons (PHIBRONs): administrative command function of, 126–27; continental U.S.–based squadrons, 127–28; forward-deployed squadrons, 128; N3 duties in and operational planning for, 125, 132–33; operational command function of, 126–27; strike group environment in, 133–35
amphibious transport dock (LPD), 10
anchoring references, 91
antisubmarine warfare (ASW) systems, 139, 145
antiterrorism force protection (ATFP) training and operations, 139, 140, 141, 143, 147
antiterrorism training module, 18, 21–22
antiterrorism training supervisor (AT TRASUP), 144
Arleigh Burke-class destroyers, 114
assistant first lieutenant (AFL), 195
assistant senior watch officer (A-SWO), 102, 107, 109
authenticity as a leader, 36–37
Avenger-class mine countermeasure ships, 214–15
aviation-capable ships, 203–4
awards and commendations, 123, 171, 199, 201

basic phase preparation, 197
battle orders, 80–81, 153, 189–90

INDEX

battle rhythm, 54, 106, 117–18, 119–20, 134, 185, 195–96, 218–19
billets: duty preferences and slating, 9–11; fleet up/single longer tour assignments, 10, 151, 152; training for specific, 8, 18, 24
Bluejacket's Manual, The, 205
Board of Inspection and Survey: deck checklist for safety gear from, 194; preparation for, 54, 166, 197; references and lessons learned from, 53, 166; relationship with, 197; SWO as coordinator for, 101
boatswain mates (BMs), 195, 197
boatswains, limited duty officer (LDO)/chief warrant officer (CWO), 195
boatswain's mate chief petty officer (BMC), 195
books and references: air department references, 203, 211; command, references on decision to pursue, 213; correspondence and administration references, 11–12, 115, 199; engineer officer/CHENG references and instructions, 160–63; evolutions/special evolutions references, 91–92, 94; first lieutenant references, 193–94; news, reading and staying up on, 75; OPS reading and references requirements, 115–16; professional reading, 14–15; vaults and security management, 158; WEPS reading and references requirements, 140–41
bridge resource management (BRM), 18, 21, 94
bridge watch hours logbook, 107
briefings and debriefings: checklist or brief for weapons evolutions, 140, 141–42, 147; debrief and capture of lessons learned after evolutions, 90–91, 96, 109; plan, brief, execute, debrief (PBED) processes, 186, 187–88; self-assessment through, 9
Brown, Rich, 225–26
Burke, Arleigh, 17

camaraderie and having fun, 55, 171, 231
career intermission program, 9
carrier air wing (CVW) helicopter maritime strike (HSM) squadrons, 204, 206

carrier strike group (CSG): air department organization for, 204; air warfare commander, 114; N3 duties in surface ship squadrons as, 127, 129–30, 133–36; training groups, 186–87
Certification of the Aviation Capability of Ships Operating Aircraft, 211
certifiers, relationship with, 53, 154, 178
chain of command: changes in operational and tactical control, 116; PTO operational and administrative chains of command, 185
challenge coin, 171
chief engineer. *See* engineer officer/chief engineer (CHENG)
chief warrant officer (CWO) boatswain, 195
China, Great Power competition with, 1, 234
circadian battle rhythm, 54, 106, 117–18, 119–20, 134, 185, 195–96, 218–19
Cole, 1
combat cargo officer (CCO), 199–200
combat element (CEL) air departments, 204
combat information center (CIC): coordination between bridge and, 86; decentralized command and command by negation in, 87–88; leading watch team from, 80–85; special evolutions support from watch team in, 83–84; TAO responsibility for, 79; TAO watchstanding in, 80; turnovers in and communication with watch team, 83
combat systems: degradation of and issues with, 154–55; diagrams with components and information about, 155; eight o'clock reports on, 158, 162–63, 175–76; microminiature electronics repair (2M) program, 152, 155, 156–57; team to maintain and manage readiness of, 152–53
combat systems maintenance manager (CSMM), 152–53, 157, 158, 159
combat systems officer (CSO), 151–59; advice for success as, 154–59; certification expectations and metrics for success, transparency about, 159; command assessment of, 29; core team relationships, 152–53; department head assignment as, 10; duties, responsibilities, and authority of, 151–52, 153, 159; equipment status updates

238

INDEX

to, 86–87; fleet up/single longer tour assignments, 10, 151, 152; relationships, on-ship and off-ship, 152–54; second tour position of, 102, 151, 152
combat systems officer of the watch (CSOOW), 158–59
combat systems training team (CSTT), 153, 183, 187
command assessment (CA): bibliography for, 15, 28; difficulty of, 27; failure of any portion of and additional attempts, 27; preparation for, 28–30; process for and scope of, 25–27; purpose of, 28; schedule for, 25–26; success in, 27, 28, 30; SWOS location for, 15, 24, 25
Command at Sea (Stavridis and Girrier), 213
command climate and culture, 40–41, 44n3, 55, 147, 148–49, 188–89, 234–36
command climate survey, 41, 44n3
command duty officer (CDO), 22, 107, 108, 118
command master at arms (CMAA), 144
command master chief (CMC), 235; communication with CO, role in, 47–48; duty section rotation role of, 108; recognition of team accomplishments in front of, 123; senior enlisted watchbill coordinator selection role of, 101
command philosophy, 219–20
command priorities, 63, 64, 65–66, 67
command qualification assessment (CQA), 216
command qualification exam (CQE): bibliography for, 15, 26–27; command assessment role of, 25; preparation for, 15; process for and scope of, 26–27; Rules of the Road exam, 15, 20–21, 26–27
commanding officer (CO): battle orders, standing orders, and intent of, 80–81, 153, 162, 186, 189–90; characteristics and leadership qualities for, 213; command as pinnacle of career, 213; communication with, 47–48, 49, 62–63; equipment status updates to, 86–87; execution of vision of, 2, 56, 69; expectations of, 22, 69–74, 165; experience as department head and development of skills for, 213; experience of, 70; organizational line of authority, 56–58; priorities of and priority-setting for department, 39;

recognition of team accomplishments in front of, 123; references on, 213; relationship with department heads, 56–57, 66–67, 68, 75–76; relationship with N3, 130–31; relationship with XO, 61–62, 65; relationships with air boss, 206–7; relationships with other COs, 221–22; special evolution expectations of, 95; support for, 56, 66–67, 68–75
command-wide programs, 64, 67
commendations and awards, 123, 171, 199, 201
commodore: early command and office call with, 219; expectations of, 221; N3 as representative of, 130; N4 as representative of, 175–76
communication: air COMMO–ship COMMO relationship, 207; CO, communication with, 47–48, 49, 62–63; consolidated reports and streamlined communication, 49; cross-department communication, 60, 61, 121, 169; duty station, communication with, 14; early command communications style, 220; email inbox, optimization of, 122, 233; flight operations communications, 210; khaki call and communication with department khaki, 52, 57, 61; management of department and effective communication, 47–50, 61; meetings with Sailors and walking the deckplates, 48–49, 74, 122–23; N3 communications, 130; N4 communications and representation of commodore, 175–76; OPS off-ship communications and message traffic responsibilities, 116–17, 118; reporting requirements and communication with bosses, 222; SWO communications about duty schedules, 108–9; tools for, 50; vaults and security management, 158; watch team, communication with, 83, 87–88; watchstanding communications and data links, 85; WEPS communications and debriefings, 147, 148–49; XO, communication with, 62–64. *See also* correspondence
communications officer (COMMO), 205, 207
Communications Security Management for Commanding Officers Handbook, 158

239

INDEX

confidence and humility, 38
conning officer virtual environment (COVE) sessions, 21
contact reports, 224
correspondence: all-but-signature standards for, 233; drafting and processing duties, 11–12, 63–64; email inbox, optimization of, 122, 233; N3 correspondence, 130; 1LT duties and writing skills for, 199; references on, 11–12, 115, 199; responding to all, 50, 233. *See also* communication
Covey, Stephen, 40, 74
crew resource management, 184–85
cruisers and destroyers (CRUDES): air boss duties on, 206–7; *Arleigh Burke*–class destroyers, 114; aviation-capable ships, 203–4; billet options on, 9, 10, 138; combat element (CEL) or detachment air departments on, 204; operations officers on, 113–14; *Ticonderoga*-class cruisers, 114
culture and command climate of department, 40–41, 44n3, 55, 147, 148–49, 188–89, 234–36
CVN NATOPS Manual, 211
Cyclone-class patrol coastal ships, 214

damage control training module, 18, 21–22
data links and communication for watchstanding, 85
deadlines, meeting, 64
deck department: air OPS–ship OPS relationship and operations of, 208, 210; department/division quarters organization, 197–98; embarkation/debarkation coordination with Marine Corps, 199–200; first lieutenant command of, 192; priorities and departmental philosophy of, 201; programs and evolutions of, 192; Sailors working in, 195, 197–98; SAR program responsibilities of, 194; schedule for and staying ahead of schedule, 195–96; walking your spaces and instilling space ownership in Sailors, 198
delegation of tasks: expectations of XO, 58, 59; identification and management of tasks, 46, 51, 58, 59; N4, task delegation by, 179; 1LT, task delegation by, 201; personal organization and, 12; during special

evolutions, 94; techniques and rules about, 12, 122
delinquent in qualification (DINQ) study, 104
department: assessment and self-assessment of, 38–39, 59; culture and command climate, 40–41, 44n3, 55, 147, 148–49, 188–89, 234–36; departmental philosophy, 201; meetings with Sailors and walking the deckplates, 48–49, 74, 122–23; model for assessment of priorities of, 40; priority-setting for, 39–40, 75, 232; vision for, 40
department heads: best practices and hints for success as, 2–3, 22, 231–36; billet options as, 9–11; bosses of, 56; career briefs, 10; career path of, 8–9; challenges related to role of, 2, 22, 236; competencies for future command opportunities, 72, 75–76; duties and responsibilities of, 22, 46, 97; experience as and development of skills for becoming a CO, 213; first tour as, 24; leading fellow department heads, 184; personal life of, getting in order, 74; preparation for, 7, 231–32; self-assessment for success as, 8–9; strength of and success of ship and captain, 2, 16, 231–32; turnover schedule, 227–29; unified department head team, 145–46; vision of for department, 40
Department of the Navy Correspondence Manual (SECNAV M-5216.5 series), 12, 115, 199
desire, drive, and determination, 30
destroyer squadrons (DESRONs): administrative command function of, 126–27; aviator assignment to, 131; continental U.S.–based squadrons, 127–28; forward-deployed squadrons, 128; N3 duties in, 125; N3 operational planning, 132–33; operational command function of, 126–27, 128; readiness squadrons, 129–30; strike group environment in, 133–36
destroyers. *See* cruisers and destroyers (CRUDES)
detachment air departments, 204
detachment maintenance officer (DETMO), 205–6, 207
division officers (DIVOs): boss of, 56; communications with, 49; formal

schooling for, 8; leadership as, 35, 36–37; logbook keeping by, 107; management responsibilities of, 45; Navy policy knowledge of, 73–74; planning off-site event with, 75; relationships with, 52, 73, 234–35; A-SWO role of, 102; warfare coordinator qualifications, 23

dock landing ship (LSD): billet options on, 10; 1LT duties on, 194, 198; Sailors working for 1LT on, 195

doctrine: development of and TTP development, 190; resources on, 185, 190; study and understanding of, 133

Doctrine for the Armed Forces of the United States, Joint Publication-1, 185

duty assignments/tours: communication during training pipeline, 14; first department head tour, 24; permanent change of stations (PCS) orders, 13–14; preferences and slating, 9–11; shore duty tours, 8–9

early command: career path and decision to pursue, 213–14, 225–26; challenges and rewards of, 225–26; command as pinnacle of career, 213; communications style for, 220; hints for successful command, 222–25; levels of command, 225; opportunities for, 214–15; priorities as, 220–21; record review and screening process, 216–17; relationships and building a network, 221–22; reporting requirements and communication with bosses, 222; reporting to ship and assuming command, 218–22; risk management and safety, 222–23; selection for, 214, 217–18; testing as the new guy, 220; training pipeline for, 218; where to start and requirements for, 215–16

education and training: billet-specific training, 8; early command pipeline, 218; formal schooling, 1–2, 7, 8–9; integrated training team, 184; logbook of special evolutions and training, 107; 1LT training and qualifications process responsibilities, 195; professional reading, 14–15; PTO training and planning role, 183–84; relational administration data management (R-ADM) system, 103–5; reporting requirements, education on, 118; self-guided learning, 7–16; simulators, 1–2, 8, 21, 92, 107, 232; specialized training, 13–14, 18, 24; strengthening weaknesses through, 231–32; waterfront town halls and training opportunities, 145; weapons personnel training and qualifications and growing experts, 143–45. *See also* Surface Warfare Officers School (SWOS)

eight o'clock reports, 158, 162–63, 165, 175–76, 234

electronic key management system (EKMS)/ key management infrastructure (KMI) manager, 158

electronics material officer, 152

Elements of Style, The (Strunk and White), 12, 63

11 September attacks, 1, 234

email inbox, optimization of, 122, 233

emotional intelligence, 37–38

engineer officer/chief engineer (CHENG), 160–72; advice for a successful tour, 162–71; billet-specific training for, 24; challenge coin for, 171; characteristics and temperament for success as, 168, 171–72; chief engineer as special evolution OOD, 95; CO expectations of, 165; coveralls, tools, and looking the part as, 164; department head assignment as, 9, 10; duties, responsibilities, and authority of, 160–62, 167, 171–72, 173, 174; equipment status updates to, 86–87; fleet up/single longer tour assignments, 10; N4 assignment after tour as, 173–74, 180; professional development as, 170–71; references and instructions for, 160–63; relationship with 1LT, 196; relationship with CSO, 153; relationships and building a network, 168–70; shipdriving skills of, 170–71; showing up ready, 162–64; taking charge, 164–68; turnover, items included in, 163–64

engineering department: air department and DETMO relationship with, 207; assessments and inspections of, 166, 167–68; camaraderie and having fun, 171; challenge coin for, 171; CHENG-specific items and information in turnover, 163–64; importance of, 160; risk decisions and final approval requirements, 167; ship-wide interest in program effectiveness, 166–67; shipyard, responsibilities in, 167–68; training and professional development in, 170–71; walking spaces with critical eye, 164–65

Engineering Department Organization and Regulations Manual (EDORM), 160–63, 167, 170, 174, 176

engineering duty officers (EDOs), 108

engineering officer of the watch (EOOW), 161

Engineering Operational Sequencing System User's Guide, 163

engineering operations casualty control (EOCC) response procedures, 160

equipment: CHENG-specific items and information in turnover, 163–64; CSO responsibility for, 151–52, 154–55; degradation of and issues with, 154–55, 165, 198–99; eight o'clock reports on, 158, 162–63, 165, 175–76, 234; first lieutenant understanding of for evolutions, 198–99; issues during special evolutions, 95; knowledge about, 58, 234; log and records about issues and actions related to, 155–56, 165; management of, 72, 234; signal paths, understanding of, 156; status updates to other department heads about, 86–87; walking spaces and special evolution readiness, 97–98

ethos, warrior, 138, 150

evolutions/special evolutions: activities during, 93–96; checklist or brief for weapons evolutions, 140, 141–42, 147; CO direction and style during, 95; communication and brief prior to, 90, 96–97; debrief and capture of lessons learned after event, 90–91, 96, 109; debriefing after, 147; definitions/examples of, 83–84, 89–90; department head as OOD for special evolutions, 89, 90–96, 99; effective execution of, 61; first lieutenant understanding of equipment for and participation in, 192, 198–99; logbook of special evolutions and training, 107; note-taking during, 95–96; OOD responsibilities for special evolutions, 89; OPS participation in, 119; preparations prior to evolution, 90–93, 96–98, 99; PTO participation in, 185–86; references for, 91–92, 94; risk management and decisions related to, 194; successful evolutions through department head support, 96–99; TAO and watch team support for, 83–84; walking the deckplates and observation of, 48; walk-through, talk-through exercises, 92; watch team support for, 83–84, 98; weapons department evolutions/significant evolutions, 140, 141–42, 147–48, 150

executive officer (XO): administration duties to support, 11; communication with, 62–64; communication with CO, role in, 47–48, 62–63; duties of, 56–57; expectations of, 56, 58–61, 66–67; experience of, 66; future XO, acting like, 66; leverage of, 65; organizational line of authority, 56–58; priorities of and command priorities, 63, 64, 65–66, 67; recognition of team accomplishments in front of, 123; relationship with CO, 61–62, 65; relationship with department head, 56–58, 66–67; relationship with TAO, 80; reporting to, 12, 57; support for, 56, 61–65, 66–67; support from, 65, 66; watchstanding training coordination with, 101, 102

expect what you inspect, 97–98

explosive safety waterfront training, 145

extra military instruction (EMI), 104

fast cruises, 106

fatigue and circadian battle rhythm, 106

feedback, self-assessment through, 9

first lieutenant (1LT), 192–202; administrative duties and writing skills of, 199, 201–2; billet-specific training for, 24, 193; characteristics and temperament for success as, 192, 202; collateral duties of, 194; delegation of tasks and time management by, 201; department head assignment as, 10; duties, responsibilities, and authority of, 192–93, 202; embarkation/debarkation coordination with Marine Corps, 199–200; evolutions, participation in and understanding equipment for, 192, 198–99; expertise of, 198–200; leadership presence and relationships important to, 195–97; leadership style of, 192, 197–98, 201, 202; organization and organizational skills of, 201–2; preparation for, 193–202; priorities and departmental philosophy of, 201; reading and references for, 193–94; risk management and decisions related to evolutions by, 194; taking care of and learning about your Sailors, 197–98, 202; training and qualifications process responsibilities of, 195; understanding and learning from Sailors working for, 195; walking your spaces and instilling space ownership in Sailors, 198

fitness reports (FITREPs): all-but-signature standards for, 233; early command and RSCA, 224; early command annotations in, 216, 217; log/record keeping and writing of, 155–56; notes of accomplishments in, 201; 1LT duties and writing skills for, 199, 201; responsibility for, 46

Fleet Operational Order, 115

fleet up/single longer tour assignments, 10, 151, 152

flight deck operations: air COMMO–ship COMMO relationship and, 207, 209; air OPS–ship OPS relationship and, 208, 210; authority for granting flight deck clearance, 210; certifications, drills, and air schedules related to training and operations, 114; OPS duties, 113, 114; ship-air team integration to support flight operations, 208–10

follow-up as leadership function, 236

force protection and terrorist attacks, 1

Girrier, Robert, 213

guided missile cruisers (CGs), 9, 220

guided missile destroyers (DDGs), 9, 10, 129–30

H-60 Wind Envelopes, 211

helicopter maritime strike (HSM) squadrons, 204, 206

Helicopter Operations from Ships Other than Aircraft Carriers, 211

homeports, duty preferences and slating, 9–11

humility and confidence, 38

immediate superior in command (ISIC): early command and relationship with, 221; engineering department assessment assistance from, 166; guidance for OPS from, 116; length of command relationship as, 127; N3 duties in surface ship squadrons as, 126, 127, 129–30; priorities of, 169; relationships with, 52, 115

information, technological advances and focusing on, 1

information technician for vault security management, 158

information warfare, 232

innovation, 42–43

instructions, deviation from, 223–24

integrated training team, 184

integrity, 36

Joint Publication-1, *Doctrine for the Armed Forces of the United States*, 185

junior watch officer, 102

khaki leadership: assessment of, 38–39; command-wide program support from, 64; communication with, 52, 57, 61; early command and crew size, 225; engineering department training for, 170; execution of department priorities by, 39–40; 1LT relationship with, 198; senior enlisted as leadership partners, 235; watchstation responsibilities of, 102

landing helicopter assault/landing helicopter dock (LHA/LHD): billet options on, 10; *LHA/LHD NATOPS Manual*, 211; N3 duties in strike group environment on, 135; Sailors working for 1LT on, 195

landing safety officer (LSO), 209–10

leadership: advice and informal lessons on, 19; CO characteristics and leadership qualities, 213; commanding your department, 58–59, 69; concept of, 33–36; culture and command climate role of, 40–41, 44n3, 55, 147, 148–49, 188–89, 234–36; development of skills for and perspective on, 33, 43–44; experience as division officer, 35, 36–37; first lieutenant leadership style, 192, 201, 202; follow-up as leadership function, 236; innovation and initiative in, 42–43; khaki leadership, 38–40; management compared to, 34, 45; natural talent for, 34–35; notes and thoughts about, 19; qualities of leaders, 36–38; senior enlisted as leadership partners, 235; skills for, 34–35, 38–43; tough calls, making, 73; training module on, 18, 22; trust and access to privileged information, 175; warfighting leadership, 43. *See also* khaki leadership

leading chief petty officer (LCPO), 205–6, 235

lean forward and anticipate challenges, 70

learning organizations, 188–89

leave/temporary assigned duty (TAD) tracker, 53–54

lessons learned: administrative changes related to, 186; application of, 179, 181; capture of, 166; debrief and capture of lessons learned after event, 90–91, 96, 109; resources on, 53, 91; sharing of, 52, 173, 178, 190

Lessons Learned Library, 91

LHA/LHD NATOPS Manual, 211

life-saving equipment, 194, 198

limited duty officer (LDO) boatswain, 195

limited duty officer (LDO)/chief warrant officer (CWO) assistant first lieutenant (AFL), 195

littoral combat ship (LCS): billet options on, 10; operations officers on, 113

littoral combat ship squadrons (LCSRONs): N3 duties in, 125; readiness squadrons, 129

main propulsion assistant (MPA), 165, 168–69, 170

main reduction gear (MRG) and MRG keys, 163, 164

maintenance: CHENG–maintenance organization relationships, 169; walking the weatherdecks and tracking maintenance responsibilities, 120

maintenance team: N4 coordination with, 178; relationship with, 52–53, 154, 196–97

management: camaraderie and having fun, 55, 171, 231; communication process, effective communication, and, 47–50, 61; consolidated reports and streamline communication, 49; drumbeats and priorities, 46–47; leadership compared to, 34, 45; programs and warfare areas management, 59; responsibilities and requirements, 45–46; stamina, planning, and effective management, 54–55; training management module, 18, 23–24; triad for, 48, 53–54, 168–69

Marine Corps, U.S.: embarkation/debarkation coordination with Marine Corps, 199–200; follow-up as leadership function in, 236

Mark VI patrol boat, 215

mast, tour of, 156

material readiness, training module on, 18, 23–24

meetings: collaborative workshops to building learning organizations, 188–89; deconfliction of issues before, 49; plan, brief, execute, debrief (PBED) processes, 186, 187–88; walking the deckplates and meetings with Sailors, 48–49, 74, 122–23; war councils, 190

mentors and mentorship, 19, 66, 201

microminiature electronics repair (2M) program, 152, 155, 156–57

mine countermeasure ship (MCM), 10, 214–15

mistakes, learning from, 188–89

Mobility-Engineering, 163

multimission tactical trainers (MMTTs), 23, 26

MyNavy Career Center, 14

NATOPS General Flight and Operating Manual, 211

Naval Aviation Safety Management System, 211

Naval Facilities Engineering Command (NAVFAC), 196

INDEX

Naval Ordnance Safety and Security Activity website, 145
Naval Ordnance Safety Precautions, 141
Naval Ships' Technical Manuals (NSTMs): "Boats and Small Craft" chapter, 194; *Electric Plant–General*, 163; *F76 Fuel System*, 163; *Propulsion Reduction Gears, Couplings, Clutches, and Associated Components*, 163; *Surface Ship Firefighting*, 163
naval surface fire support (NSFS) training and operations, 139, 144
naval surface squadrons (SURFRONs), 125, 129
Naval Surface Warfare Center, 145
navigation, seamanship, and shiphandling (NSS): command assessment of knowledge about, 25, 26, 29–30; competencies for future command opportunities, 72; pierwork assessment, 21, 29–30; resources on, 20; Rules of the Road exam, 15, 20–21, 26–27; Rules of the Road lessons, 20–21; shipdriving skills, 170–71; training module on, 18, 20–21
Navigation, Seamanship, and Shiphandling Trainer (NSST), 29, 92
Navigation Rules and Regulations Handbook, 15, 116
navigator (NAV), 118–19
Navy, U.S.: diversity of experiences of a career in, 8–9; knowledge about, 73–74; MyNavy Career Center, 14
Navy and Marine Corps Awards Manual, 199
Navy Doctrine Library, 190
Navy enlistment classification (NEC) management, 144
Navy Performance Evaluation System, 116, 199
Navy Personnel Command website, 199
Navy Tactics, Techniques, and Procedures—Underway Replenishment, 194
news, reading and staying up on, 75
Nietzsche, Friedrich, 34–35

Office of the Chief of Naval Operations Navy Personnel Conventional Ammunition and Explosives Handling Qualification and Certification, 141
officer in charge (OIC, air boss), 205–7
officer of the deck (OOD): back-up and support from TAO for, 86; department head as OOD for special evolutions, 89, 90–96, 99; duties and responsibilities of, 89, 99; relationship with TAO, 80; requalification as, 89; special evolutions responsibilities, 89, 99; training for, 8; watchstanding as, 21, 89
one ship, one fight mentality, 147
operational task messages (OPTASKs), 23, 26
operations officer (OPS), 113–24; advice for a successful tour, 115–23; afloat duty compared to shore duty responsibilities, 114; air department duties, 205–6, 207; air OPS–ship OPS relationship, 208, 210; billet-specific training for, 24; collaboration and relationships as, 113; communications and off-ship communications responsibilities, 116–17, 118; department head assignment as, 9, 10; duties, responsibilities, and authority of, 113–15, 123–24; equipment status updates to, 86–87; off-ship relationships and network of, 115; platform-specific duties of, 113–14; reading and references requirements, 115–16; relationship with N3, 130, 131; relationship with WEPS, 143; representation of ship and captain by, 115–17; schedule-related authority and responsibilities, 117–18; special evolutions, participation in, 119; walking the weatherdecks and tracking maintenance responsibilities, 120; work day routine for, 121–23
organization and organizational skills: communication during training pipeline, 14; departmental trackers for, 53–54, 179, 199, 201; personal organization, 12; planner or calendar for, 121, 202. *See also* delegation of tasks

peers, relationships with, 51, 52, 60, 72, 75
permanent change of stations (PCS) orders, 13–14
PERS-41 website: billet options on, 9–10; bridge watch hours submission to, 107; career briefs on, 10; early command process and instructions on, 215, 217

245

PERS-43 website, 211
personnel: ammunition and explosives handling QUAL/CERT programs, 139, 143–44; identification and monitoring redlines, 120; issues during special evolutions, 95; NEC management and building bench depth, 144; subordinates, standing by, 149; turnover and rotation of watchstanders, 98; walking spaces and special evolution readiness, 97–98. *See also* Sailors
personnel qualification standard (PQS) program, 103–4
philosophy, command, 219–20
philosophy, departmental, 201
physical fitness routine, 12–13, 19, 75
Picasso, Pablo, 43
pierwork assessment, 21, 29–30
plan, brief, execute, debrief (PBED) processes, 186, 187–88
plan of action and milestone (POA&M), 54, 166, 179
planning board for training (PB4T), 60–61, 143–44, 157, 158
plans and tactics officer (PTO), 181–91; advice for a successful tour, 183–90, 233; characteristics and temperament for success as, 181; closing the seams, 183–85; CO creation of, 10, 113–14; duties, responsibilities, and authority of, 153, 181–83, 191; evolution, participation in, 185–86; flexibility of role of, 181–82, 187, 191; planning competencies, 185–87; relationship with CSO, 153; relationships important to, 181, 186–87; second tour position of, 102, 113, 181; SWO duty of, 184–85; training mindset and building a learning organization, 187–89; warfare tactics and owning the fight, 189–90
Plans and Tactics Officer Roles and Responsibilities, 181, 182–83
plans and tactics (PT) department, 152, 158
plans/planning: departmental trackers for, 53–54, 179, 199, 201; expanding planning horizon, 70; innovation and planning for change, 42–43; N3 operational and readiness planning, 132–33, 136–37; planning off-site event, 75; stamina, planning, and effective management, 54–55; time for planning, 74; time management techniques and skills, 12, 60–61, 122, 201; vision and, 40; WEPS long-term planning, 143–44

plant control officer (PCO), 95, 161, 170–71
platforms and systems: command assessment of knowledge about, 26, 28–29; duty preferences and slating, 9–11; MMTT exercises and assessments on, 23, 26; N4 expertise on, 176, 177–78, 179; OPS platform-specific duties, 113–14; threats lessons and capabilities of, 20; training for specific, 18, 24; training on, 17–18, 23. *See also* ships and ship types
port, references for entering/exiting, 91
Princeton, 1
prize crew training and operations, 141
professional development, 74–75, 170–71
programs: command-wide programs, 64, 67; management of, 59, 72
prospective engineering officer (PEO) course, 24

quad/tri chart, 50

reading. *See* books and references
recovery, assist, secure, and traverse (RAST) system, 207
Redlines, 163
relational administration data management (R-ADM) system, 103–5
relationships: air boss–CO, 206–7; air COMMO–ship COMMO relationship, 207, 209; air department relationships, 203, 207–8; air OPS–ship OPS relationship, 208, 210; building strong relationships, 51–53, 55; camaraderie and having fun, 55, 171, 231; with certifiers and trainers, 53, 154, 178; CHENG relationships and network, 168–70; CHENG–1LT, 196; CHENG–CSO, 153; CHENG–maintenance organizations, 169; CHENG–N4, 169, 177–78; CO–department head, 56–57, 66–67, 68, 75–76; cross-department relationships, 60, 121, 145–46, 153, 169, 181, 196; CSO relationships, 152–54; with

department heads on other ships, 154; division officer–department head, 52, 73, 234–35; early command relationships and network, 221–22; emotional intelligence and, 37–38; with family and friends, 75; with khaki leaders, 52; with maintenance team, 52–53, 154, 196–97; N3 relationships with CO, XO, and OPS, 130–31; N3 waterfront network, 136; N4 relationships, 175, 177–78; off-ship relationships, 52, 72, 153–54, 196–97; 1LT relationships and network, 196–97; OPS off-ship relationships and network, 115; with peers, 51, 52, 60, 72, 75; PTO relationships and network, 186–87; PTO–CSO, 153; on-ship relationships, 51, 72, 152–53; TAO–key watch stations, 80; WEPS–CSO, 153; WEPS–OPS, 143; WEPS–resource providers, 144; XO–department head, 56–58, 66–67; XO–TAO, 80

reporting senior's cumulative average (RSCA), 224

Requirements for Air-Capable and Amphibious Assault Ships to Operate Aircraft, 211

right thing, fidelity to, 36

risk management, 136–37, 167, 194, 222–23

Rules of the Road exam, 15, 20–21, 26–27

Rules of the Road lessons, 20–21

Russia, Great Power competition with, 1, 234

safe and safe combination, 164

safety: afloat safety officer course, 18, 21–22; gun lay sat and safe fire bearing, 147–48; life-saving equipment and other safety gear, 194, 198; 1LT as safety officer, 194; OPS as safety officer, 115; PTO planning for, 187; risk management and, 222–23; walking the deckplates and compliance with procedures, 48; weapons safety responsibilities, 139–40

safety and occupational health (SOH) programs, 166–67

Safety Center, 166

Safety Process for Navy Gun and Ammunition Systems, 141

Sailors: camaraderie and having fun, 55, 171, 231; collaborative approach to mistakes and failures by, 188–89; command-wide program support from, 64; esprit de corps, 122–23, 171; formality and standard of behavior for, 195; liberty for watchstanders, 107–8; Navy policy knowledge of, 73–74; not yelling at, 235; pride and tradition of rates, 195; recognition of accomplishments of, 123, 171, 199, 201; subordinates, standing by, 149; taking care of and learning about, 72, 122, 197–98, 202, 235; training and competencies of, tracking, 120; understanding and learning from, 195; walking the deckplates and meetings with, 48–49, 74, 122–23; walking your spaces and instilling space ownership in, 198; watchstanding qualifications of, 101, 102, 103–5

schedules: anxiety from uncertainty about, 123; battle rhythm, 54, 106, 117–18, 119–20, 134, 185, 195–96, 218–19; changes to, 118, 218–19; draft plan of the day, 119–20; duty section rotations and schedule, 108–9; early command and planning your day, 224–25; OPS ownership of, 116–17; roadmap for extended planning horizon, 233; turnover schedule, 227–29

seamanship. *See* navigation, seamanship, and shiphandling (NSS)

search and rescue (SAR) program, 194

self-care and stress relief, 12–13, 19, 75

senior enlisted watchbill coordinator (SEWBC), 101, 102, 108

senior watch officer (SWO), 100–110; advice for, 103–10; communications about duty schedules, 108–9; duties, responsibilities, and authority of, 100, 110; experience and seniority of, 101, 110; organizational relationships, 100; PTO as, 184–85; relief of, 102–3; selection of, 101; team to support, 101–3; watchstander supervision by, 98, 100

September 11 attacks, 1, 234

Shipboard Aviation Facilities Resume, 211

shipboard operations officer. *See* operations officer (OPS)

shipboard plans and tactics officer. *See* plans and tactics officer (PTO)

247

INDEX

shipdriving skills, 170–71

shiphandling. *See* navigation, seamanship, and shiphandling (NSS)

ships and ship types: advocacy and ambassador roles for, 73; aviation-capable ships, 203–4; duty preferences and slating, 9–11; histories and namesakes of ships, 14; lethal response as difference between ship and warship, 138; N4 expertise on, 176, 177–78, 179; OPS platform-specific duties, 113–14; relationship building aboard, 51–53; surface ship squadrons, 125, 126–30; threats lessons and capabilities of, 20

ship's electronics readiness team (SERT) meetings and plan, 153, 157–58

ship's maintenance and material officer (SMMO), 52–53

shore duty tours, 8–9

simulators, 1–2, 8, 21, 92, 107, 232

single longer tour/fleet up assignments, 10, 151, 152

Small Arms Training and Qualification, 141

spaces, walking and owning, 48–49, 59, 120, 198, 232

special evolutions. *See* evolutions/special evolutions

staff operations officer (squadron N3), 125–37; administrative/readiness functions, 126–30, 136–37; advice for a successful tour, 130–37; characteristics for success as, 125; commodore representative role of, 130; duties, responsibilities, and authority of, 125, 126–27, 137; impact and influence of, 125; operationally focused functions, 132–36; OPS team, effective use of, 131; relationships with CO, XO, and OPS, 130–31; risk management across squadron by, 136–37; strike group environment duties of, 133–36; waterfront network, 136; workload distribution to N-heads, 132

staff readiness officer (N4), 173–80; adding value to ships as, 177–78; advice for a successful tour, 174–79; assignment after tour as CHENG, 173–74, 180; challenges related to role of, 173–74, 180; characteristics and temperament for success as, 179; commodore representative role of, 175–76; communications and commodore expectations, 175–76; duties, responsibilities, and authority of, 173–75, 179, 180; engineering department assessment assistance from, 166; expertise of and knowledge about ship platforms and configurations, 176, 177–78, 179; planning and delegation of tasks by, 179; relationship with CHENG, 169, 177–78; relationships important to, 175, 177–78; trust and access to privileged information by, 175

stamina, planning, and effective management, 54–55

Standard Operating Procedures for Special Incident Reporting, 116

Standard Organization and Regulations of the U.S. Navy (SORM, OPNAVINST 3120.32 series): administration matters direction in, 12; combat systems officer duties in, 151–52; department head duties in, 22, 46, 97; engineer officer duties in, 160–61, 174; executive officer duties in, 56–57; first lieutenant duties in, 192–93; officer of the deck duties in, 89; operations officer duties in, 114–15; senior watch officer duties in, 100; staff operations officer duties in, 126; staff readiness officer duties in, 174–75; tactical action officer duties in, 79–80; weapons officer duties in, 138–40

Standard Subject Identification Code Manual, 12, 115–16

standing orders, 80–81, 162, 186

Stavridis, James, 213

steady strain approach, 54

stress relief and self-care, 12–13, 19, 75

strike warfare (STW) training and operations, 139, 144, 145

Strunk, William, 12, 63

Surface and Mine Warfighting Development Center (SMWDC), 74, 182, 186–87, 190

surface development squadrons (SURFDEVRONs), 125, 129

"Surface Force Command Requirements," 215–16

Surface Force Training and Readiness Manual (SFTRM), 115, 139, 163, 176, 194

Surface Ship Navigation Department Organization and Regulations Manual (NAVDORM), 90
surface ship squadrons, 125, 126–30
surface warfare mariner skills logbook, 107
surface warfare officers: career briefs, 10; career path of, 8–9
Surface Warfare Officers School (SWOS), 13–14; continuum of training at, 1–2; department head school at, 1, 7; engineering course at, 160; execution of orders to, 13–14; graduation from department head school, 24; history and overview of, 17–18; location of, 13, 17; preparation for department head school at, 18–20; quality of training at, 1–2, 8; scope of training at, 17, 18, 20–24; social engagements with classmates at, 19–20; week one and threats, 20
system test officer (STO), 152, 153, 157, 158, 159

tactical action officer (TAO), 79–88; advice for a successful watch, 85–88; back-up and support for OOD by, 86; complacency, guarding against, 88; decentralized command and command by negation in CIC, 87–88; duties, responsibilities, and authority of, 79–80, 88; leading watch team, 80–85; relationship with XO, 80; relationships with key watch stations, 80; ship-air team integration to support flight operations, 209–10; special evolutions support from, 83–84; tactical assessment during CA, 29; training for, 17, 18, 22–23, 231–32; watchstanding as, 21, 22–23, 80–84
tactical assessment, 25, 26, 29
tactics, techniques, and procedures (TTP), 183, 185, 190
Tag-Out User's Manual, 163
talk-through, walk-through exercises, 92
teams and teamwork: assessment of performance of, 38–39; camaraderie and having fun, 55, 171, 231; collaboration and success of ship, 2, 7, 59–60, 71, 74; combat systems officer team, 152–53; combat systems training team (CSTT), 153; communication and performance of, 47, 48–49, 61; department head team, 145–46; effective execution of evolution by, 61; expectations of XO, 59–60; expertise of and knowing your people, 58; good team transformation into great team, 148–49; integrated training team, 184; OPS team, effective use of, 131; recognition of accomplishments of, 123, 171; ship-air team operations, 203, 211; SWO team, 101–3; watch team, 80–85; working hours and staying late, 55
temporary assigned duty (TAD) tracker, 53–54
terrorism and force protection, 1. *See also specific antiterrorism entries*
threat exam, 29
threats: battle orders, standing orders, and priority of, 81; command assessment of identification of, 26; module on, 20
360-degree review, 26, 27
Ticonderoga-class cruisers, 114
time management techniques and skills, 12, 60–61, 122, 201
trackers, departmental, 53–54, 179, 199, 201
trainers, relationship with, 53, 154, 178
training. *See* education and training
training management, module on, 18, 23–24
training officer (TRAINO), 101, 118–19
triad, command, 220
triad, department, 48, 53–54, 168–69
trust, 97–98, 175, 225
turnover schedule, 227–29
type commander, 169, 176, 206, 216, 218
Type Commander Near Miss Report, 91

underway replenishment references, 91
undesignated seamen, 195

vault inventory and security management, 158
visit, board, search, and seizure (VBSS) training and operations, 139, 141

walk-through, talk-through exercises, 92
war councils, 190
warfare areas management, 59
warfighting development centers, 186–87
warfighting leadership: competencies for future command opportunities, 72; focus

on warfighting, 234; importance of skills for, 43
warrior ethos, 138, 150
watch team replacement plan (WTRP), 53, 59, 98
watchbills: approval of, 100; business rules about teams, 109; clean copies and pen-and-ink changes to, 106; department head as OOD on, 89, 95; duty exemptions and who stands duty, 108; duty section rotations, 108–9; mishaps related to errors, 110; pranks and practical jokes in, 109; preparation, review, and routing of, 98, 100, 101, 103–5, 109; R-ADM system and construction of, 103–5; special evolution inclusion on, 22, 89–90; SWO communications about duty schedules, 108–9; templates for, 104–5; timing and publicity of, 109; validation drills, 106
Watchstander's Guide, 163
watchstanding: advice for a successful watch, 85–88; assuming the watch, 81–84; communication with watch team, 83, 87–88; communications and data links for, 85; complacency, guarding against, 88; CSOOW watchstanding, 158–59; decentralized command and command by negation, 87–88; fatigue and circadian battle rhythm, 106; leading watch team, 80–85; liberty for watchstanders, 107–8; 1LT responsibilities for, 195; OOD watchstanding, 21, 89; Rules of the Road knowledge for, 21; senior watch officer (SWO), 100–110; special evolution support from watch team, 83–84, 98; strength and weaknesses of watch team, 85–86; TAO watchstanding, 21, 22–23, 80–84; training and qualifications for, 8, 101, 102; turnover and rotation of watchstanders, 98; who stands duty, 108
waterfront town halls and training opportunities, 145
weapons and ammunition: ammunition and explosives handling QUAL/CERT programs, 139, 143–44; ammunition replenishment planning and onload/offload process, 143, 146–47; eight o'clock reports on, 158, 162–63, 175–76; evolutions and significant evolutions with, 140, 141–42, 147–48, 150; explosive safety waterfront training, 145; gun lay sat and safe fire bearing, 147–48; lethal response as difference between ship and warship, 138; procurement of and safety related to, 139–40; references on, 140–41; responsibilities for, 138; responsibility for/person in charge of evolutions, 142; waterfront town halls and training opportunities, 145
weapons officer (WEPS), 138–50; advice for a successful tour, 140–49; billet-specific training for, 24; checklist or brief development for department evolutions, 140, 141–42, 147; communications and debriefings, 147, 148–49; department head assignment as, 9; duties, responsibilities, and authority of, 138–40, 150; evolutions/significant evolutions planning and safety, 140, 141–42, 147–48, 150; feedback on effectiveness of, 138; NEC management and building bench depth, 144; personnel training and qualifications and growing experts, 143–45; planning/long-term planning by, 143–44; reading and references requirements, 140–41; relationship with CSO, 153; relationship with OPS, 143; relationships with resource providers, 144; subordinates, standing by, 149; tone set by for weapons department, 147, 148–49; waterfront town halls and training opportunities, 145
well deck operations, 113
Wet Well Operations Manual, 194
White, E. B., 12, 63
working hours and staying late, 55
workout routine, 12–13, 19, 75
world events, staying informed about, 75

Zephyr, 223

ABOUT THE EDITORS

RADM Fred W. Kacher has deployed multiple times at sea and commanded Expeditionary Strike Group SEVEN, Destroyer Squadron SEVEN, and USS *Stockdale* (DDD 106). An author of numerous articles on naval affairs and recipient of the Elmo Zumwalt Award for Visionary Leadership and the U.S. Navy League's John Paul Jones Award for Inspirational Leadership, he has also served ashore at the White House and the Pentagon. A graduate of the United States Naval Academy and Harvard's Kennedy School, he is also the author of the *Newly Commissioned Naval Officer's Guide,* 2nd edition (Naval Institute Press, 2018), and co-author of the *Naval Officer's Guide to the Pentagon* (Naval Institute Press, 2019).

CAPT Joseph A. Gagliano is a surface warfare officer, naval strategist, and politico-military specialist. At sea, he has served as the commander of Task Force 65, commodore of Destroyer Squadron 60, commanding officer and executive officer in USS *Independence* (LCS 2), and combat systems officer and weapons officer in USS *Cole* (DDG 67). Ashore, he has served as the director for defense policy and strategy for the National Security Council at the White House, a strategist on the Joint Staff in the Asia political-military affairs directorate, and the strategic planning team leader for OPNAV N00X. Captain Gagliano holds a PhD and a master's degree in international relations from the Fletcher School of Law and Diplomacy at Tufts University and a master's degree in national security and strategic studies from the U.S. Naval War College. He is also the author of *Shiphandling Fundamentals for Littoral Combat Ships and the New Frigates* (Naval Institute Press, 2015).

ABOUT THE EDITORS

CDR Samantha A. O'Neil is a surface warfare officer who served at sea as a division officer in USS *Curtis Wilbur* (DDG 54), USS *Pearl Harbor* (LSD 52) and as the chief engineer in USS *Preble* (DDG 88) and USS *Cowpens* (CG 63), where she was the recipient of the Navy and Marine Corps Association Leadership Award. Ashore, she served as a company officer at the United States Naval Academy and as a staff member in the Commander's Action Group at Commander, Naval Surface Force Pacific. As a Navy reserve officer, she served as executive officer of the Navy Reserve Commander, Naval Surface Force Pacific Headquarters unit and executive officer of the Navy Reserve Surface and Mine Warfighting Development Center headquarters unit. She is a graduate of the United States Naval Academy, the University of Maryland, and the U.S. Naval War College.

The Naval Institute Press is the book-publishing arm of the U.S. Naval Institute, a private, nonprofit, membership society for sea service professionals and others who share an interest in naval and maritime affairs. Established in 1873 at the U.S. Naval Academy in Annapolis, Maryland, where its offices remain today, the Naval Institute has members worldwide.

Members of the Naval Institute support the education programs of the society and receive the influential monthly magazine *Proceedings* or the colorful bimonthly magazine *Naval History* and discounts on fine nautical prints and on ship and aircraft photos. They also have access to the transcripts of the Institute's Oral History Program and get discounted admission to any of the Institute-sponsored seminars offered around the country.

The Naval Institute's book-publishing program, begun in 1898 with basic guides to naval practices, has broadened its scope to include books of more general interest. Now the Naval Institute Press publishes about seventy titles each year, ranging from how-to books on boating and navigation to battle histories, biographies, ship and aircraft guides, and novels. Institute members receive significant discounts on the Press' more than eight hundred books in print.

Full-time students are eligible for special half-price membership rates. Life memberships are also available.

For more information about Naval Institute Press books that are currently available, visit www.usni.org/press/books. To learn about joining the U.S. Naval Institute, please write to:

Member Services
U.S. Naval Institute
291 Wood Road
Annapolis, MD 21402-5034
Telephone: (800) 233-8764
Fax: (410) 571-1703
Web address: www.usni.org

www.ingramcontent.com/pod-product-compliance
Ingram Content Group UK Ltd.
Pitfield, Milton Keynes, MK11 3LW, UK
UKHW041912140426
5217IPUK00001B/4